ILEX FOUNDATION SERIES 16

ERIN AND IRAN

ERIN AND IRAN

CULTURAL ENCOUNTERS BETWEEN THE IRISH AND THE IRANIANS

Edited by
H. E. Chehabi and Grace Neville

Ilex Foundation
Boston, Massachusetts

Distributed by Harvard University Press
Cambridge, Massachusetts, and London, England

Erin and Iran: Cultural Encounters between the Persians and the Iranians
Edited by H. E. Chehabi and Grace Neville

Published by Ilex Foundation, Boston, Massachusetts

Distributed by Harvard University Press, Cambridge, Massachusetts and London, England

Production editor: Christopher Dadian
Cover design: Joni Godlove
Printed in the United States of America

Cover images are original illustrations by Glynnis Fawkes, adapted from:

front cover   Ceramic frieze tile, Iran, lustre, Rustam rescues Bizhan, late 12th–early 13th century, Dallas Museum of Art

back cover   Gundestrup Cauldron, Denmark, hammered silver, partially gilded, probably 2nd–1st century BCE, National Museum of Denmark

Library of Congress Cataloging-in-Publication Data

Erin and Iran : cultural encounters between the Irish and the Iranians / edited by H.E. Chehabi and Grace Neville.
    pages cm. -- (Ilex Foundation series ; 16)
  Includes bibliographical references.
  ISBN 978-0-674-08828-3 (alk. paper)
  1. Comparative literature--English and Persian. 2. Comparative literature--Irish and Persian. 3. Comparative literature--Persian and Irish. 4. Comparative literature--Persian and English. 5. English literature--Irish authors--History and criticism. 6. Irish literature--History and criticism. 7. Persian literature--History and criticism. 8. Ireland--Relations--Iran. 9. Iran--Relations--Ireland. I. Chehabi, H. E., editor. II. Neville, Grace, editor.
  PR129.P38E85 2015
  891'.5509--dc23
                        2015017908

CONTENTS

Contributors

Houchang Esfandiar Chehabi is a professor of international relations and history in the Frederick S. Pardee School of Global Studies at Boston University. His main research interests are Iranian cultural history and Iran's transnational relations. He is the author of *Iranian Politics and Religious Modernism* (1990) and the main author of *Distant Relations: Iran and Lebanon in the Last 500 Years* (2006). He has edited or co-edited six volumes, most recently (with Farhad Khosrokhavar and Clément Therme) *Iran and the Challenges of the Twenty-First Century: Essays in Honour of Mohammad-Reza Djalili* (2013). His articles have appeared in *Aus Politik und Zeitgeschichte, Daedalus, Gastronomica, Government and Opposition, International Journal of the History of Sport, International Journal of Middle East Studies, Iranian Studies, Journal of Persianate Studies, Persica, Political Science Quarterly, Yemek ve Kültür*, and numerous edited volumes.

Olga Davidson earned her PhD in 1983 from Princeton University in Near Eastern studies. She is on the faculty of the Institute for the Study of Muslim Societies and Civilizations, Boston University, where she has served as Research Fellow since 2009. From 1992 to 1997 she taught at Brandeis University. Since 1999, she has been Chair of the Board, Ilex Foundation. Her research interests center on comparative approaches to the study of Classical Persian poetry and prose, including the comparison of evidence from the visual arts. She is the author of two books: *Poet and Hero in the Persian Book of Kings* (1994, 2006, 2013) and *Comparative Literature and Classical Persian Poetry* (2000, 2013), both of which have been translated into Persian and distributed in Iran. Her articles include "The *Haft Khwân* Tradition as an Intertextual Phenomenon in Ferdowsi's *Shâhnâma,*" *Bulletin of the Asia Institute* (1990); "The Text of Ferdowsi's *Shâhnâma* and the Burden of the Past," *Journal of the American Oriental Society* (1998), and "The Burden of Mortality: Alexander and the Dead in Persian Epic and Beyond," *Epic and History*, ed. David Konstan and Kurt Raaflaub (2010).

Dick Davis is emeritus professor of Persian at Ohio State University, where he was chair of the Department of Near Eastern Languages and Cultures from 2002 to 2012. He has written scholarly works on both English and Persian literature, as well as eight volumes of his own poetry. He has been the recipient of numerous academic and literary awards, including both the Ingram Merrill and Heinemann awards for poetry; his publications include volumes of poetry and verse translation chosen as books of the year by *The Sunday Times* (UK) 1989; *The Daily Telegraph* (UK) 1989; *The Economist* (UK) 2002; *The Washington Post* 2010, and *The Times Literary Supplement* (UK) 2013. He has published numerous book-length verse translations from medieval Persian, most recently, *Faces of Love: Hafez and the Poets of Shiraz* (2012). He is a Fellow of the Royal Society of Literature, and has been called, by the *Times Literary Supplement*, "our finest translator from Persian."

M. R. Ghanoonparvar is professor emeritus of Persian and comparative literature at The University of Texas at Austin. Ghanoonparvar has also taught at the University of Isfahan, the University of Virginia, and the University of Arizona and was a Rockefeller Fellow at the University of Michigan. He has published widely on Persian literature and culture in both English and Persian and is the author of *Prophets of Doom: Literature as a Socio-Political Phenomenon in Modern Iran* (1984), *In a Persian Mirror: Images of the West and Westerners in Iranian Fiction* (1993), *Translating the Garden* (2001), *Reading Chubak* (2005), and *Persian Cuisine: Traditional, Regional and Modern Foods* (2006). His translations include Jalal Al-e Ahmad's *By the Pen*, Sadeq Chubak's *The Patient Stone*, Simin Daneshvar's *Savushun*, Ahmad Kasravi's *On Islam and Shi'ism*, Sadeq Hedayat's *The Myth of Creation*. Davud Ghaffarzadegan's *Fortune Told in Blood*, Mohammad Reza Bayrami's *The Tales of Sabalan*, and Bahram Beyza'i's *Memoirs of the Actor in a Supporting Role*. His edited volumes include *Iranian Drama: An Anthology*, *In Transition: Essays on Culture and Identity in Middle Eastern Societies*, Gholamhoseyn Sa'edi's *Othello in Wonderland* and *Mirror-Polishing Storytellers*, and Moniru Ravanipur's *Satan Stones* and *Kanizu*. His most recent books and translations include *The Neighbor Says: Letters of Nima Yushij on Modern Persian Prosody*, Ja'far Modarres-Sadeqi's, *The Horse's Head*, (2011), and *Red Olive: The Memoirs of Nahid Yusefian*. He is working on two forthcoming books *Iranian Films and Persian Fiction* and *Literary Diseases in Persian Literature*.

Todd Lawson is emeritus professor of Islamic religious thought at the University of Toronto, where he taught for 25 years. He has written on the historical development of the Qur'an and Qur'an commentary, and on more purely literary features of the Qur'an, and has published numerous articles on these and related topics. His two most recent books are *The Qur'an and the Crucifixion* (2009) and *Gnostic Apocalypse in Islam* (2012). He is co-editor, with Sebastian Günther, of the two-volume *Roads to Paradise: Studies in Islamic Eschatology* (Brill) to appear early in 2015.

David Lewis James (1941–2012) earned his PhD from the University of Durham in Islamic art. From 1969 to 1989 he was Islamic curator at the Chester Beatty Library and Gallery of Oriental Art in Dublin. His books include *Islamic Art: An Introduction* (1974), *Arab Painting* (1978), *Islamic Masterpieces of the Chester Beatty Library* (1981), *Masterpieces of the Holy Quranic Manuscripts* (1987), *Qur'āns of the Mamlūks* (1988), *The Master Scribes: Qur'ans of the 10th to the 14th centuries AD* (1992), *After Timur: Qur'ans of the 15th and 16th centuries* (1992), *Manuscripts of the Holy Qur'ān from the Mamluk Era* (1999), *Early Islamic Spain: The History of Ibn al-Qūṭīya* (2009), and *A history of early Al-Andalus: the Akhbār majmū'a* (2012). He articles appeared in *Art about Ireland, Arts & the Islamic World, Bulletin of John Rylands University Library, Bulletin of the School of Oriental and African Studies, Humaniora Islamica, Islamic Art, Journal of the Royal Society of Antiquaries of Ireland, Kunst und Antiquitäten, Manuscripta Orientalia,* and *Muqarnas.*

Brendan McNamara is a doctoral student in the Study of Religions Department at University College, Cork. His thesis concerns the construction of discourse around religion, outside of mainstream Christianity, at the turn of the twentieth century in Britain. He is the author of *Connections: Early Links Between the Bahá'í Faith and Ireland* (2007).

John McDonald earned his PhD in classics from Cornell University in 2014. The title of his dissertation was "Orpheus and the Cow: Indo-European Inheritance and Virgilian Variation in Georgics 4." His major research interests are the Indo-European heritage of Indo-Iranian, Greco-Roman, and Celtic literary and religious traditions, cultural exchanges between the ancient Near East and the Greco-Roman world, and the adoption and adaptation of the classics in medieval and modern Irish literature.

Joseph Falaky Nagy received his PhD in Celtic languages and literatures from Harvard University, in 1978. He is professor of Celtic and folklore/mythology in the Department of English, University of California, Los Angeles. His main research interests are medieval Celtic literatures, Indo-European studies, and comparative mythology. He is the author of *Conversing with Angels and Ancients: Literary Myths of Medieval Ireland* (1997) and *The Wisdom of the Outlaw: The Boyhood Deeds of Finn in Gaelic Narrative Tradition* (1985) and editor of *Writing Down the Myths* (2013); his articles have appeared in *Celtica, Éigse, Ériu, Folklore, Studia Celtica,* and *Zeitschrift für celtische Philologie.*

Grace Neville studied French and Irish at University College Cork, l'Université de Caen, and l'Université de Lille 3. For over 30 years, she lectured in French at University College Cork where she was also Head of Department and, from 2008–12, Vice-President for Teaching and Learning. Her research areas include Franco-Irish relations (medieval-modern period), women's writing, and language legislation. Since retiring from UCC in 2012, she has been an invited member of numerous committees in Paris at the Ministère de l'Education Nationale, the Ministère de l'Enseignement Supérieur et de la Recherche, the ANR (Agence Nationale de la Recherche), and l'AERES (Agence d'Evaluation de la Recherche et de l'Enseignement Supérieur). She is Chair of the Strategic Orientation Committee at Sorbonne Universités (2014–19).

Oliver Scharbrodt is professor of Islamic studies at the University of Chester. He taught at the School of Oriental and African Studies in London and at University College Cork in Ireland. His research interests lie in the intellectual history of modern Islam, the role of mystical, esoteric and millenarian traditions of Islam in the modern world and the historical and contemporary presence of Islam in Europe. He is the author of *Islam and the Baha'i Faith: A Comparative Study of Muhammad 'Abduh and 'Abdul-Baha 'Abbas* (London: Routledge, 2008) and co-authored *Muslims in Ireland: Past and Present* (Edinburgh: Edinburgh University Press, 2015).

Introduction

H. E. Chehabi and Grace Neville

IN THE SPRING OF 1981 Ireland suddenly burst onto the consciousness of politically interested Iranians when the revolutionary authorities who had taken power two years earlier renamed Tehran's Winston Churchill Street "Bobby Sands Street." The street, located behind the British embassy, had received its name in 1943 on the occasion of the Tehran Conference when the prime minister met with Franklin D. Roosevelt and Joseph Stalin to plot strategy in their common struggle against the Axis powers. Upon the outbreak of World War II in 1939, like Ireland, Iran had declared its neutrality, but Germany's attack on the Soviet Union in 1941 turned Iran into a strategic corridor for conveying supplies to the Western powers' new ally, and so Churchill ordered British troops to violate Iran's neutrality and occupy the country, while the Soviet army invaded from the north. Churchill was again prime minister when in 1953 the British government plotted with the CIA and the Iranian army to overthrow Prime Minister Mohammad Mosaddeq, at whose instigation the Anglo-Iranian Oil Company had been nationalized. By naming the street after an IRA activist who had died in a British prison after a long hunger strike, Iranian revolutionaries not only removed a reminder of repeated British meddling in Iranian affairs, but also demonstrated what they believed to be anti-imperialist solidarity.

Seventy years earlier, it was Iran that had made the news in Ireland. From 1905 to 1911 Iran underwent a constitutional revolution that aimed to abolish an old despotic order deemed responsible by progressive forces for the country's vulnerability to European intervention. At first Britain supported the constitutionalists, but when the British began conniving with the Russians to undermine the constitutionalists' efforts, Irish nationalists and the MPs of the Irish Parliamentary Party at Westminster vociferously criticized the British government's policies in Iran.[1]

These two episodes show how events in a distant land can capture the fancy of politically articulate citizens and lead them to conceive imagined

---

1. Mansour Bonakdarian, "Erin and Iran Resurgent: Irish Nationalists and Iranian Constitutional Revolution," in H. E. Chehabi and Vanessa Martin, eds., *Iran's Constitutional Revolution: Politics, Cultural Transformations and Transnational Connections* (London: I. B. Tauris, 2010), 291–318 and 467–76.

communalities with people about whom they know very little.[2] In the case of Ireland and Iran the obvious *tertium comparationis* is resentment against British policies: "800 years of oppression" and "the hidden hand of England" are stock phrases in the rhetoric of Irish and Iranian nationalism, respectively.

But there is more to the story, at least on the Irish side. In the nineteenth century, Irish, Iranian, and Indian nationalists were all captivated by the notion of an "Aryan" origin of their respective nations.[3] Strictly speaking, "Aryans" meant little more than speakers of Indo-European languages, a linguistic family encompassing Sanskrit, Persian, English, and Gaelic (among others) whose existence had been firmly established by the early nineteenth century. For many nationalists, however, peoples speaking related languages had to share the same origin, hence the appearance of the notion of an "Aryan race." Iranian nationalists, citizens of a country that had never been formally colonized but whose sovereignty was forever precarious, hoped that Aryan origins might render their quest for equality in an international system of states dominated by Europeans more credible: in 1911 the Iranian delegate at the First Universal Races Congress in London offered a "categorical denial" that there was "among our people any natural hostility to Europeans, who are, after all, *of one and the same race with ourselves.*"[4] While Iranian Aryans stressed their common roots with the British by whom they aspired to be recognized as equals, Irish Aryans were more concerned with forging anti-imperialist alliances in the struggle against British domination. Although for obvious reasons India featured more prominently in this endeavor than Iran, the latter did catch the imagination of some Irish literati and activists.[5] For instance, Lady Francesca Wilde, a nationalist poet (and Oscar Wilde's mother), writing under the *nom de plume* "Speranza," had this to say about Iran:

2. On this "nationalist cosmopolitanism" see Mansour Bonakdarian, "Iranian Nationalism and Global Solidarity Networks 1906–18: Transnationalism, Globalization, and Nationalist Cosmopolitanism," in H.E. Chehabi, Peyman Jafari and Maral Jefroudi, eds., *Iran in the Middle East: Transnational Encounters and Social History* (London: I.B. Tauris, 2015), 77–119.

3. On Ireland see Edward A. Hagan, "Aryan Myth: a Nineteenth-Century Anglo-Irish Will to Power," in Tadgh Foley and Seán Foley, eds., *Ideology and Ireland in the Nineteenth Century* (Dublin and Portland, OR: Four Courts Press, 1998), 197–205; Tony Ballantyne, *Orientalism and Race: Aryanism in the British Empire* (Houndmills: Palgrave, 2002), 19 and 35–38; and Joseph Lennon, *Irish Orientalism: A literary and Intellectual History* (Syracuse: Syracuse University Press, 2004), 328–33. On Iran see Reza Zia-Ebrahimi, "Self-Orientalisation and Dislocation: The Uses and Abuses of the Aryan Discourse in Iran," in *Iranian Studies* 44:4 (2011): 445–72 and David Motadel, "Iran and the Aryan Myth," in Ali M. Ansari, ed., *Perceptions of Iran: History, Myths and Nationalism from Medieval Persia to the Islamic Republic* (London: I.B. Tauris, 2014), 119–45.

4. Quoted in Bonakdarian, "Erin and Iran Resurgent," 306. Emphasis added.

5. Ibid., 303–08.

> The source of all life, creed and culture now on earth, there is no reason
> to doubt, will be found in *Iran*, or Persia as we call it, and in the ancient
> legends and language of the great Iranian people, the head and noblest of
> the Aryan races. Endowed with splendid physical beauty, noble intellect,
> and a rich, musical language, the Iranians also had a lofty sense of the
> relation between man and the spiritual world.[6]

Note that at a time when most Europeans used the name "Persia," she
preferred "Iran," which had always been used in Iran and India and which is
indeed of the same root as the term "Aryan."[7]

The essays collected in this volume offer glimpses of such cultural
encounters. Part I focuses on mythology. The existence of common themes
in Celtic and Iranian mythology has long been known;[8] the most famous
example being the parallel between the story of Cúchulainn killing his son
Connla, as narrated in the Ulster Cycle, and the story of Rostam killing his
son Sohráb in the *Shāhnāmeh*,[9] the "Book of Kings." The three essays in this
section break new ground. In "The 'Conqueror Worm' in Irish and Persian
Literature," Joseph Falaky Nagy argues that, like Sheherezade's storytelling,
the *Tóruigheacht Dhairmada agus Ghráinne* provides an overarching frame
within which back stories (and back stories to back stories) are accommo-
dated. The story of the "conquering worm" is one such story, with analogues
across Irish and Persian literature. Similarities abound across these narratives, including the threat to authority ultimately posed by these unmanageable creatures. In the second chapter, "Building Bulls and Crafting Cows:
Narratives of Bovine Fabrication from Iran, Ireland and In-between," John
McDonald provides a comparative analysis of the construction of cows

6. Lady Wilde, *Ancient Legends, Mystic Charms, and Superstitions of Ireland* (Boston: Ticknor
and Co., 1887), 3.

7. Although it is sometimes suggested that the toponyms Éire and Iran are etymologi-
cally related, today there is a wide consensus that they are not. The reason for this is that
the earliest versions of Eire, transmitted in Greco-Roman sources, clearly show more than
one vowel before the /r/ (Ierne, Iwerne – this is why the Roman name of the province was
Hibernia): the vowels later contracted to give the long e of Éire, but archaic forms like Ierne
are not really compatible with the name of Iran. It is thought that Eire continues a Proto-Indo-
European form that started with a sound *p (*pīwerih̥) and meant something like "fat, full,
providing abundance." As to the name Iran, its earlier form is *ērān* (in the title of the Sasanian
kings) and the word is thought to go back to *aryānām* "[the land] of the Aryans" (genitive
plural), where *Arya- is the self-denomination of ancient Iranians and Indo-Aryans. E-mail
communication from Professor Alexander Nikolaev (Boston University), 29 November 2014.

8. For an early study see Patrick K. Ford, "The Well of Nechtan and 'La Gloire Lumineuse',"
in Gerald James Larson, ed., *Myth in Indo-European Antiquity* (Berkeley: University of California
Press, 1974), 67–74.

9. Connell Monette, "Indo-European Elements in Celtic and Indo-Iranian Epic Tradition:
the Trial of Champions in the *Táin Bó Cúailgne* and the *Shahnameh*," *The Journal of Indo-European
Studies* 32 (2004): 61–78.

within three traditions between which he posits a cognate relationship: Indo-Iranian, Greek, and Celtic. Within these respective traditions, the function of these contextually conditioned cows is linked to sovereignty (legitimate, contested, undermined). In this context, rich interpretations are enabled via a comparative reading of such texts from all three traditions. In the next chapter, "Parallel Heroic Themes in the Medieval Irish *Cattle Raid of Cooley* and the Medieval Persian *Book of Kings*," Olga Davidson, analyzes two texts, the Irish *Cattle Raid of Cooley* and the Persian *Book of the Kings*, in which the struggle to recover lost or fragmented texts becomes part of the narrative and is ultimately recounted within the texts as part of the actual performance of these texts. She argues that this is characteristic of societies in which oral and written cultures co-exist and overlap.

Part II contains studies of literary encounters and parallels. In "A Trout in the Milk: *Vis and Ramin* and *Tristan and Isolde*," Dick Davis argues that *Tristan and Isolde* is ultimately a retelling of the Parthian romance *Vis and Ramin*. Similar plots aside, the short phonetic distance between the names Iseut and Viseh and, indeed, between Erin and Iran, the frontloading of meaning onto the names Tristan and Ramin, the peripheral location of Ireland and Iran for medieval Europe, and the role played by the "empty" but meaningful space (sea and desert) are circumstantial elements that make such a hypothesis plausible. In the next chapter, "'From Hafiz': Irish Orientalism, Persian Poetry, and W. B. Yeats," Oliver Scharbrodt explores the reception of Persian mystical poetry in literary and intellectual circles in late nineteenth- and early twentieth-century Ireland, with particular reference to the poetry of W. B. Yeats. The chapter highlights "Eastern" influences that existed within the socio-cultural context of the Dublin of the period. Yeats's interest in India and in Hindu Vedantic philosophy is widely known, but this article highlights the impact of work derived from Hafiz on Yeats and his contemporaries, who were particularly struck by the apparent reconciliation between sexuality and mysticism which they identified within such texts. Todd Lawson then offers us a comparative study of two immensely different texts in his chapter "Joycean Modernism in a Nineteenth-Century Qur'an Commentary? A Comparison of the Bab's *Qayyūm al-asmā'* with Joyce's *Ulysses*." James Joyce's seminal novel and Ali Mohammad Shirāzis's commentary on a key chapter of the Qur'an evince intriguing similarities: both are located within strong texts (the Odyssey, the Qur'an) with which they engage from inside, both narratives take place on a single day, and both authors paid dearly for challenging authority: Joyce by exile and the Bab by death. In the final chapter of this section, "Sharing Poetic Sensitivity and Misery: Encounters of Iranians with the Irish in Travel Writings and Fiction," M. R. Ghanoonparvar examines a series of Persian-language fictional and non-fictional narratives that feature Ireland or Irish characters. One common trait shared by these very different texts is their generally positive and sympathetic attitude towards Ireland and the Irish.

The theme of Part III is travelogues. In "An Indo-Persian in Ireland, anno 1799," H. E. Chehabi offers a new translation of the section in Mirzā Abu Tāleb Khān Esfahāni's's Persian travelogue of his long sojourn in Europe that deals with Ireland. This account offers interesting glimpses of Cork and Dublin, as seen through the eyes of a colonial subject of the British Empire who was warmly received wherever he went. "An Irish Visitor to the Court of the Shah of Persia in 1835: Extract from the Unpublished Diary of Sir Francis Hopkins of Athboy," is a reprint of an article by the late David James. Hopkins accompanied the British Ambassador, Henry Ellis, on his mission to Tehran in 1835. The diary starts with the journey from the Ottoman-Persian border onwards to Tehran, and ends with an account of his reception by Mohammad Shah Qajar. The reprint departs from the original article only in that the transliteration of Persian words and names was changed to conform to the overall system used in this book. In the tenth and final chapter of this book, "An Irishwoman in Tehran, 1849–1853: Identity, Religion, and Empire," Brendan McNamara focuses on the first travelogue on Persia published by a woman, the Irish-born Catholic, Mary Woulfe Sheil, wife of Justin Sheil, the British ambassador to the court of the Shah. Her text reveals much about herself and her husband, but offers little towards advancing cultural literacy with respect to mid-nineteenth century Persia. For Sheil, Persia is a strange, decayed land in need of the modernizing, "civilizing" influence of England. She downplays her Irishness more than her Catholicism. On publication in 1856, her work was much criticized, especially because its author was a woman.

Most of the papers collected in this volume are based on a conference held at University College Cork on 22 October 2011. At UCC funding was provided by the School of Asian Studies, the UCC Library, Ionad Bairre – the Teaching Centre at UCC, and the Irish Research Council for Humanities and Social Sciences. Additional financial support came from Boston University, the Ilex Foundation, and the Iran Heritage Foundation. We are grateful to all of these institutions. Much of the organizing work was done at UCC by Mary O'Rourke, and we thank her for her cheerful efficiency. We also thank the editors of *Studies: An Irish Quarterly Review* for permission to reprint David James, "An Irish Visitor to the Court of the Shah of Persia," *Studies* 60, No. 238 (1971): 139–154. Finally, we should like to express our gratitude to Farhad Atai, Christopher Dadian, John McDonald, and Sunil Sharma for their help in the last stage of the preparation of the manuscript.

Part I

Mythology

1

The "Conqueror Worm" in Irish and Persian Literature

Joseph Falaky Nagy

OUR MAIN SOURCE for one of the most famous tales from medieval Irish tradition, the Early Modern Irish text *Tóruigheacht Dhiarmada agus Ghráinne* (*The Pursuit of Diarmaid and Gráinne*, or TDG for short) cannot resist the temptation to sidetrack the reader/listener with stories that delve into the past of the characters and situations that constitute the foreground of the main tale it tells. The earliest version of this text to have survived, preserved in a manuscript written in 1651,[1] is somewhat abbreviated compared to later versions,[2] but the predilection for back-stories is fully on display. The main story of TDG is about Diarmaid ua Duibhne, the "star" of the older hero Fionn mac Cumhaill's war-band, and what happens to him after he is honor-bound by Fionn's young bride Gráinne (the daughter of Cormac, the high-king of Ireland) to elope with her. This overarching narrative serves in effect as a frame-tale, which, in conjunction with the narrative inserts, sometimes approaches the complexity of Sheherazade's storytelling.

One of these story excursions, exemplary of the riches TDG offers the reader,[3] is actually a back-story to a back-story. It is a bizarre account of a monstrous worm, a tale that to my knowledge is told nowhere else in extant Irish literature, although there may be an ironic reference to this creature in a passage from another text, to be considered at the end of this study. The story unfolds as follows:

Fionn, furious about the humiliation of his wife's having left him for the

1. Nessa Ní Shéaghdha, ed. and tr., *Tóruigheacht Dhiarmada agus Ghráinne: The Pursuit of Diarmaid and Gráinne*, Irish Texts Society 48 (Dublin: Published for the Irish Texts Society by the Educational Company of Ireland, 1967).

2. Caoimhín Breatnach, "The Transmission and Text of *Tóruigheacht Dhiarmada agus Ghráinne*: A Re-Appraisal," in Sharon J. Arbuthnot and Geraldine Parsons, eds., *The Gaelic Finn Tradition* (Dublin: Four Courts, 2012), 139–50.

3. Tomás Ó Cathasaigh, "Tóraíocht Dhiarmada agus Ghráinne," in Pádraig Ó Fiannachta, ed., *An Fhiannaíocht*, Léachtaí Cholm Chille 25 (Maynooth: An Sagart, 1995), 45–46.

most valuable member of his team, spends a good deal of the story venge-
fully pursuing the couple himself, but he also sends others forth on what
proves to be a vain quest to kill Diarmaid and return Gráinne to Fionn. For
example, when, coincidentally, two sons of a man who fought on the side
of those who killed Fionn's father come to Fionn asking for reconciliation,
he offers peace to them on the condition that they fetch Diarmaid's head
or a handful of berries from a magical rowan tree guarded by a one-eyed
giant. The heroic pair, having accepted the offer, track down Diarmaid and
in chivalrous fashion introduce themselves to him, declaring their mission.
Diarmaid, responding courteously in kind, explains to the young warriors
that they are between a rock and a hard place. Not only would it be impossible for such relative newcomers to the heroic arena to overcome him, but
they would be incapable of overcoming the obstacles the alternative mission would pose, simple though it may seem. Diarmaid also points out to his
would-be opponents, who have now become his advisees, that this would
not be the first time Fionn has drawn his enemies into what would appear to
those in the know to be a hopeless position. He recounts a similar situation
from the past, back when Diarmaid was still a trusted member of Fionn's
retinue:

A warrior named Conán, the son of the Liath Luachra, yet another enemy of Fionn's father, comes to Fionn seeking reconciliation. The price
dictated, in this case, is for Conán to bring Fionn a head of the multi-headed,
overgrown "worm" (the word used is *cnuimh*, a variant of the more common
cruimh) which dwells in the head of Cían, son of Oilill Ólom. (The latter is said
in earlier texts to have been a king of the southern half of Ireland, but in TDG
he is not specifically so described.) What follows in the text (summarized
below) is Diarmaid's reminiscence of what he learned about the worm and
its remarkable life. Diarmaid does not tell this story-within-a-story-within-
a-story in his own words but those of his fellow hero Oisín, the son of Fionn,
who told it to Conán back then as a warning about how difficult it would be
for him to fulfill Fionn's request:

Approaching a branch full of sloes, the pregnant Sadhbh, Oilill's wife,
is overwhelmed with a craving for the berries. Her husband, traveling together with Sadhbh in a chariot, shakes the branch, and she thus obtains
her fill of the fruit. Later, when their child is born (named Cian), a protuberance appears on his forehead and grows as he matures. Embarrassed by his
deformity, the mature Cian swaddles his head so that the protuberance will
be less noticeable. Cian cruelly slays anyone whom he has asked to shave
him and/or cut his hair, after the unfortunate designated barber undoes
the wrapping on Cian's head and views the unseemly bump. One day, Cian,
seeking revenge on one of Fionn's warriors in the wake of a false report of an

insulting lack of hospitality shown to Cian's servant, invites himself to the warrior's home for a shave and a haircut. Not intimidated by the murderous intent he suspects on the part of his guest, Fionn's man not only removes the covering from Cian's head but, curious to know what lies therein, slashes the exposed bump with his knife. Out jumps a large worm, leaping onto and winding itself tightly around the top of Cian's nearby spear. Reluctant simply to kill the beast (as both his barber and his father propose), Cian asks his mother what should be done, since, as he states, the worm (like Cian himself) came from her belly. Sadhbh confirms Cian's suspicion that the worm may have an intimate connection with the lifespan of its twin-of-sorts, so that to kill it, she says, may be to harm Cian as well. Hence, the family decides to keep the worm in a box and feed it to keep it alive (and Cian safe).

The worm in time grows too big for the box, and so a house is built for it. It grows one hundred voracious heads, each big enough to swallow an armed man. Hearing of this marvel, Cian's foster brother, the son of a king, comes for a visit to view the monster. As he does so, the worm takes note (and takes offense?), savagely tearing off one of the foster brother's legs. Consequently, all the women and lesser members of the household, who presumably had been tending to the creature, flee in panic from the worm's house. This turning-point incident makes it clear to everyone that the creature engendered by Sadhbh's craving has become an unmanageable monster. The insult and injury done to Cian's royal kinsman prove too much even for Cian's mother, who now agrees with her husband and son that the worm must be killed. But how? Adverting to a trick usually played by sundry characters in Celtic storytelling tradition on enemies too fearsome to be confronted directly, Cian's people build a fire under the house of the worm, hoping to burn the monster to death. But defeating their expectations, with a leap even more spectacular than that with which he erupted out of Cian's head, the worm escapes from the flames and lands near a cave. He makes it his lair, one that even Fionn and his men are loath to approach, for fear of the hard-to-kill worm.

Oisín's story (as relayed by Diarmaid) does not dissuade the courageous Conán from accepting Fionn's challenge to confront the worm. He in fact succeeds in killing it, though the feat is only accomplished with Diarmaid's special spear, which the latter graciously loans to Conán. If any weapon could slay the monster, Diarmaid claims, his could.[4]

Whether Diarmaid would have been able to dissuade the brothers from

---

4. The passage I am summarizing from the 1651 version of TDG specifically names the *Ga Dearg* – "Red Spear," elsewhere in TDG said to be Diarmaid's weapon – as the instrument used by Conán to slay the worm, but the necessity of using it is a plot complication supplied in a different version of TDG: see Breatnach, "The Transmission," 40.

pursuing their quest by employing the *exemplum* of Conán (perhaps not the best case to cite, since it ends in success for *that* would-be-hero on a quest) we will never know for certain. His lover Gráinne, overhearing the conversation between Diarmaid and the young seekers, inquires about the rowan tree from which they are supposed to obtain fruit. Once she hears the back-story Diarmaid tells about the tree and its guardian (information the brothers already have, thanks to Oisín), Gráinne, announcing her pregnancy, insists that she must have some of the berries too – a craving that her man must satisfy (as Oilill craved Sadhbh's craving). Hence, the mission to the rowan tree now becomes Diarmaid's task, and the two brothers will in effect have Diarmaid do their work for them. After he slays the tree-guardian, there are plenty of berries for everyone. Diarmaid instructs the brothers, now his veritable protégés, to return to Fionn with the fruit and with the false story that they themselves slew the giant. Diarmaid and Gráinne, meanwhile, take shelter in the top of the tree, where the berries are sweetest. Fionn, upon receiving the berries from the brothers and detecting the scent of Diarmaid on the fruit, discerns that the young men are lying and sets out for the rowan tree himself, bringing the story closer to the pivotal encounter between the betrayed husband and his wife's reluctant lover.

Heretofore hardly noticed, there is a remarkable family resemblance between Cian's *cruimh*, at the center of a story unattested elsewhere in the pre-modern Irish literary record, and Haftvād's luck-bringing *kerm* 'worm' (the Persian and English words are cognate with the Irish) featured in the tenth-century Persian epic *Shāhnāmeh* ("the Book of Kings") by Abolqāsem Ferdowsi,[5] as well as in other early Persian sources.[6] Whether this correspondence reflects the parallel development of an inherited Indo-European story pattern or the "oikotypification" (local adaptation) in Persian and Irish tradition of a more widespread narrative complex is a question that will not be pursued here. I do, however, intend to show that whatever their relationship, aligning our reading of the two stories in the spirit of the other comparative studies in this volume brings out shared key elements that we would miss if each tale were examined in isolation.[7]

---

5. Dick Davis's translation of the story as preserved in Ferdowsi's text is my source: Dick Davis, trans., *Shahnameh: The Persian Book of Kings* (New York: Viking, 2006), 544–53. I gratefully acknowledge Elizabeth Thornton, a fellow teacher in the GE 30 "Never-ending Stories" UCLA cluster course, for having introduced me to the story of Haftvād in her lectures to the class on Persian mythology.

6. *Encyclopaedia Iranica*, s.v. "Haftvād" (by A. Shapur Shahbazi).

7. Back in 1941, the folklorist Alexander H. Krappe noted the similarity among the ominously growing worms or snake-like creatures featured in the Irish story, the Persian legend, a Scandinavian analog (discussed below), and other traditional stories, in "Sur un épisode de la

What follows is a summary of Ferdowsi's account of the Irish inverte-brate's less nasty but equally troublesome distant cousin.

The daughter of an insignificant poor man named Haftvād ('Having Seven Sons') finds a worm in an apple she had started to eat at the beginning of the task of spinning her daily portion of cotton. Cinderella-like in her being overlooked by her parent, who is interested only in his sons after whom he is named, the girl calls upon the worm as her good-luck charm to enable her to spin as well and as much cotton as possible. Her wish is granted, and, keeping the worm in her spindle case and feeding it daily with pieces of the apple, the unnamed girl becomes a one-person source of wealth for her parents and brothers. With the riches provided to him by his daughter's industry and the worm's *bakht* ('good fortune'), Haftvād buys himself an army, builds an impregnable fortress on a mountain-top, and along with his sons even challenges the rule of the king of Iran, Ardeshir. Meanwhile, while the girl remains the creature's chief guardian, Haftvād makes sure that the worm, which has grown as big as an elephant, is fed, well cared for, and protected in the fort on high.

Ardeshir, thwarted in his military attempts to suppress this grave threat to his sovereignty, decides to resort to trickery, knowing that Haftvād's success is intimately connected to the worm. Disguised as merchants, he and a select band of his men enter the mountain fastness and ply the attendants of the worm with wine, until they fall asleep. Then the invaders melt lead, feed the worm with the molten metal, and thus kill it. With the death of the monster, Haftvād's fortune and royal ambitions collapse, and Ardeshir goes on to enjoy a long and successful reign.

One scholar has described the Persian story as a cross between two international folktale-types, namely, "The Dragon Slayer" (ATU 300) and a story pattern most famously exemplified by "Rumpelstilskin" (ATU 300),[8] wherein the discreet enabler of a woman's exceptional productivity as a spinner turns into a serious nuisance.[9] In both the Irish tale and in Ferdowsi's account, there is certainly a dragon-like creature: specifically, a worm

Saga de Ragnar Lodbrók," *Acta Scandinavica Philologica* 15 (1941): 326–38. But Krappe, interested primarily in identifying an international motif, did not discuss the possible relevance of these monstrous beings to the thematic frameworks of the stories where he found them.

8. Hans-Jörg Uther, *The Types of International Folktales: A Classification and Bibliography, Based on the System of Antti Aarne and Stith Thompson*, 3 vols, Folklore Fellows Communications 284–86 (Helsinki: Suomalainen Tiedeakatemia, Academia Scientiarum Fennica, 2004), 1: 174–76, 285–86.

9. Kinga Ilona Márkus-Takeshita, "From Iranian Myth to Folk Narrative: The Legend of the Dragon-Slayer and the Spinning Maiden in the Persian Book of the Kings," *Asian Folklore Studies* 60 (2001): 203–14.

Ardeshir feeds molten lead to the worm. Page from fifteenth-century manuscript of the *Shāhnāmeh*. Los Angeles County Museum of Art.

that grows monstrously large and ultimately needs to be killed. There is, however, no "magic spinner" in the TDG episode comparable to Haftvād's daughter. Nevertheless, woman's work is highlighted in the Irish tale, as the activity or condition by which a sinister element slips into the social realm, but it is a more biological than cultural aspect of female life, and the "little" woman behind the "big" worm is a wife and mother instead of a daughter. Sadhbh, the pregnant queen with a craving for sloes, unwittingly plays host to the *cruimh* that finds its way into her womb, a receptacle far more private than the girl's spindle case into which the *kerm* is welcomed. Later, concerned about the possible threat to her son's life, Sadhbh protects the invasive worm from being killed after it is gruesomely released from its next incubation, in her son's head. For Sadhbh to make sure that the increasingly threatening worm stays alive and comfortable is for her to overplay her maternal role. In guarding Cian, her child, against possible harm, she seeks to assure an outcome perhaps less ambitious but still akin to the prosperous future that Haftvād's daughter, in conjunction with *her* worm, seeks to obtain for her father and her family.

A comparison of the two tales shows other important shared themes. It is the main female character in each case who plans and makes the decision leading to the strange situation of the creature's being solicitously pampered. Insulated from harm, the worm, almost a parody of a spoiled child or potentate, grows in size – but in neither case does it grow in intelligence or cunning. On the one hand, the Irish worm shows just how viciously mindless it is when it lashes out at his "twin's" kinsman, whom the worm, if it could think, might almost view as *its own* foster brother. The *cruimh* does, however, possess enough sense to leap out of the fort in which his former guardians hope to burn him to death. On the other hand, Haftvād's worm lacks even the sense to suspect or resist Ardeshir's feeding it molten metal. Cunning monsters these are not.

And yet, in each story the worm undeniably "turns," as the saying goes.[10] However lowly and insignificant the creature and its secret sharers are when they enter the story (with Cian still anonymously in the womb, and Haftvād mired in poverty), they ultimately achieve a dizzying level of success and control that, unfortunately, exposes the worms' beneficiaries to the irresistible temptation to exploit their circumstances and resort to tyranny. The commoner Haftvād does not simply enjoy the untold wealth the worm provides but, overstepping his bounds, uses it to fund subversive dreams of

10. Wolfgang Mieder, Stewart A. Kingsbury and Kelsie B. Hardered, eds., *A Dictionary of American Proverbs* (New York: Oxford University Press, 1992), 679. Even a worm turns (when stepped on, for example) and can offer resistance.

conquest and empire. And, given the traditional Irish requirement that a king be without physical blemish, Cian, the "host" whose appearance is disfigured by the parasite lurking within his head, has no more right to aspire to sovereignty than does Haftvād. Nevertheless, he turns his defect into an excuse to behave like an unjust monarch, imagining insult where it does not exist, abusing the principles of hospitality, and being the terror of those he designates as his barbers.

The tyrannical rise of the worm and its human counterpart poses an untenable challenge to the *status quo* that neither the narrative traditions to which our stories respectively belong, nor the ideological structures that provide their underpinnings, can tolerate. To put it in the terms actually used in the *Shāhnāmeh* episode, the rightful king Ardeshir comes close to being nearly defeated by the upstart Haftvād because a person's arbitrary *bakht* 'good luck' nearly negates a king's inherited *farr*, a royal attribute that is supposed not only to secure the throne for him but to guarantee the proper ordering of the world and its inhabitants in general.[11] In Irish terms, it is the worm's attack on Cian's foster brother that makes the situation intolerable, tearing as it does at the very fabric holding society together. Not only is the mutilation an outrage against the social institution of fosterage but an assault on the symbolism of the sovereign body – for it is not just any foster brother but a royal one whose leg the worm lops off.

The violent responses these actions elicit from the (successful or would-be) "dragon-slayers" in these stories are amply justified. Yet they are faintly redolent of the same subversiveness the worms-to-be-slain represent. This paradox of the dragon-slayer's coming to resemble the dragon is hardly unusual in stories of heroic endeavor, but there is a particular irony to the "fighting fire with fire" strategies employed in our two tales. Ardeshir as much as admits that his disguising himself as a merchant in order to gain access to the worm and kill it is hardly the standard royal-heroic way to counter so grave a threat. Even though he is not the first hero in the *Shāhnāmeh* to resort to this ploy, the king's deciding to disguise himself as a merchant accompanied by two mysterious (supernatural?) helpers who come to his aid at the nadir of his reign, is awkward, to say the least. The embarrassment is compounded by the disguised king's slyly emphasizing to the guardians of the worm that he has come to pay homage to the creature to whom he owes his own good fortune, and from whom he hopes to obtain more.

Unwilling to confront Cian's mega-worm directly, the would-be dragon-slayers in TDG resort to a trick usually associated with craven villainy in Celtic (and Scandinavian) storytelling tradition: they set the house in which the worm dwells on fire. This structure, which already exists before the Mun-

---

11. Márkus-Takeshita, "From Iranian Myth to Folk Narrative": 206, 212.

stermen decide to destroy its chief occupant, is not built with this purpose in mind, but it still evokes the motif of the "iron house," the construction of which, grimly perverting the guest-host relationship, creates an oven of sorts for the unwitting guests whom the builders invite.[12] And, while Cian's killing of the worm can be characterized as "clean," there is the conspicuous complication of another hero's weapon being needed by the monster-slayer to do the deed. Furthermore, given the guile underlying Fionn's offer to Conán and the double choice he sets before the two sons of Fionn's father's enemy, not to mention Fionn's deceptive behavior toward Diarmaid in fateful interactions yet to come in TDG, there is no lack of treachery in the narrative frame housing the story of the killing of the worm.

The later royal career of Ardeshir shows no sign of any negative aftereffects of his encounter with the worm or lingering damage done to his reputation by the ruse to which he resorts in order to kill it. As for Conán, however, there is a curious tradition preserved in an earlier Irish text that both affirms and diverges from his story as told in TDG. The *Acallam na Senórach*, a thirteenth-century composition that dwarfs the later TDG in both its size and its willingness to take on additional narrative baggage, introduces Conán as an enemy of Fionn's who wishes to be at peace with him. No surprise so far, but in this account he resorts to trickery to obtain what he wants, capturing Fionn from behind when he is alone and forcing him to come to terms. As his gift upon being accepted in Fionn's company, Conán requests and receives a fort hidden by the surrounding mountains – an impregnable shelter for a man who has made many enemies, like the home in which Haftvād and his worm dwell. There is, however, no monstrous vermin to be slain in Conán's secure dwelling, and yet an even deadlier worm waits to "attack" Conán there and bring the hero's life to an embarrassing end. Caílte mac Rónáin, the main storyteller of the *Acallam*, declares, as perhaps the most outstanding detail in Conán's dossier, that he was one of only four men in Finn's band of warriors who died in bed (in his fortress), on account of a poisonous worm that somehow penetrated his head and killed him within a day (*cruimh neime do ghabh 'na chin ⁊ fuair bás ón trath co araili*).[13] Thus perhaps the worm, or a second-generation worm on behalf of its kind, has its revenge after all, at least according to the Irish member of what I have treated as a pair of narrative multiforms.

12. On this motif, and possibly analogous instances of house-burnings in Norse tradition, see Patrick Sims-Williams, *Irish Influence on Medieval Welsh Literature* (New York: Oxford University Press, 2011), 262–77. The author does not include this particular story in his survey.

13. Whitley Stokes, ed., *Acallamh na Senórach*, in Whitley Stokes and Ernst Windisch, eds., *Irische Texte: Mit Übersetzungen und Wörterbuch*, Vierte Serie. 1. Heft (Leipzig: Hirzel, 1900), 101–02.

We may be able to infer that the "worm *redux*" motif is not unique to the Irish oikotype of this story pattern from the outcome of the story of Ragnarr Loðbrók,[14] a Danish king of the Viking era whose legendary dragon-slaying was already being compared by a scholar in the nineteenth century to that of Ardeshir.[15] Ragnarr embarks on his heroic and royal career by slaying a snake (or a pair of snakes) grown monstrously large under the care of a chieftain's daughter, who subsequently becomes his first wife. Here too, the prosperity of the "pet" owner is intimately connected with the continued life and growth of the creature. When it is given to the girl by her father as a pretty gift, she places it on top of some gold in a box. The pile of precious metal mystically grows along with the snake, even after the latter no longer fits in the box or even the girl's private quarters. As in the Persian and Irish analogs, cleverness and concealment are required in the encounter with this pet-turned-monster: Ragnarr invents a way to make his clothes resistant to the flood of venomous blood that erupts after he kills the snake.

Many years after his youthful triumph, Ragnarr encounters more serpentine nemeses, at the end of his career. He is thrown by an enemy into a snake-pit, where he dies after his magical talisman-shirt is taken away from him. The irony is perhaps not lost on Ragnarr himself: "My bane I did not expect from a worm / But fate is oft not the thing we thought."[16] The shadow of the worm, moreover, resurfaces among the next generation of characters in the Ragnarr legend, in the peculiar physical characteristics of two of his sons by his second wife, Áslaug, the daughter of Sigurðr, the greatest dragon-slayer in Norse tradition: the one is "boneless," and the other has a serpent-shape in his eye.[17]

In Ferdowsi's chronicle, no wormlike creature appears later on in Ardeshir's life, but, in the opposite chronological direction, one of the most notorious of Ardeshir's predecessors, the tyrannical Zahhāk, out of whose

14. On the legend of Ragnarr and its multiforms, see Rory McTurk, *Studies in* Ragnars Saga Loðbrókar *and its Major Scandinavian Analogues*, Medium Aevum Monographs, New Series, 15 (Oxford: Society for the Study of Mediaeval Languages and Literature, 1991) and Elisabeth Ashman Rowe, *Vikings in the West: The Legend of Ragnarr Loðbrók and His Sons*, Studia Medievalia Septentrionalia 18 (Vienna: Fassbaender, 2012).

15. Felix Liebrecht, "Die Ragnar Lodbroksage in Persien," *Orient und Occident* 1 (1862): 561–67; Márkus-Takeshita, "From Iranian Myth to Folk Narrative": 213 n4.

16. From the thirteenth-century Icelandic saga *Ragnars saga loðbrókar*, in Margaret Schlauch, tr., *The Saga of the Volsungs, The Saga of Ragnar Lodbrok, together with The Lay of Kraka* (New York: The American-Scandinavian Foundation, W.W. Norton & Company, 1930), 239.

17. See Carolyne Larrington, "Þóra and Áslaug in *Ragnars saga loðbrókar*: Women, Dragons and Destiny," in Martin Arnold and Alison Finlay, eds., *Making History: Essays on the Fornaldarsögur* (London: Viking Society for Northern Research, 2011), 60–65.

shoulders serpents grew, which he fed on human brains,[18] clearly anticipates the would-be usurper Haftvād and his worm. And so, in light of Conán's worm-ridden postlude as noted in the *Acallam*, and the afterlife of the serpent theme in the Ragnarr legend, we may well ask: did any epigones of Zahhāk or Haftvād insinuate their way into the line of Ardeshir's successors? Even the mere possibility of such slithery irruptions profoundly disturbs the "motley drama" of life, as we have seen, and as the angels viewing the show of human "mimes" discover, in an allegorical poem by Edgar Allan Poe from which this contribution borrows its title:

> ... But see, amid the mimic rout,
> A crawling shape intrude!
> A blood-red thing that writhes from out
> The scenic solitude!
> It writhes! – it writhes! – with mortal pangs
> The mimes become its food,
> And seraphs sob at vermin fangs
> In human gore imbued.
>
> Out – out are the lights – out all!
> And over each quivering form,
> The curtain, a funeral pall,
> Comes down with the rush of a storm,
> While the angels, all pallid and wan,
> Uprising, unveiling, affirm
> That the play is the tragedy, "Man,"
> And its hero the Conqueror Worm.[19]

18. M. Rahim Shayegan, *Aspects of History and Epic in Ancient Iran: From Gaumāta to Wahnām*, Hellenic Studies 52 (Washington, DC: Center for Hellenic Studies, 2012), 139–55.

19. "The Conqueror Worm," Edgar Allen Poe, *Collected Works. Volume 1: Poems*, ed. T. O. Mabbott (Cambridge MA: Belknap Press of Harvard University Press, 1969), 325–26.

2

Building Bulls and Crafting Cows:

Narratives of Bovine Fabrication from Iran, Ireland, and In-between

John McDonald

IT GOES WITHOUT SAYING that the cow played and to some extent still plays a significant role in both the practical and the artistic domains of Iranian society and of Irish society.[1] When it comes to Iranian literature, the cow is literally definitive: according to a passage of the *Zādspram*, Ohrmazd created a large (*wuzurg*), presumably fantastically large ox whose task it was to designate with its hoof the border between Iran and Turan, and to reiterate the frontier every time a dispute arose.[2] The medieval Irish literary corpus does not provide a patently compatible narrative, but perhaps a similarly fundamental link between cow and country can be said to be at work in the conclusive clash of the bulls in *Táin Bó Cúailnge*, a text that is just one representative, however preeminent, of an entire genre consisting of cattle raids in name and in content alike.[3] The result of this taurine tussle is that the Donn, who has slaughtered the Findbennach and sports on his horns his rival's remnants, proceeds to roam about Ireland, depositing here and there a gobbet of the Findbennach's mutilated carcass, and it is

1. Although this chapter is concerned with portrayals of cows in pre-modern and mostly verbal art, I am loath to deny at least passing mention of the astonishing representation of the Iranian admiration for this animal in the form of the intense attachment that Masht Hasan, the tragic hero of Dariush Mehrjui's influential film *Gāv*, displays toward his extraordinarily beloved bovine.

2. Philippe Gignoux and Ahmad Tafazzoli, ed. and trans., *Anthologie de Zādspram: Édition critique du texte pehlevi* (Paris: Association pour l'avancement des études iraniennes, 1993), 58–59; Edward West, trans., *Pahlavi Texts*, vol. 5 (Oxford: Clarendon Press, 1897), 135–38. The narrative is also more briefly related in the *Dēnkard*. See Marijan Molé, *La légende de Zoroastre selon les textes pehlevis* (Paris: Klincksieck, 1967), 24–27; E. West, *Pahlavi Texts*, vol. 5, 32–33.

3. The first member of the phrase *táin bó* "cattle raid" is the verbal noun of the compound verb *do-aig* "drive off, away," the cognates of the root of which express the action of rustling cows in other Indo-European languages as well. See Ranko Matasović, *A Theory of Textual Reconstruction in Indo-European Linguistics* (New York: Peter Lang, 1996), 79–80.

with reference to these somatic segments that the Irish name the various locations at which they are abandoned.[4]

Of course any community that is considerably invested in cattle is bound to steer their storytelling in the direction of bovine topics, but ethno-linguistic groups owing something to Indo-European heritage exhibit particular correspondences when it comes to vocabulary, narrative, ritual praxis, semiotic conventions, and conceptual ideology concerning cows. Such correspondences are most extensively and in some cases exclusively exhibited by Indo-Iranian, Greek, and Celtic cultures. A case in point is the association of cows with the dawn and sun, which is articulated to one degree or another by various cultures of Indo-European ancestry, but most thoroughly elaborated in Indo-Iranian, Greek, and Celtic.[5] This general association is reinforced by a number of specific details. So, for example, treatments of the dawn cows consistently characterize them as being lactiferous. Calvert Watkins confirmed the traditional status of this tendency when he established an etymological match between Vedic and Irish, both of which are exercising the same hereditary metaphor in referring to the milk of the matutinal cows by means of one of the Indo-European words for water (Vedic *vā́r*, Irish *fír* < IE *$\ast\underset{\scriptscriptstyle\sim}{u}eh_1r$-).[6]

In this chapter I pursue a different, although sometimes intersecting category of bovine lore located in these same three traditions.[7] The narratives in question feature the fabrication of cows.[8]

4. Bruce Lincoln perceives in this episode of toponymic aetiology an attenuated bovine cosmogony, and so rather relates it to an event in another Pahlavi text; see Bruce Lincoln, *Priests, Warriors and Cattle: A Study in the Ecology of Religions* (Berkeley: University of California Press, 1981), 87–90. For a Celticist's favorable assessment of Lincoln's interpretation see Tomás Ó Cathasaigh, "Mythology in *Táin Bó Cúailnge*," in Hildegard Tristram, ed., *Studien zur Táin Bó Cúailnge* (Tübingen: Gunter Narr Verlag, 1993), 121–22.

5. Many studies have treated this topic. I recommend Deborah Boedeker, *Aphrodite's Entry into Greek Epic* (Leiden: Brill, 1974), 59–61; Enrico Campanile, *La ricostruzione della cultura indoeuropea* (Pisa: Giardini, 1990), 130–38; Douglas Frame, *The Myth of Return in Early Greek Epic* (New Haven: Yale University Press, 1978), 44–47, 56; Michael Janda, *Eleusis: das indogermanische Erbe der Mysterien* (Innsbruck: Institut für Sprachen und Literaturen der Universität Innsbruck, 2000), 214–15; David Sick, "Mit(h)ra(s) and the Myths of the Sun," *Numen* 51 (2004): *passim*, especially 437–44; Calvert Watkins, "The Milk of the Dawn Cows Revisited," in Kazuhiko Yoshida and Brent Vine, eds., *East and West: Papers in Indo-European Studies* (Bremen: Hempen, 2009); and Martin West, *Indo-European Poetry and Myth* (Oxford: Oxford University Press, 2007), 218, 223–24.

6. For his most recent treatment of this topic see Watkins, "The Milk of the Dawn Cows Revisited," 225–26, 230–31. The metaphor is synchronically defunct in Irish, where *fír* means only milk, but the language remains marked, since the word occurs in this context alone.

7. What I mean by intersecting is that the narratives to be investigated in this chapter sometimes contain solar or auroral elements, which I shall indicate in footnotes at the appropriate junctures.

8. In this study I limit myself to data from traditions of Indo-European heritage, but I am

Fabricated Bovines from Iran

Let us begin with one of the most famous, albeit enigmatic cows of Iranian literature: *the* Cow, whose importance is often conveyed by a majuscule, of the *Avesta*. This Cow is described on several occasions as having been composed by a character called Gə̄uš Tašan, whose appellation means none other than "the Cow's Craftsman."[9] The deed is most memorably referenced in the initial stanza of *Yasna* 29. Here the *gə̄uš uruuā*, which we can content ourselves for present purposes with translating as "soul of the Cow,"[10] complains to her creator that she is being abused by a group of inimical individuals, and poses the questions: *kahmāi mā θβarōždum kə̄ mā tašat* "For whom did you craft me? Who fashioned me?"[11] As Stephanie Jamison observes, these queries, as well as other statements referring to the same act of bovine craftsmanship, are among the mere handful of past-tense passages in the *Gāthās*, which otherwise concern themselves with matters present and future.[12] We might say that the grammatical anteriority of these utterances is indicative of their relative antiquity.

In fact what we have here is a demonstrably Indo-Iranian scenario: the *Ṛg Veda*, the *Avesta*'s most proximate textual relative, contains two comparanda to Gə̄uš Tašan's act of fabrication. The agents in this case are the Ṛbhus, a triad of prodigious artisans. Among their various creative feats, the

---

all the while aware that a broader scope might provide further relevant material. To mention just one instance of bovine craftsmanship in an extra-Indo-European literary tradition: in the Finno-Karelian *Kalevala*, the smith Ilmarinen, as one of a series of lackluster efforts building up to the invention of his *chef d'œuvre*, the mysterious *sampo*, fabricates several defective items, including a heifer, on account of the impudence of which he therefore smashes and tosses it back into the forge as fuel for his next endeavor. See Francis Magoun, trans., *The Kalevala, or Poems from the Kalevala District* (Cambridge, MA: Harvard University Press, 1963), 60. However, I would point out that certain elements of the *Kalevala* appear to have been adopted from the mythological traditions of various neighboring Indo-European cultures. A case in point is the *sampo* itself, long thought to be linguistically and conceptually related to Sanskrit *skambha* "(cosmic) pillar." See József Erdődi, "Finnische *sampo*, Ai. *skambha*," *Indogermanische Forschungen* 3 (1932): 214–19.

9. On the identity of this individual see Jean Kellens, "Qui est Gə̄uš Tašan?," in B. G. Fragner, C. Fragner, G. Gnoli, R. Haag-Higuchi, M. Maggi and P. Orsatti, eds., *Proceedings of the Second European Conference of Iranian Studies* (Rome: Istituto Italiano per il Medio ed Estremo Oriente, 1995), 347–57.

10. For a discussion of this phrase and its significance see Helmut Humbach, Josef Elfenbein, and Prods Oktor Skjærvø, ed. and trans., *The Gāthās of Zarathushtra, and the Other Old Avestan Texts*, vol. 2 (Heidelberg: Winter, 1991), 29–30.

11. Compare the similar statements at *Yasna* 12.7, 37.1, 44.6, 47.3, and 51.7.

12. Stephanie Jamison, *The Rig Veda between Two Worlds* (Paris: Collège de France, 2007), 36–37.

Ṛbhus *tákṣan dhenúṃ* "fashioned a milch cow."[13] The validity of the notion that we are in the midst of the Vedic equivalent of Gāuš Tašan's activity is bolstered by a linguistic correspondence: the verb that routinely describes the Ṛbhus's execution of their bovine accomplishment is *takṣ-*, which is the Sanskrit cognate of Avestan *taš-*, the verb of the second question that the Cow asks Gāuš Tašan. Furthermore, the second member of the designation Gāuš Tašan is a nominal derivative of this same verbal root.

The second Vedic correlate to our Avestan situation is contained in the verses that describe the creation of a variety of items, including a cow, by a group of deities headed by the divine craftsman Tvaṣṭṛ, who is synchronically portrayed as being in rivalry with the Ṛbhus, but who to a certain extent functionally overlaps with them.[14] In this instance we should look to the verb of the first question with which the Cow interrogates Gāuš Tašan, because both Tvaṣṭṛ's name and the Avestan form *θβarōždum* are derived from another Indo-European verbal root meaning "fashion." Ahura Mazdā, moreover, refers to the Cow's creator as a *θβōrəštā* "fashioner,"[15] which form is *mutatis mutandis* equivalent to the Vedic theonym Tvaṣṭṛ. The *Ṛg Veda* thus appears to distribute over two distinct but isofunctional narratives the same verbal elements that *Yasna* 29 serially combines, suggesting that we are dealing with reflexes of a common Indo-Iranian narrative of bovine artistry, in which the description of the principal action alternately or jointly employs the verbal roots **tetk̂-* (> Avestan *tašat̰*, Tašan; Vedic *takṣan*), and **tu̯erk̂-* (> Avestan *θβarōždum*, *θβōrəštā*; Vedic Tvaṣṭṛ).

Accounts of bovine craftsmanship also occur in Middle and Classical Persian literature. When it comes to the former, our text is the *Bundahišn*, several episodes of which reflect traditions of Indo-European provenance. In one such episode, numerous plants and animals are generated from the slaughter of the primordial ox Ewagdād (Avestan *gāv- aēvō.dātā-*), an event that appears to be founded on an inherited narrative, given that primeval bovines have a creative role to play in several cosmogonies informed by the Indo-European mythico-religious repertoire.[16] So we should not be astonished to find hereditary bovine lore at work elsewhere in this same text.

The passage of the *Bundahišn* that interests us is that which recounts

13. *Ṛg Veda* 1.20.3c. Compare the similar statements at *Ṛg Veda* 1.110.8, 1.111.1, 4.34.9, and the anticipation of the deed at 1.161.3. The correspondence is recognized by Humbach et al.; see *The Gāthās of Zarathushtra*, vol. 2, 31.

14. *Ṛg Veda* 10.65.10–11. In fact Tvaṣṭṛ is referred to as an Ṛbhu in this very passage.

15. *Yasna* 29.6.

16. Lincoln, *Priests*, 72–73. It is this same apparently Indo-European tradition of bovine cosmogony that Lincoln argues informs the aftermath of the battle of the bulls in *Táin Bó Cúailnge* as mentioned in footnote 4.

the unsuccessful machinations of a figure whose name is generally rendered Nō(k)targā.[17] Due to the inherent ambiguities that plague the Pahlavi script, notoriously difficult to interpret on account of the numerous possible phonetic values that a single character can be used to convey, it is impossible to determine the true composition of this personage's onomastic identity. The situation is so bad in this particular instance that in the most recent edition of the *Bundahišn*, the individual in question appears as Wadīrgā![18] For simplicity's sake, I chose Nō(k)targā, which is the one most often employed in scholarly discussions of this figure.

Georges Dumézil describes the Nōktargā episode as "complexe, obscur en plus d'un point, mais clair sur celui qui nous importe."[19] The same can be said for what we expect to accomplish with it. To summarize the immediately pertinent events: the *xwarrah* (Avestan *x*ʸ*arənah*, Modern Persian *farr*), that complicated entity whose presence legitimizes the sovereignty of Iranian rulers, departs from Frēdōn and conceals itself at the base of a reed growing in the body of water Frāxkard (Avestan Vouru.kaša). Nōktargā wants to transfer the *xwarrah* into his sons, and in order to do so, he uses sorcery to perform some sort of creative act involving a cow. The reason I speak of this deed in such a roundabout way is that the Pahlavi rendering again allows for more than one interpretation of what is being communicated: Nōktargā either concocts a cow for the purpose of tillage (*warzīdan*), or he transforms a cow into a goat (*buz dād*).[20] That being said, in either case we have a creative process involving a cow, even if we should choose to understand her as being the starting point rather than the end product. And even then the cow, whether or not she has been mutated into a nanny goat, continues to be referred to as a cow as the narrative progresses, so that we are still in the realm of an act of primarily, if not entirely bovine fabrication.[21]

17. Behramgore Tehmuras Anklesaria, ed. and trans., *Zand-Ākāsīh: Iranian or Greater Bundahišn*. (Bombay: Rahnumae Mazdayasnan Sabha, 1956), 298–99; Fazlollah, Pakzad, ed., *Bundahišn: Zoroastrische Kosmogonie und Kosmologie* (Tehran: Centre for the Great Islamic Encyclopedia, 2005), 399; E. West, *Pahlavi Texts*, vol. 1 (1880), 138–39.

18. Pakzad, *Bundahišn*, 399. Justi already similarly understood this name to be Wītirsā. Ferdinand Justi, *Iranisches Namenbuch* (Marburg: Elwert, 1895), 373.

19. Georges Dumézil, *Mythe et épopée*, vol. 2 (Paris: Gallimard, 1971), 220.

20. Pakzad, *Bundahišn*, 399 fn255, assesses both readings as being reasonable.

21. See also Dumézil, *Mythe et épopée*, vol. 2, 327 fn2 and Andrew Welburn, *From a Virgin Womb: The Apocalypse of Adam and the Virgin Birth* (Leiden: Brill, 2008), 125–26, 202–03; both note the similar sequence of the *xwarrah* entering a botanical host, cows consuming the latter, and a woman consuming the cows' milk in the *Dēnkard*'s narrative of Zoroaster's conception (Molé, *La légende de Zoroastre selon les textes pehlevis*, 20–33; E. West, *Pahlavi Texts*, vol. 5, 25–28). Furthermore, the final segment of Nōktargā's name, as well as that of the names of numerous other characters at this stage of the *Bundahišn*'s narrative, is apparently the Iranian cow word. See *Encyclopaedia Iranica*, s.v. "Barmāya" (by Djalal Khaleghi-Motlagh) and s.v. "Ferēdūn," (by

In any event Nōktargā conducts his cow, superficially caprine or otherwise, to the patch of reeds including the one containing Frēdōn's *xwarrah*, and feeds the reeds to her, so that the cow eventually ingests and absorbs the *xwarrah*. Nōktargā then milks the cow and feeds the milk to his children. His scheme, however, does not turn out as planned. The *xwarrah* refuses to enter his sons, whom it apparently considers unworthy recipients. Instead, it comes to reside inside his daughter, the precise shape of whose name is again not totally certain, but which is probably Farānak, or something very close to this.[22]

This last turn of events is one of the factors that motivates Dumézil's interest in the episode, since in Farānak's reception of the *xwarrah* we appear to have an Iranian reflex of the association of legitimate sovereignty with specifically female figures that occurs more fully developed in Indic and Celtic.[23] Dumézil's observation is very significant for our topic, and we shall return to it in due order.

For the moment, however, let us turn to our Classical Persian comparandum: the *gorz-e gāv-sar* 'cow-headed mace' that Ferdowsi tells us Faridun commissions in preparation for his combat with the malevolent monarch Żaḥḥāk.[24] That the *gorz* represents a meaningful combination of cow and craftsmanship is indicated by the fact that a cow and a craftsman are hovering about at the very point in the narrative at which its construction takes place. The cow in question is the spectacular specimen Barmāye, on whose milk the infant Faridun is nursed by his mother Farānak.[25] It is after Farānak

---

Ahmad Tafazzoli). However if we are indeed dealing with a shift from cow to goat, we might rather compare Polyphemus's goats and sheep in *Odyssey* 9. As Boedeker (*Aphrodite's Entry*, 60 fn1, 90–91) and Frame (*The Myth of Return*, 66–69) have demonstrated, the composition and significance of the Cyclops episode is informed by the mythological dossier of the Indo-European auroral-solar cows.

22. Infuriated by the failure of his project, Nōktargā desires to harm Farānak, but she secures safety for herself by dedicating her prospective first-born son to the divinity Ōšbām, whose name is the Middle Persian word for dawn. On the apparent antiquity of the formation of this word see M. West, *Indo-European Poetry*, 219. On the hereditary status of the cow as the appropriate animal for extracting the *xwarrah* from its aquatic refuge see Appendix A of this chapter.

23. Dumézil, *Mythe et épopée*, vol. 2, 326–27, 350–51.

24. Djalal Khaleghi-Motlagh, ed. *Shāhnāmah*, vol. 1 (New York: Bibliotheca Persica, 1988), 71. For actual artefacts with the *gorz* as their model see Prudence Harper, "The Ox-headed Mace in Pre-Islamic Iran," *Acta Iranica* 24 (1985): 247–59.

25. Khaleghi-Motlagh, *Shāhnāmah*, vol. 1, 63. For the incorporation of the bovine associated with Faridun into the tradition of auroral-solar cattle, see the turquoise saddled and bridled bull with rising suns on its sides described by A. S. Melikian-Chirvani, "The Wine-Bull and the Magian Master," in *Recurrent Patterns in Iranian Religions: From Mazdaism to Sufism*, ed. Philippe Gignoux (Paris: Association pour l'avencement des études iraniennes, 1992), 120.

has disclosed Ẓaḥḥāk's slaughter of Barmāye that her son resolves to design the *gorz* and to meet his ophidian opponent with this weapon in hand,[26] so that it is difficult to avoid the impression of some sort of relationship between Barmāyeh and the bovine morphology that Faridun requires of this apparatus.[27]

As for the craftsman, in addition to the anonymous artisans that Ferdowsi describes as fashioning the *gorz*, the blacksmith Kāveh has also just arrived on the scene,[28] and in fact in other versions of the *Shāhnāmeh* tradition, it is Kāveh himself who crafts this tool.[29] Such variants convey the inherited state of affairs, since Kāvya Uśanā, Kāveh's Vedic onomastic and functional relative, is one of the creators of the *vajra*, which is the *gorz*'s Indic etymological and functional equivalent.[30]

Furthermore, the Nōktargā episode also indicates that Faridun's *gorz* is more than incidentally boomorphic. Recall that the *xwarrah* consumed by Nōktargā's constructed cow was previously possessed by Frēdōn, who is of course none other than Faridun's Middle Persian correlate.[31] Recollect, moreover, that the name of the daughter of Nōktargā whom Frēdōn's *xwarrah* enters via the cow's milk is Farānak, or something quite close to that, and that according to Ferdowsi, Farānak is also the name of Faridun's moth-

---

26. Khaleghi-Motlagh, *Shāhnāmah*, vol. 1, 65–66.

27. Zirak's prophecy implies such a connection, see ibid., 61, lines 101–02. According to the recitation of a *naggāle-xān* quoted and discussed by Daryaee (Touraj Daryaee, "Kāve the Black-Smith: An Indo-Iranian Fashioner?," *Studien zur Indologie und Iranistik* 22 [2001]: 13) it takes two years to complete the construction of the *gorz*; the Ṛbhus similarly spend a year crafting their cow (*Ṛg Veda* 4.33.4). The *gorz*' biological correlate Barmāye might also be said to resemble the Ṛbhus's cow to the extent that she is impressively motley and so compared to a peacock (Khaleghi-Motlagh, *Shāhnāmah*, vol. 1, 62 line 115 and 65 line 169); the Ṛbhus's cow is *viśvárūpām* "omnicoloured" (4.33.8b).

28. Khaleghi-Motlagh, *Shāhnāmah*, vol. 1, 69.

29. For the text and discussion thereof see Daryaee, "Kāve the Black-Smith": 13.

30. Olga Davidson, *Poet and Hero in the Persian Book of Kings*, 3rd edition (Boston: Ilex Foundation, distributed by Harvard University Press, 2013), 80–81. The *vajra* is never described as boviform, but remember that Tvaṣṭṛ, to whom the *Ṛg Veda* alternately assigns the construction of this weapon (1.32.2, 5.31.4), also creates a cow. We might also want to consider *Ṛg Veda* 1.55.1, in which Indra sharpens the *vajra* as a bull (viz. its horns).

31. While this Frēdōn brushes up against a narrative of bovine craftsmanship and Faridun is directly involved in one, the Vedic congener of these characters, Trita, is on the one hand likened to a craftsman (*Ṛg Veda* 5.9.5) and on the other releases imprisoned cows, and his equivalent in Classical Indian literature, who is a carpenter, does the same. On the common onomastic ancestor shared by all of these figures see Lincoln, *Priests*, 104–32. Another reflex of the same precursor is the Pahlavi hero Srīd, who plays a crucial role in the fate of the ox created by Ohrmazd mentioned in the opening paragraph of this chapter. On the evolution of the latter narrative see Dumézil, *Mythe et épopée*, vol. 2, 224–25.

er, who nourishes her son on the milk of the magnificent cow Barmāyeh.[32] So in the *Bundahišn* Frēdōn's *xwarrah* enters first the milk of a bovine artifact and then a woman named Farānak, and in the *Shāhnāmeh* Faridun is raised by his mother Farānak on the milk of a cow, and then goes on to commission the construction of a bovine device.

Fabricated Bovines from Greece

Now let us travel from Iran to Ireland, but let us do so via Greece, so that upon arriving in Ireland we will be satisfying the methodological principle of Indo-European studies known as the *tertium comparationis*, the third point of comparison. Greek mythology offers multiple occasions on which bulls are built and cows are crafted. With respect to the former variety of artisanship, the divine smith Hephaistos forges a team of bronze, fire-breathing bulls for the Colchian tyrant Aeetes.[33] It is these same brazen bulls with which Aeetes challenges Jason to plough and sow a field with dragon's teeth if he is to take away the Golden Fleece, a situation that recalls the use of the likewise metallic *gorz* in a similarly draconine context.

When it comes to crafting cows, the most famous, or rather infamous case is an event in the prologue to the mythological biography of the Minotaur, a narrative complex that practically bristles with inherited bovine elements.[34] To mention just one beyond that in question: after having defeated the semi-taurine Minotaur, Theseus invents the dance called the *géranos* "crane."[35] The same combination of animals occurs in the name and iconography of the Gaulish cultic entity Tarvos Trigaranus ('Bull of the Three Cranes'), who is so designated and depicted on the Gallo-Roman Pilier

32. Compare Welburn, *From a Virgin Womb*, 202 fn. 45.

33. Apollonius Rhodius *Argonautica* 3.230. Hephaistos also makes an adamantine plough for use with the bronze bulls as an offering to the sun god Helios (3.233), and Aeetes, the bulls' recipient, is himself a son of Helios, so that these creatures appear to owe something to the Indo-European tradition of solar cattle. In other respects Hephaistos's extensive animal artisanry is informed by Near Eastern traditions. See Christopher Faraone, *Talismans and Trojan Horses: Guardian Statues in Ancient Greek Myth and Ritual* (Oxford: Oxford University Press, 1992), 18–35.

34. These include the bovine detail of Theseus's underwater adventure discussed in Appendix A and the name of the Athenian maiden mentioned in footnote 38. For a bovine narrative inherited from Indo-European with which Minos is involved outside of the confines of the Minotaur portion of his mythological biography see Paul-Louis Van Berg, "Spit in My Mouth, Glaukos: A Greek Indo-European Tale about Ill-gotten Knowledge," in Karlene Jones-Bley et al., eds., *Proceedings of the Sixteenth Annual UCLA Indo-European Conference* (Washington: Institute for the Study of Man, 2005), 78–79.

35. Plutarch, *Life of Theseus*, 21.

des Nautes as a bull with two birds perched on his back and one on his head.[36]
Now the manner of the Minotaur's conception is as follows:[37] Poseidon, en-
raged that Minos has failed to sacrifice to him a bull designated for that
purpose, enlists Aphrodite to cause Minos's wife Pasiphae to become smit-
ten by irrepressible lust for the animal.[38] Desperate to satisfy her zoophilic
impulse, Pasiphae contracts Daedalus to construct a hollow wooden cow,
from the interior of which she might enjoy the bull's amorous attentions.[39]
This mechanism produces the desired result, and the Minotaur is the hybrid
offspring of this trans-species union.

Fabricated Bovines from Ireland

Now for our third point of comparison. An invention strikingly similar to
Daedalus's bovine contraption in particular occurs in the *dindsenchas*, the

36. Many studies offer this comparison, and almost none of them acknowledge previous
scholarship, so that I have not been able to ascertain with whom it originates. The earliest
author whom I know to have presented it in language suggesting that he considers himself to
be the first to do so is Arthur Cook; see his "The Cretan Axe-cult outside Crete," in Percy Allen
and John de Monins Johnson, eds., *Transactions of the Third International Congress for the History
of Religions*, vol. 2 (Oxford: Clarendon Press, 1908), 186–87. The correspondence is analyzed in
greater depth in Bernard Sergent, *Celtes et Grecs*, vol. 2 (Paris: Payot, 2004), 271–77. Anne Ross
remarks that the birds depicted as roosting on Tarvos Trigaranus are not really cranes, but
rather more like egrets; see Anne Ross, "Esus et les trois 'grues'," *Études Celtiques* 9 (1961): 409.
On bovines and aquatic birds as a natural pairing see Jeremy McInerney, *The Cattle of the Sun:
Cows and Culture in the World of the Ancient Greeks*, (Princeton: Princeton University Press, 2010),
7 and 254 fn24. For a vestigial Iranian reflex of this apparently hereditary concatenation of
cow and crane see Appendix B of this chapter.

37. Apollodorus *Bibliotheca* 3.1.3–4; similarly recounted by Diodorus Siculus (4.77); otherwise explained by Hyginus *Fabulae* 40.

38. Pasiphae is a daughter of Helios (cf. Jean Haudry, *La religion cosmique des Indo-Européens*
[Paris: Les Belles Lettres, 1987], 204–05). Furthermore, there is also a dawn cow of sorts in
the Minotaur's mythological profile: various versions of this narrative consistently name one
of the Athenian adolescents whom Minos demands as an annual sacrifice to the Minotaur
Eeriboia, e.g. Bacchylides (David Campbell, *Greek Lyric*, vol. 4, [Cambridge, MA: Harvard University Press, 1992], 216–17). As Janda (*Eleusis*, 214–15) points out, this name is the univerbated
equivalent of the Vedic phrase *usríyāḥ...gávo* "dawn cows" and its variants, which are of formulaic status in the *Ṛg Veda*. Compare Bacchylides's other bovine archaism in the same poem
proposed in Appendix A.

39. The cow fashioned by Daedalus is compared to that composed by the Ṛbhus by Adalbert Kuhn, "Die Sprachvergleichung und die Urgeschichte der indogermanischen Völker,"
*Zeitschrift für Vergleichende Sprachforschung auf dem Gebiete des deutschen, griechischen und latein-
ischen* 4 (1855): 112–13. Although I follow Kuhn in identifying Indo-European heritage as the
basis for Daedalus' bovine device, many other aspects of Daedalus and his ilk rather derive
from Near Eastern concepts and narratives, on which see Sarah Morris, *Daidalos and the Origins
of Greek Art* (Princeton: Princeton University Press, 1992).

abundantly engaging textual tradition of Irish toponymic aetiology, multiple narratives of which reflect inherited material; in fact several *dindsenchas* narratives involving cows other than the one we are about to consider also possess Indo-Iranian and Greek equivalents.[40] The narrative that interests us for the time being, the *dindsenchas* of Carn Uí Néit, tells of the extermination of the dysfunctional despot Bres.[41] The latter demands as tribute from his subjects an exorbitant amount of milk, so the god Lug, who is variously associated with craftsmanship (as are his Welsh, Continental Celtic and folkloric brethren[42]), orchestrates the construction of three hundred hollow wooden cows, into the cavities of which are inserted artificial udders consisting of pails full of poisonous pseudo-milk apparently consisting of bog sludge.[43] To scramble the title of Dylan Thomas's play, what we are dealing with, after a fashion, is milk under wood. Bres, who is under a variously explained obligation to drink this mock milk, consumes the lethal substance and inevitably perishes at Carn Uí Néit.[44]

40. We shall see in Appendix A the Indo-European ancestry of the Bóand *dindsenchas*. See Calvert Watkins, *How to Kill a Dragon: Aspects of Indo-European Poetics* (Oxford: Oxford University Press, 1995), 412 for a comparative remark on the Bóguine *dindsenchas*.

41. Edward Gwynn, ed. and trans., *The Metrical Dindsenchas*, vol. 3 (Dublin: Academy House, 1913), 218; Robert Macalister, ed. and trans., *Lebor Gabála Érenn: The Book of the Taking of Ireland*, vol. 4 (Dublin: Irish Texts Society, 1941), 228–29; Whitley Stokes, "The Prose Tales in the Rennes *Dindsenchas*," *Revue Celtique* 15 (1894): 438–40. John Carey notes that the Carn Uí Néit *dindsenchas* and *Cath Maige Tuired* are exceptional in their presentation of Bres as an illegitimate sovereign, but for our purposes it is sufficient to examine his portrayal in the texts under examination. John Carey, "Myth and Mythography in *Cath Maige Tuired*," *Studia Celtica* 24–5 (1989–90): 57.

42. William Gruffydd, ed. and trans., *Math vab Mathonwy* (Cardiff: University of Wales Press, 1928), 65–80, 142–56, 234–43; Thomas O'Rahilly, *Early Irish History and Mythology* (Dublin: Dublin Institute for Advanced Studies, 1946), 308–17; Patrick Ford, *Math uab Mathonwy* (Belmont: Ford and Bailie, 1999), xxii-iv.

43. Lug's folkloric equivalent is similarly related to a craftsman who owns or is associated with a marvelous cow. See Gruffydd, *Math vab Mathonwy*, 65–80, 142–56. For a comparison of these Celtic cows with their Indic equivalents see John Leavitt, "The Cow of Plenty in Indo-Iranian and Celtic Myth," in Karlene Jones-Bley, Martin Huld and Angela Della Volpe, eds., *Proceedings of the Eleventh Annual UCLA Indo-European Conference* (Washington, DC: Institute for the Study of Man, 2000), 209–24. Given that the smith's fabulous cow is consistently named Glas, the meaning of which spans green, blue, and grey, I wonder whether she might have something to do with Babe, the magical blue ox who is the constant companion of the prodigious lumberjack Paul Bunyan. For other craftsmen associated with cows, see Appendix C of this chapter.

44. Perhaps the relationship between milk and violent death to be found elsewhere in Irish is involved here. Nikolaeva argues that milk in such contexts is just a kenning for blood (Natalia Nikolaeva, "The Drink of Death." *Studia Celtica* 35 [2001]: 303–05), but then there is the death of Suibhne, who is murdered as he is drinking milk out of his cow-dung bowl, see James O'Keeffe, ed. and trans., *Buile Suibhne Geilt* (London: Irish Texts Society, 1913), 142–45. Cohen

The narrative of the Carn Uí Néit *dindsenchas* is at odds with the more familiar fate of Bres recounted in *Cath Maige Tuired*, in which the vanquished wretch manages to convince the victors to spare his life, although it is worth noting that this alternate tradition of Bres's deposition also involves lactiferous cows. Here he does not require from his vassals an enormous quantity of milk, but rather the poet Coirpre, embittered by Bres's meager hospitality, utters vituperative verses expressing his expectation that Bres's resources, including cow's milk, should become depleted, the recitation of which curse effects the anticipated dearth.[45] Furthermore, one of the pieces of knowledge that Bres offers in exchange for his life is the method by which the cows of Ireland could be kept in a perpetually lactiferous state.[46]

To the extent that they are hollow and wooden, the cows engineered by Lug are remarkably reminiscent of that fashioned by Daedalus, which is also both ligneous and vacuous.[47] Lug and Daedalus's cows are also involved with a common factor of deceit: both are synthetic, but meant to be mistaken for animate. So we might suspect some degree of Classical influence in the composition of the Carn Uí Néit *dindsenchas*. In fact we know that the Irish were well acquainted with the myth of Pasiphae, Daedalus, and the crafted cow, which the *Scél in Mínaduir* narrates in considerable detail.[48] That being said, the tendency in the Irish handling of Classical literature is to incorporate elements native to the Gaelic literary tradition.[49] In the current context of our interest in cows, it will be expedient to mention a constituent that has

---

rather assigns Suibhne's milk a purificatory property; see David Cohen, "Suibhne Geilt," *Celtica* 12 (1976): 123.

45. Elizabeth Gray, ed. and trans., *Cath Maige Tuired: The Second Battle of Mag Tuired* (Naas: Irish Texts Society, 1982), 34. Compare what happens during the reign of Conn: Richard Best, ed. and trans., "The Adventures of Art Son of Conn, and the Courtship of Delbchaem," *Ériu* 3 (1907): 154–55.

46. Gray, *Cath Maige Tuired*, 66. Just as the mendacious "milk" consumed by Bres in the *dindsenchas* is a sham, so too Sayers has argued that there is something fishy about the incessant flow of milk that Bres claims he can induce in *Cath Maige Tuired*. William Sayers, "Bargaining for the Life of Bres in *Cath Maige Tuired*," *Bulletin of the Board of Celtic Studies* 34 (1986): 32.

47. Nōktargā's cow is biological, and so presumably graced with organs, and yet she is also intended to function as a receptacle.

48. Barbara Hillers, "*Sgél in Mínaduir*: Dädalus und der Minotaurus in Irland," in Erich Poppe and Hildegard Tristram, eds., *Übersetzung, Adaptation und Akkulturation im insularen Mittelalter* (Münster: Nodus, 1999): 131–44. The author of the Irish *Aeneid* omits Virgil's description of the doors of Apollo's temple and so their depiction of Pasiphae copulating with the bull; however he does maintain the catalogue of women who have perished on account of passion, including Pasiphae: George Calder, ed. and trans., *Imtheachta Aeniasa: the Irish Aeneid* (London: Irish Texts Society, 1907), 86, line 1370.

49. For a study of the ways in which the Irish transform the Classical tradition see Frederick Ahl, "Uilix Mac Leirtis: the Classical Hero in Irish Metamorphosis," in Rosanna Warren, ed., *The Art of Translation: Voices from the Field* (Boston: Northeastern University Press, 1989): 173–98.

been introduced into the Irish adaptation of Statius's *Achilleid*, in which the eponymous hero enters into combat with characteristically Celtic aquatic bulls.[50] On the other hand, it seems to me that in likening the eyes of the Donn and Findbennach to great balls of fire, and the swelling of their cheeks and nostrils to that of a smith's bellows, the *Táin* is reproducing a description of Hephaistos's fire-breathing bulls, whose igneous exhalation Apollonius compares to flames emerging from a furnace fanned by the leather bellows of a smith.[51] As with the mythology of the Minotaur's conception, we know that the Irish were familiar with these brazen bulls.[52] In any event, whether or not Daedalus's invention has affected Lug's, I proceed with the assumption that the fundamental content of the Carn Uí Néit *dindsenchas* at the very least reflects an indigenous narrative, the merit of which impression I shall now demonstrate.

Fabricated Bovines and Suspect Sovereignty

At this point we have met with fabricated bovines in three different textual traditions of Indo-European heritage, a distribution indicative of a cognate relationship. But does an appreciation of the apparently familial filiation of this clan of kindred kine improve our understanding of their function within their respective narratives? I would argue that it does, because these cows populate parallel thematic contexts. In almost every instance we are in the midst of a narrative concerned with the elimination of an illegitimate sovereign, or the failure of an aspiring illegitimate sovereign, as the case may be. In our *Bundahišn* episode, the reason that Nōktargā devises his cow is that it allows him to extract for his sons the *xwarrah* from its place of concealment in Frāxkard, which we know from the *Avesta* is where this entity hides when it wants to avoid those unworthy of possessing it.[53] The *xwarrah*, however, shuns the boys and instead infuses itself into the daughter, a receptacle, apparently, of legitimate sovereignty, as female figures tend to be in Indic and Celtic ideology, which is one of the circumstances on account of which Dumézil studied this passage.

When it comes to the *gorz*, recall that Faridun commissions this instru-

---

50. Donncha Ó hAodha, ed. and trans., "The Irish Version of Statius' *Achilleid*," *Proceedings of the Royal Irish Academy* 79 (1979): 98–99; 128–29. As pointed out in Appendix A, Greek mythology also possesses a tradition of aquatic bovines, but these do not figure in Statius.

51. Apollodorus *Bibliotheca* 3.1299–1303; cf. Ovid *Metamorphoses* 7.106–10; Cecile O' Rahilly, ed. and trans., *Táin Bó Cúailnge from the Book of Leinster* (Dublin: Dublin Institute for Advanced Studies, 1967), 271.

52. Brent Miles, *Heroic Saga and Classical Epic in Medieval Ireland* (Cambridge: D.S. Brewer, 2011), 72–74.

53. See Appendix A.

ment specifically for his encounter with the maleficent monarch Ẓaḥḥāk, and that with it he succeeds in defeating the despot. Furthermore, the *gorz*'s animate correlate Barmāye also seems to function as a tool for stamping out attempts at illicit hegemony: after Frēdōn has defeated the monstrous Māzandars, who had invaded the region Xwanērah, he apparently binds his enemies to the hooves of Barmāyūn, which is the form of Barmāye's name in all literature prior to the *Shāhnāmeh*.[54] A hoof of Barmāye's Avestan kin, the ox of *Yašt* 17 to whom the adjective *barǝmāyaona-* is applied,[55] similarly serves to protect a victim from her aggressors: it is under the hoof of this ox that the goddess Aši, who is being pursued by the hostile Turanians and Naotarids, seeks to conceal herself.[56]

We come upon something quite similar to the function of the *gorz* in our *dindsenchas* cows, which are also mechanisms for bringing about the dethronement and death of a deficient sovereign. In fact their architect Lug explicitly figures as a representative of regal authority in the *Baile in Scáil*, in which he appears as the consort of the young woman who is identified as the Sovereignty of Ireland (*flaith hÉrenn*), and in which he himself predicts for Conn the length of the latter's reign, as well as that of each future king of Tara.[57] The false milk of Lug's cows accentuates their role in terminating Bres's defective dominion: a persistent aspect of the Irish ideology of kingship is that during the reign of a magnanimous monarch, milch cows are exuberantly productive, whereas during that of a depraved potentate, their yield becomes utterly inadequate, which we have already seen is just what happens during Bres's stint as sovereign in *Cath Maige Tuired*.[58] With an eye

54. *Encyclopaedia Iranica*, s.v. "Ferēdūn" (by A. Tafazzoli), 532. The translation of Edward West (*Pahlavi Texts*, vol. 4 [1892], 218) is confusing, if not confused. Khaleghi-Motlagh proposes that Ferdowsi's modification of the cow's name is metrically conditioned, see *Encycopaedia Iranica*, s.v. "Barmāya". The punishment of the Māzandars is reminiscent of that of Dirke, which is also part of a narrative about the reestablishment of legitimate sovereignty (Apollodorus, *Bibliotheca* 3.5.5).

55. Justi, *Iranisches Namenbuch*, 256.

56. Darmesteter draws the patent comparison between Aši's bovine method of concealment together with her subsequent attempt to hide under the throat of a ram and that by which Odysseus manages to escape the Cyclops' cave. James Darmesteter, trans., *The Zend-Avesta*, vol. 2 (Oxford: Clarendon Press, 1883), 281. For some other correspondences between Homeric heroes and the content of *Yašt* 17 see Prods Oktor Skjærvø, "Eastern Iranian Epic Traditions III: Zarathustra and Diomedes – An Indo-European Epic Warrior Type," *Bulletin of the Asia Institute* 11 (2000): 176–78.

57. Kevin Murray, ed. and trans., *Baile in Scáil: the Phantom's Frenzy* (London: Irish Texts Society, 2004), 34.

58. For scarcity of milk as the mark of another flawed ruler see the reference to Conn in footnote 45. Tymoczko suggests that the woman selling milk in Joyce's *Ulysses* represents the sovereignty of Ireland, whose anthropomorphic personification conventionally performs her

to this symptom, the bogus bog-milk of Lug's counterfeit cows becomes an expression of Bres's rotten rule.

In fact Irish *fír* "truth," an essential criterion in the constitution of a Celtic king, is homophonous with *fír* "milk," the rare word we met in brief near the beginning of this chapter. That these homonyms were subject to wordplay is demonstrated by the *Bretha Nemed*'s description of the cauldron of judgment, into which one *inoimbligh fíor* "milks truth," a phrase that could also be esoterically interpreted as meaning "milks milk."[59] Tomás Ó Cathasaigh has observed that *Cath Maige Tuired* emphasizes the absence of veracity in Bres's kingship:[60] so the latter admits to his own *anfír* "injustice," literally "non-truth," his father counsels him not to seize control of Ireland by means of injustice (*anfír* again), and the Dagdae accuses Bres of uttering the antithesis of the ruler's truth (*ní fíor flathu*).[61] It is accordingly suitable that a sovereign whose conduct is characterized by *anfír* "non-truth" should be made to drink poison masquerading as milk, which could equally be styled *anfír* "non-milk."

The case of the Avestan Cow's complaint to Gāuš Tašan is somewhat more difficult to assimilate into this analysis.[62] However, remember that the

---

role by offering the sovereign at hand a drink, as she does in *Baile in Scáil*, see Maria Tymoczko, *The Irish Ulysses* (Berkeley: University of California Press, 1994), 108–09. Dumézil contrasts the lactic crises in which Bres is implicated with the abundant earth-cow of the benevolent monarch Pṛthu's reign: Georges Dumézil, *Servius et la Fortune: essai sur la fonction sociale de louange et de blâme et sur les éléments indo-européens du cens romain* (Paris: Gallimard, 1943), 239.

59. Edward Gwynn, "An Old-Irish Tract on the Privileges and Responsibilities of Poets," *Ériu* 13 (1942): 26 line 11. Apparently this is not the only instance of lacteal wordplay in this passage; see Patrick Henry, "The Caldron of Poesy," *Studia Celtica* 14–15 (1979–80): 115. The wordplay between *fír* "truth" and *fír* "milk" is in the immediate sense the result of fortuitous synchronic homophony, but ultimately has its basis in an inherited conceptual concatenation: Sanskrit *ṛta* "truth," which expresses the same complex of concepts as the Irish king's *fír* (Calvert Watkins, "*Is tre fír flathemon*: Marginalia to *Audacht Morainn*," *Ériu* 30 [1979]: 181–98), is similarly connected with cows and their milk (e.g. *Ṛg Veda* 1.73.6, 4.1.13); compare the recurring proximity of *aša*, the Avestan cognate of Sanskrit *ṛta*, and the Cow in *Yasna* 29, and the frequency with which *aša* occurs in the liturgy of the *jīwām* "consecrated milk"; see *Encyclopaedia Iranica*, s.v. "Jiwām" (by Firoze Kotwal and Jamsheed Choksy).

60. Tomás Ó Cathasaigh, "*Cath Maige Tuired* as Exemplary Myth," in Pádraig de Brún, Seán Ó Coileáin and Pádraig Ó Riain, eds., *Folia Gadelica* (Cork: Cork University Press, 1983), 2–3.

61. Gray, *Cath Maige Tuired*, 36 lines 213 and 220, 30 line 111.

62. For a fully developed discussion of the bovine component of *Yasna* 29 see Martin Schwartz, "Gathic Compositional History, *Yasna* 29, and Bovine Symbolism," in Siamak Adhami, ed., *Paitimāna: Essays in Iranian, Indo-European, and Indian Studies in Honor of Hanns-Peter Schmidt* (Costa Mesa: Mazda Publishers, 2003), 220–43. The Ṛbhus's act of bovine craftsmanship, the significance of which seems to me to be incompatible with the thematic consistency of the other narratives discussed in this chapter, is the subject of the final chapter of my dissertation, *Orpheus and the Cow*.

motivation for the Cow's conversation with her creator is that she is being maltreated by some pernicious persons, and is encouraging her protector to make greater efforts in repelling them. Bruce Lincoln once argued that *Yasna* 29 is a charter myth, the content of which is intented to facilitate the coordination of two intersecting spheres of sovereignty, on the one hand that of the sacerdotal stratum of ancient Iranian society, and on the other that of the warrior class, both of which are fundamentally dependent on cattle, and which are consequently bound to quarrel over these animals.[63] In fact the Cow tells her interlocutor that she wishes for him to possess *īšā. xšaθrīm* "vigorous sovereignty," the second segment of which is cognate with Old Persian *xsāyaθiya*, the title of the Achaemenid king, and with Modern Persian *shāh*.

The comparative perspective therefore teaches us that the participation of constructed cows in their respective narratives has been conditioned by context, so that rather than thinking of these instances of bovine fabrication in isolation, we should have in mind a particular kind of thematic complex, of which crafted cows are an intrinsic component. Our Greek comparandum also belongs here, for although Daedalus does not fabricate his cow with the intent of compromising Minos's tyranny, Pasiphae's request for its invention is triggered by the erotic insanity to which Aphrodite subjects her in order to punish Minos for his failure to sacrifice to Poseidon the bull that is rightfully his. So the wooden cow ultimately has its roots in a divine plot to damage Minos's personal life, and perhaps in so doing to corrupt his sovereignty by cuckolding him.[64] Furthermore, when it does come time for Minos to get his just desserts, Daedalus is merely one step removed from the manner of his death, since it is the daughters of Daedalus's protector, the Sicilian king Cocalus, who kill Minos when the latter comes to Sicily, demanding that Daedalus be surrendered to him.[65]

63. Bruce Lincoln, "The Myth of the 'Bovine's Lament'," *Journal of Indo-European Studies* 3 (1975): 337–62; and idem, *Priests*, 134–62. Lincoln, having since become disenchanted with the Indo-European enterprise and now doing rather different work, has withdrawn many of his previous claims. See his more recent study of the passage of the *Bundahišn* related to the Avestan lament of the Cow, in the conclusion of which he explicitly distances himself from the Indo-European perspective: Bruce Lincoln, *Theorizing Myth: Narrative, Ideology and Scholarship* (Chicago: University of Chicago Press, 1999), 183–91.

64. That Pasiphae's intercourse with the bull is to be understood as a threat to Minos's rule is confirmed by the rationalizing version of the myth explicated by Plutarch (*Theseus* 16, 19) according to which Pasiphae never had sex with a bull, but was rather having an affair with Minos's general Tauros "Bull," who had acquired for himself a dangerous amount of power, and who was an arrogant personality to boot, so that Minos invites Theseus to defeat and thus humiliate his overweening officer in an athletic competition.

65. Jason similarly uses Hephaistos's bronze bulls to the detriment of Aeetes. He does so

Given the decidedly negative impact that Daedalus and his cow have on the tyrannical Minos both immediately and in the long run, it is perhaps somewhat peculiar that the historical Sicilian tyrant Phalaris of Akragas reputedly ordered the construction of a hollow bronze bull, in which he imprisoned his enemies and roasted them alive, and which was constructed in such a way that it transmuted the howling of the victim within into a bovine bellow.[66] As Thomas Dunbabin observes, Akragas was a Rhodian colony, so that Phalaris's macabre machine has a benign antecedent in the animated bronze oxen of Rhodes that are said to have bellowed terribly (*kakòn mukôntai*)[67] in warning when enemies approached.[68] Yet with this abhorrent apparatus to his name, would Phalaris not have run the risk of associating himself with Daedalus, and by extension with the deficient Minos who, after all, met his end on Sicilian soil? In fact Daedalus, Phalaris, and the author of Minos's undoing convene in the context of the krater found and dedicated by Phalaris to Athena Lindia, on the rim of which vessel was inscribed *Daídalos édōke xeínión me Kōkálōi* "Daedalus gave me as a token of friendship to Cocalus," and to the base of which Phalaris added an inscription of his own.[69] Maybe it occurred to Phalaris that his internecine instrument could kindle in the imagination of his subjects an association with Daedalus's device, but

---

with the help of Aeetes's daughter Medea, with whom he then elopes, much in the same ways as Minos's daughter Ariadne helps Theseus slay the Minotaur and then absconds with her paramour.

66. Diodorus Siculus 9.19.

67. Anders Drachmann, ed., *Scholia vetera in Pindari carmina* vol. 1 (Leipzig: Teubner, 1903), 233.

68. Thomas Dunbabin, *The Western Greeks* (Oxford: Clarendon Press, 1948), 320. The oxen of Rhodes apparently have a Cretan comparandum in Talos, the bronze giant forged by Hephaistos for Minos, whose duty was to patrol the perimeter of the island, and whom Apollodorus says that some people believed to have been a bull (*Bibliotheca* 1.9.26). If there is any authenticity to the tradition of a taurine Talos, then we should consider Hesychius's gloss, which tells us that in the Cretan dialect *talôs* means "sun."

These bovine sentinels correspond in both form and function to the aforementioned ox made by Ohrmazd and its task of maintaining the border between Iran and Turan. A relationship between border and bovine also occurs in Dido's delineation of Carthage by means of strips of oxhide. For an Indo-European *tertium comparationis* we might consider the *Gylfaginning*'s account of the method according to which Gefjon creates Zealand, to which Dido's deed is frequently approximated. However there might also be a Phoenician dimension to the narrative of the foundation of Carthage (on which see Edward Lipiński, *Itineraria Phoenicia* [Leuven: Peeters, 2004], 477–84), so that we could be dealing with a tradition the distribution of which extends beyond Indo-European. See also Faraone, *Talismans and Trojan Horses*, 31 fn34, where it is noted that Assurbanipal claims to have possessed animated apotropaic metallic oxen, guardians that sound remarkably similar to the oxen of Rhodes.

69. Carolyn Higbie, *The Lindian Chronicle and the Greek Creation of Their Past* (Oxford: Oxford University Press, 2003), 32–33.

if the accounts of Phalaris's personality are anything akin to the truth, he was apparently as brazen as his bull. We might say that he recognized the connotative risk of his contrivance, but that it did not cow him.

So I have endeavored to establish the presence of contextually conditioned crafted cows in Iranian, Hellenic, and Hibernian tradition, members of the same three branches of Indo-European that also most fully manifest other correspondences in the realm of bovine lore. In light of this threefold distribution, and in light of the particular cultures involved, it strikes me as appropriate to conclude by recapitulating a likewise triadic entity that we have already met in passing: Tarvos Trigaranus, the Gaulish bull with his three cranes. In 281 B.C.E. the Gauls, under the leadership of Brennos, invaded northern Greece, and apparently even made a stab at plundering Delphi. During this period of contact, the Greeks seem to have gained some knowledge of Celtic mythico-religious traditions. A case in point might be the occurrence of the term *trigéranos* in a fragment of the comic playwright Philemon, who was in the middle of his literary output at just this time. As noted by Joseph Vendryes, in this remarkable *hapax*, which refers to an exotic beast (*thēríon*), we appear to be dealing with none other than our Gallic bull and his three feathery friends, with the vocalism of the Celtic crane word (cf. Brittonic *garan*) having been slightly modified and thus transformed into its transparent Greek cognate *géranos*.[70] How very fitting for the topic at hand that the Athenian interlocutors of Philemon's fragment make mention of Tarvos Trigaranus because they are considering sending such a curious creature as a gift to Seleucus,[71] founder of the dynasty that would govern parts of the Iranian world for many years, and whose half-Persian

70. Joseph Vendryes, "Sur un passage du comique Philémon: le *Tarvos Trigaranos* en Grèce," *Revue Celtique* 28 (1907): 123–7. The manuscripts also yield *trugéranos*, which Meineke prefers and suggests could be a haplologized compound of *trugṓn* "turtle-dove" and *géranos*; see August Meineke, ed. *Fragmenta Comicorum Graecorum*, vol. 4 (Berlin: Reimer, 1841), 15–16. In considering the idea that the Greeks received some exposure to Gaulish bovine mythico-religious traditions, Vendryes notes the meaning of the name of the distinguished Galatian king Deiotaros "Divine Bull," scion of the same marauding Gauls who invaded Greece and then settled in Galatia sometime thereafter. It is a neat, if specious fact that the agricultural author Diophanes of Nicaea dedicated to Deiotaros his farming manual, which must have included a section on the care of cattle, as is known to be the case for Cassius Dionysius's *Georgica*, of which Diophanes's work is an abridgement.

71. One might comfortably expect this taurine tribute to be warmly welcomed by Selecus, who is depicted on his coinage as having bull's horns, perhaps in imitation of Dionysus. See Julien Tondriau, "Dionysos, dieu royal: du Bacchos tauromorphe primitif aux souverains hellénistiques Neoi Dionysoi," in *Mélanges Henri Grégoire*, vol. 4 (Bruxelles: Secréteriat des Éditions de l'Institut, 1952), 461. Hellenic aesthetics are also apparent in sculpted bulls from Achaemenid Persia; see Trudy Kawami, "Greek Art and Persian Taste: Some Animal Sculptures From Persepolis," *American Journal of Archaeology* 90 (1986): 260, 265–66.

ruler Antiochus I, son and successor of Seleucus, was about to face a Gaulish invasion of his own.[72]

Appendix A

That the cow is the appropriate animal for extracting the *xwarrah* from its aquatic refuge is also suggested by a related situation in the Irish literary tradition. The Avestan correspondent to the Nōktargā episode is the adventures of the *xᵛarənah* in *Yašt* 19 where, having fled from Ātar and Aži Dahāka and having entered Vouru.kaša, it is seized by Apąm Napāt. The Turanian Fraŋrasyan then makes three attempts to obtain the *xᵛarənah*; on each occasion it escapes him and generates a new body of water in the process. As shown by Dumézil, pursued by Patrick Ford, and mentioned by Olga Davidson,[73] the Irish narrative equivalent to this section of *Yašt* 19 is the *dindsenchas* tradition of the goddess Bóand,[74] wife of Nechtan, Apąm Napāt's etymological and functional congener. Bóand apparently seeks her husband's spring in order to obtain from it the *imbas forosna* "illuminating wisdom," an essence that furnishes those who possess it with poetic inspiration, and that belongs to the same clan of stimulating substances as the likewise luminous and hydrophilic *xᵛarənah*, which is associated not only with sovereignty, but also with intellectual illumination (note, however, that the second metrical version of the Bóand *dindsenchas* assigns to her a different motivation). However only Nechtan and his three cupbearers have license to access the spring, and so when Bóand approaches it, its waters rise up and attack her in three successive waves. She flees this aqueous assault, and the River Boyne, of which Bóand is the eponym, is generated in her wake.

What needs to be added to Dumézil's analysis for our purposes is that the first segment of Bóand's name is the Celtic cow word, and its overall formation is probably inherited from the Indo-European mythico-religious

---

72. Antiochus defeated the Gauls in 278 B.C.E. and apparently in so doing earned the title Soter. The inverse of this apparent migration of Gaulish bovine lore into an Iranian context via the Classical world would occur when Mithraism made its way into the provinces of Rome, including Gaul. For numerous Gaulish representations of the Mithraic tauroctony, including one from none other than Mons Seleucus; see Vivienne Walters, *The Cult of Mithras in the Roman Provinces of Gaul* (Leiden: Brill, 1974), 73–75.

73. Dumézil, *Mythe et épopée*, vol. 3 (1973), 21–38; Patrick Ford, "The Well of Nechtan and 'La Gloire Lumineuse'," in Gerald James Larson, ed., *Myth in Indo-European Antiquity* (Berkeley: University of California Press, 1974), 67–74; Davidson, *Poet and Hero*, 106 and eadem, *Comparative Literature and Classical Persian Poetics: Seven Essays*, 2nd edition (Boston: Ilex Foundation, distributed by Harvard University Press, 2013), 48.

74. Gwynn, *The Metrical Dindsenchas*, vol. 3, 26–39; Whitley Stokes, ed. and trans, "The Bodleian *Dinnshenchas*," *Folklore* 3 (1892): 500; and idem, "The Rennes *Dindsenchas*," *Revue Celtique* 15 (1894): 315–16.

onomasticon.[75] Cows are also an important component in the episode of the *Táin* that, as Olmsted has demonstrated, corresponds to the events of the Bóand *dindsenchas*.[76] No comparable bovine element occurs in *Yašt* 19, but Apām Napāt, the Vedic version of Apạm Napāt, is recurringly connected with cows; for instance, he is identified as a bull, and a milch cow inhabits his hydrous abode.[77] This cow's specifically lactiferous constitution resumes an image illustrated earlier on in the same hymn, in which Apām Napāt is portrayed as sucking the breast milk of the waters, here personified as lactating goddesses, elsewhere compared to milch cows.[78]

Poseidon, Apạm Napāt's Greek relative, is also pervasively associated with bovines, including similarly submarine ones.[79] In fact Bruce Louden argues that Theseus experiences the Greek equivalent of the Apạm Napāt episode of *Yašt* 19 when he proves to Minos his divine parentage by jumping overboard and descending to Poseidon's oceanic dwelling.[80] In Bacchylides's account of this myth, the poet describes Poseidon's wife Amphitrite as *boôpin* "cow-eyed."[81] Although this adjective is a conventional expression for female facial beauty, especially for that of Hera, perhaps its occurrence here is informed by Poseidon's hereditary affiliation with cows. Its frequent application to Hera also probably has its origin in her substantial connection with bovine myths and rituals.[82] Note, moreover, that when Bacchylides uses *boôpis* to describe Artemis,[83] yet another goddess variously related to cattle, he does so specifically when describing how Proetus sought the assistance of Artemis on account of the madness of his daughters, who had come to conceive of themselves as cows, and promised to repay the goddess with a sacrifice of twenty oxen.

We might also want to consider Callistratus's description of a depiction of Athamas's madness,[84] in which Ino flees from her deranged husband toward the sea, clutching a suckling Palaimon to her liberally lactating breast,

75. Enrico Campanile, "Old Irish *Bóand*," *Journal of Indo-European Studies* 12 (1985): 477–79.

76. Garrett Olmsted, *The Gods of the Celts and the Indo-Europeans* (Budapest: Archaeolingua, 1994), 203–04.

77. *Ṛg Veda* 2.35.13, 2.35.7.

78. E.g. *Ṛg Veda* 1.32.2; cf. *Yasna* 38.3–5.

79. Apollodorus *Bibliotheca* 2.5.7, 3.1.3; Euripides *Hippolytus* 1214.

80. Bruce Louden, "Bacchylides 17: Theseus and Indo-Iranian Apam Napat," *Journal of Indo-European Studies* 27 (1999): 57–78.

81. See Campbell, *Greek Lyric*, vol. 4, 224–25.

82. See Haudry, *La religion cosmique*, 145–49 and Joan O'Brien, *The Transformation of Hera: A Study of Ritual, Hero and the Goddess in the Iliad* (Lanham: Rowman and Littlefield, 1993), 134–56. Bovine lore is also at work in its occurrence as an epithet of Euruphaessa; see Matasović, *A Theory of Textual Reconstruction*, 44.

83. Campbell, *Greek Lyric*, vol. 4, 182–85.

84. *Ekphraseis* 14.

while Amphitrite emerges from the water into which Ino is about to plunge herself. Compare Pausanias for another approximation of Amphitrite and Palaimon, and Nonnos for focus on the lactiferous breast of Ino, for whom Athamas, moreover, mistakes a nursing nanny goat.[85] There appears to be a bovine background to Ino's marine submersion, which Christopher Faraone discusses in combination with 1) the similar dive of Dionysus, Ino's other nurseling, whom Lycurgus treats like a bullock, goading the god toward the sea; 2) the likewise briny bound of Lycurgus's brother Boutes "Cowherd"; 3) the Argive myth-ritual complex of Dionysus *Bougenēs* "Bovine-born" conducted at the Lernaian lake; and 4) the passage of the gold *lamella* from Pelinna in which the initiate becomes a bull and leaps into milk.[86] The propinquity of Ino and Amphitrite in the painting seen by Callistratus might reflect a connection between the latter and breast milk that would find its match in the milky mammae of Apām Napāt's entourage of busty goddesses.

To return to Bóand, she is on the one hand portrayed as being unworthy of receiving the *imbas* of Nechtan's spring, and so corresponds to Nōktargā's sons, whom the *xwarrah* rejects. However ultimately she does become a recipient of the *imbas* to the extent that the latter is contained in the waters of the nominally bovine Boyne, which are an extension of those of Nechtan's spring, and which poets drink as a means of enhancing their creative capabilities. In this respect the bovine goddess corresponds to Nōktargā's cow, which he uses to remove and contain the *xwarrah*, which Farānak attains by drinking the cow's milk.

Another Irish narrative related to the Nōktargā episode is the folktale in which the poet Cearúl Ó Dála becomes invested with his talent by imbibing the beestings of a cow that has grazed on a cluster of rushes visited by a mysterious cloud,[87] in which chain of events we have a match for Farānak becoming imbued with the *xwarrah* after consuming the milk of the cow that Nōktargā has pastured on the patch of reeds into which the *xwarrah* had introduced itself.

Appendix B

We seem to be in the presence of a bizarre Iranian permutation of the apparently hereditary collocation of cow and crane in the tradition that Ẓaḥḥāk's

85. Pausanias 2.1.7; Nonnos *Dionysiaca* 5.560–1, 10.7–12.

86. Christopher Faraone, "Rushing into Milk: New Perspectives on the Gold Tablets," in Radcliffe Edmonds, ed., *The "Orphic" Gold Tablets and Greek Religion: Further Along the Path* (Cambridge: Cambridge University Press, 2011), 223–224.

87. T. O'Rahilly, *Early Irish History*, 331–32 fn4; Dáithí Ó hÓgain, *Myth, Legend and Romance: An Encyclopaedia of Irish Folk Tradition* (New York: Prentice Hall, 1991), 335.

palace was shaped like a crane and so named,[88] a fact that Dumézil actually mentions in connection with Tarvos Trigaranus and his cranes, although without reference to the common bovine element that I am proposing.[89] The quasi-cows of our Persian comparandum are Jamshid's daughters, the princesses Arnavāz and Shahrnavāz, whom Ẓaḥḥāk has imprisoned in his fortress, and who are liberated by Faridun. In the Avestan equivalent of this scenario, Faridun's onomastic and functional correspondent Thraētaona conquers Aži Dahāka, Ẓaḥḥāk's etymological and functional correlate, and recovers Saŋhauuācī and Arənauuācī, the sisters of Yima, Jamshid's Avestan relative. However Trita, the Vedic congener of Faridun and Thraetaona, releases cows from Vṛtra, the Indic cousin of Ẓaḥḥāk and Aži Dahāka. Perhaps the morphologically bovine *gorz*, with which Faridun deals Ẓaḥḥāk a blow in his crane-shaped castle, maintains a relic of the cow-crane composite. In support of a diachronic understanding of Jamshid's daughters as erstwhile cows, Widengren notes that al-Bīrūnī does not mention Faridun rescuing the princesses from Ẓaḥḥāk, but rather relates that he releases rustled cattle.[90]

With this alternation between cows and women in Indo-Iranian tradition we might compare the fact that both cows and women are simultaneously stolen in medieval Irish literature, and often in contexts in which other archaisms are also involved. So the coincidental theft of cows and women is announced in the *Táin* by the severed head of Súaltaim, the behavior of whose detached member Joseph Nagy has shown reflects an Indo-European tradition,[91] and the voice of which intones an inherited formulaic syntagm.[92] In *Aided Con Roí*, the text's eponym simultaneously abducts Blathnat and seizes the cows of Iuchna, which are reflexes of the Indo-European lactiferous dawn cows.[93]

Appendix C

Other mythological craftsmen whose profiles owe something to Indo-European heritage are also associated with cows. So Tvaṣṭṛ has a cow with a secret name,[94] and Hephaistos babysits Herakles's herd while the latter box-

88. *Encyclopaedia Iranica*, s.v. "Crane" (by Hūšang Aᶜlam).

89. Georges Dumézil, *Horace et les Curiaces* (Paris: Gallimard, 1942), 132–33.

90. Geo Widengren, *Die Religionen Irans* (Stuttgart: Kohlhammer, 1965), 46.

91. Joseph Nagy, "Hierarchy, Heroes and Heads: Some Indo-European Structures in Greek Myth," in Lowell Edmunds, ed., *Approaches to Greek Myth* (Baltimore: John Hopkins University Press, 1990), 215–20.

92. Matasović, *A Theory of Textual Reconstruction*, 78.

93. Watkins, "The Milk of the Dawn Cows Revisited": 228.

94. *Ṛg Veda* 1.84.15.

es with Eryx, and transforms himself into an ox as he flees from Typhoeus.[95] Dumézil, although without reference to the bovine element in either case, compared the combination on the Pilier des Nautes of Tarvos Trigaranus and Esus, who is represented as a woodcutter, with the Indic myth of Indra, the carpenter and the tricephalic cattle rustler,[96] but he later rejected his own proposal.[97] In light of the confluence of cow, crane and craftsman in both the Minotaur's mythological complex and in the event of Ẓaḥḥāk's defeat (see Appendix B), it seems to me that Dumézil's analysis of the Pilier des Nautes is to be revived.

To return to Lug, note that he is variously juxtaposed with cows,[98] as well as the fact that the folkloric form of his mother Eithne is implicated in the aforementioned narrative in which Lug's folkloric outcome is involved with a cow,[99] and that Eithne's namesakes in medieval Irish literature are themselves consistently connected with cows. So Eithne is a byname of the cow goddess Bóand,[100] and the Eithnes of *Altrom Tige Dá Medar* and *Esnada Tige Buchet* are variously involved with lactiferous cows.[101]

95. Apollodorus *Bibliotheca* 2.5.10; Antoninus Liberalis *Metamorphoses* 28.

96. Dumézil, *Horace et les Curiaces*, 133.

97. Georges Dumézil, *Heur et malheur du guerrier: aspects mythiques de la fonction guerrière chez les Indo-Européens* (Paris: Presses Universitaires de France, 1969), 139 fn.1.

98. See Sergent, *Celtes et Grecs*, vol. 2, 79–81.

99. Gruffydd, *Math vab Mathonwy*, 65–80.

100. Osborn Bergin and R.I. Best, ed. and trans., "Tochmarc Étaín," *Ériu* 12 (1934–8): 142 and John Carey, "Eithne in Gubai," *Éigse* 28 (1995): 160–01.

101. Margaret Dobbs, ed. and trans., "Altromh Tighi da Medar," *Zeitschrift für celtische Philologie* 18 (1930): 206–15; Lilian Duncan, ed. and trans., "Altram Tige Dá Medar," *Ériu* 11 (1932): 194–98, 214–17; Mary Hayden, ed. and trans., "The Songs of Buchet's House," *Zeitschrift für celtische Philologie* 8 (1912): 226–29; and Whitley Stokes, ed. and trans., "The Songs of Buchet's House," *Revue Celtique* 25 (1904): 28–29.

3

Parallel Heroic Themes in the Medieval Irish *Cattle Raid of Cooley* and the Medieval Persian *Book of Kings*

Olga Davidson

IN THIS CHAPTER I concentrate on two stories, one that is Irish and one that is Iranian, both of which reflect the attempts of medieval literati to bridge the gap between their own respective literate cultures and the earlier cultures of oral traditions that reflect myths associated with heroes and kings. I contend that these oral traditions are the shared heritage of the Irish and the Iranian civilizations.

I start with the Irish story known as *Dofallsigud Tána Bó Cuailnge* ("Concerning the Revelation of the *Táin Bó Cúailnge*"), which is attested in a variety of medieval Irish sources.[1] The term *Táin Bó Cúailnge*, meaning "The Cattle Raid of Cooley," refers not only to a celebrated event in Irish myth but also to a monumental composition, often described as "epic," about some of Ireland's greatest heroes and kings. When I make a distinction here between an *event* and a *composition*, I am following the lead of Joseph Nagy, who has shown that there was an oral tradition of narrating *The Cattle Raid of Cooley* and that, in terms of this tradition, the title refers both to the event and to the "epic" composition about the event.[2] Even more than that, as we will see, the term *Táin Bó Cúailnge* or *The Cattle Raid of Cooley* can refer to a book containing this "epic" composition. In the story I am about to consider, which is entitled *Dofallsigud Tána Bó Cuailnge* and which can be translated as "Concerning the Revelation of the *Táin Bó Cúailnge*," the concept of such a book becomes a metaphor for the "epic" composition itself. The creation of such a metaphor could come about, as I will argue, only if the oral traditions of composing and performing *The Cattle Raid of Cooley* could coexist with the

---

1. For a survey of the medieval Irish texts that reflect this story, see Joseph F. Nagy, "Orality in Medieval Irish Narrative: An Overview," *Oral Tradition* 1:2 (1986): 292.

2. Joseph Falaky Nagy, "How the Táin Was Lost," *Zeitschrift für celtische Philologie* 49–50 (1997): 603–09.

writing traditions of medieval Irish society. As we can see from the historical evidence of surviving medieval Irish manuscripts, written versions of this composition known as *The Cattle Raid of Cooley* are preserved primarily in two major "recensions,"[3] one of which is attested in the *Book of Leinster* (twelfth century CE) and has been edited by Cecile O'Rahilly,[4] while the other of the two is most prominently attested in the *Book of the Dun Cow* (*Lebor na hUidre*, eleventh century CE) and has also been edited by the same scholar.[5]

So let me now turn to the content of the Irish story known as *Dofallsigud Tána Bó Cuailnge*, which as we have already seen means "Concerning the Revelation of the *Táin Bó Cúailnge*." This specific story of the "revelation," as we will now see, explains in terms of both writing traditions and oral traditions the genesis of the story known as *The Cattle Raid of Cooley*. Given the singular importance of this overall story for the history of medieval Irish myths about heroes and kings, I propose that the specific story about the "revelation" of the overall story can be considered a "charter myth."[6]

I quote in Item 1 the core of the story as translated by Thomas Kinsella:

Item 1. From the *Dofallsigud Tána Bó Cuailnge* ("Concerning the Revelation of the *Táin*"):

The poets of Ireland one day were gathered around Senchán Torpéist, to see if they could recall the *Táin Bó Cúailnge* in its entirety. But they all said they knew only fragments [*bloga*]. Senchán asked which of his pupils, in return for his blessing, would travel to the land of Letha to learn the version of the *Táin* that a certain sage took eastward with him in exchange for the book Cuilmenn. Emine, Ninéne's grandson, set out for the east with Senchán's son Muirgen. It happened that the grave of Fergus mac Roich was on his way. They came upon the gravestone at Enloch in Connacht. Muirgen sat down at Fergus's gravestone, and the others left him for a while and went looking for a house for the night. Muirgen chanted a poem to the gravestone as though it were Fergus himself. He said to it:

"If this your royal rock were your own self mac Roich
halted here with sages searching for a roof
Cúailnge we'd recover plain and perfect Fergus."

3. J. F. Nagy, "Orality": 278.

4. Cecile O'Rahilly, ed. and trans., *Táin Bó Cúailnge from the Book of Leinster* (Dublin: Dublin Institute for Advanced Studies, 1967).

5. Cecile O'Rahilly, ed. and trans., *Táin Bó Cúailnge: Recension I* (Dublin: Dublin Institute for Advanced Studies, 1976).

6. On the concept of "charter myth," see E. R. Leach, "Critical Introduction," to M. I. Steblin Kamenskij, *Myth* (translated by M. P. Coote) (Ann Arbor: Karoma, 1982), 5.

A great mist suddenly formed around him – for the space of three days and nights he could not be found. And the figure of Fergus approached him in fierce majesty, with a head of brown hair, in a green cloak and a red-embroidered hooded tunic, with gold-hilted sword and bronze blunt sandals. Fergus recited for him the whole *Táin*, how everything had happened from start to finish. Then they went back to Senchán with their story, and he rejoiced over it. However, there are some who say that the story was told to Senchán himself after he had gone on a fast to certain saints of the seed of Fergus. This seems reasonable.[7]

Joseph Nagy, in his 1986 essay, "Orality in Medieval Irish Narrative," has put together an illuminating commentary on this remarkable passage, and he surveys related passages referring to the story of the lost book of the *Táin*.[8] I quote his incisive wording about a central message that he finds embedded in this story in all its variations: "as the story of Senchán's embarrassment over the *Táin* shows, the written word is no substitute for the poet's *mebair glan* 'pure memory', or the numinous oral tradition behind it."[9]

As Nagy has demonstrated in his analysis of this myth, the reason for Senchán's embarrassment is that neither this chief poet nor any of the other poets of Ireland knows the complete version of *The Cattle Raid of Cooley*. As we see from Nagy's analysis of the story in all its variations, when we take all the surviving versions into account, there are further important details that go far beyond the core of the story as I quoted it from Kinsella's translation. I quote here a fuller version of the narrative as retold by Nagy:[10]

In the tale about the rediscovery of the *Cattle Raid of Cuailgne* ... we find the implicit message that the availability of written texts can corrupt the *filidecht* [or the art of *fili* 'poet'] and the storyteller's *mebair* [or 'memory'] ... The chief poet [*ardfhili*] of Ireland, Senchán Torpéist, and a delegation of his *áes dána* (craftsmen) force themselves upon the Connacht king Gúaire Aidne in an attempt to test his well-known generosity. After the "heavy hosting" of the artisans has become intolerable, Gúaire [or his brother Marbán] devises a ruse for getting rid of them: Senchán and his company are asked to tell the story of the *Cattle Raid of Cuailgne*. The professional tradition-bearers are forced to admit that it is not in their memory (*mebair* ...), and that the

---

7. Thomas Kinsella, trans., *The Táin: From the Irish Epic Táin Bó Cúailnge* (Oxford: Oxford University Press, 1969), 1–2. I have slightly modified the translation.

8. J. F. Nagy, "Orality": 292–94.

9. Ibid., 292.

10. Ibid., 294.

written text of the *Táin* has been given away in exchange for a copy of Isidore's *Etymologiae!* Senchán and his companions thus lose the right to impose upon Gúaire any longer, but in order to preserve his honor as a *fili* and fulfill the request of his audience, Senchán goes in search of the story of the Cattle Raid. The chief poet, or his son Muirgen, finally obtains it when he goes to the grave of Fergus mac Róich, one of the heroes of the story, and brings him back to life with a poetic composition, in which this hero of long ago is addressed as if he were alive. In the company of his bardic audience, the resurrected Fergus, who is noted for his storytelling within the story of the *Táin* itself (it is he who narrates the boyhood deeds of Cú Chulainn ...), chants the account of the Cattle Raid ... from beginning to end. The gigantic Fergus cannot be heard when he is standing, so he sits or lies down as he tells the tale. This live oral performance lasts three days and three nights, during which time the mortal auditor ... remains shrouded in a magical mist. Afterwards, Senchán has the tale written down, and so it is captured once again for posterity.

Nagy adds a most important further observation:

> The revenant Fergus, who is asked by the poet in search of an old story to lie or sit down so that his tale may be heard, reclines like the composing poets described [in later sources] ... But for Fergus, this passive position facilitates the transmission of his memory of a traditional tale to his audience, while for the poet, the passive position is conducive to supernatural inspiration and the creation of a new poem.[11]

I focus here on one particular detail in the story: the concept of a *blog* or "fragment" of a body of writings that has disintegrated. As the story indicates, the poets of Ireland knew only *bloga* or "fragments" of *The Cattle Raid of Cooley*, not the whole thing in its entirety. Following the lead of Joseph Nagy, his brother Gregory Nagy has argued that this concept of a fragmentation of an integral composition, as we see it narrated in the medieval Irish story concerning the "revelation" of the overall story of *The Cattle Raid of Cooley*, is a traditional theme found in the charter myths of many cultures.[12] I quote this formulation with reference to the myth of the "revelation":[13]

11. Ibid.,294.

12. Gregory Nagy, "The Sign of the Hero: A Prologue," in Jennifer K. Berenson Maclean and Ellen Bradshaw Aitken, eds. and trans., *Flavius Philostratus: Heroikos* (Atlanta: Society of Biblical Literature, 2001), 33–34, expanding on Gregory Nagy, *Homeric Questions* (Austin: University of Texas Press, 1996), 70–74.

13. G. Nagy, "The Sign," 33–34.

In terms of the myth, this book of narratives, the *Táin*, is equivalent to
an integral epic performance. The myth narrates how this book was
once lost and how the assembled poets of Ireland "could not recall it
in its entirety," since they knew only "fragments" [*bloga*]. In a quest
to find the lost integral book, the poet Muirgen happens to travel
past the tomb of Fergus mac Roich, one of the chief heroes featured
in the narrative of the *Táin*. It is nighttime. Muirgen sits down at the
gravestone of the tomb, and he sings an incantation to this gravestone
"as though it were Fergus himself."[14] Responding to the incantation,
Fergus himself appears in all his heroic glory, and he "recited for him
[= to Muirgen] the whole *Táin*, how everything had happened, from
start to finish."[15]

The point of this charter myth is that the corpus of the *Táin* is reintegrated in performance, and thus the "lost book" is finally recovered, even
resurrected.[16] Greek traditions show a variety of comparable metaphors
about a book (or a library of books) as a corpus destined for resurrection.[17]
Following Joseph Nagy,[18] I would add to these Greek examples an Indic parallel noticed by Dan Melia, whom I quote here: "The strange little story of the
'Finding of the Táin' is almost identical to the first book of the *Mahābhārata*,
which tells how a king found the only surviving man to have heard the story
from the disciple of the man who composed it."[19]

Having started with the Irish story about the "revelation" of the book
about *The Cattle Raid of Cooley*, the surviving manuscripts of which date back
to the eleventh and twelfth centuries CE, I now proceed to consider the corresponding Iranian story, dated to the late tenth and early eleventh century
CE. It comes from a collection of versified stories attributed to the poet Ferdowsi and known as the *Shāhnāmeh* ("Book of Kings"), which was meant as a
comprehensive narrative about all the greatest kings and heroes of Iranian
civilization. The Iranian story that I am about to analyze, like the Irish story,
can be considered a "charter myth," since it explains the genesis of the Book
of Kings as an overall collection of stories and even as an overall book. And

14. Kinsella, trans, *The Táin*, 1.

15. Ibid., 1–2.

16. G. Nagy, "The Sign," 33–34; Gregory Nagy, *Greek Mythology and Poetics* (Ithaca NY: Cornell University Press, 1990), 70.

17. Gregory Nagy, "The Library of Pergamon as a Classical Model," *Pergamon: Citadel of the
Gods: Archaeological Record, Literary Description, and Religious Development*, ed. Helmut Koester
(Harrisburg PA: Trinity Press International, 1998), 196–98.

18. J. F. Nagy, "Orality," 284.

19. Daniel F. Melia, "Some Remarks on the Affinities of Medieval Irish Saga," *Acta Antiqua
Academiae Scientiarum Hungaricae* 27 (1979): 260–261.

here too, as in the Irish example, the composition and the book are treated in identical language.

In the *Shāhnāmeh*, the poet tells the story of the genesis of an archetypal "Book of Kings" that became the ultimate source of his own monumental poem:

Item 2. From the *Shāhnāmeh* of Ferdowsi:

فــــراوان بــدو انـــدرون داسـتـان   یکـی نـامـه بـود از گه بـاسـتان

از او بهـره ای نـزده هـر بخردی   پراکنده در دست هر مویدی

دلـیر و بـزرگ و خـردمـند و راد   یکـی پهـلـوان بـود دهـقـان نـژاد

گذشـتـه سخـنها همـه بـاز جست   پـژوهـنـنـدهٔ روزگــار نخست

بیـاورد کایـن نـامـه را یـاد کرد   ز هـر کشـوری سـالـخـورد

وزان نـامـداران فـرُّخ مهان   بپرسیدشـان از کیـان جهان

که ایـدون بمـا خـوار بگذاشتند   که گیتـی بـه آغـاز چـون داشتند

برایشـان همـه روز کند آوری   چـه گونه سر آمـد بنیک اختری

سخنهای شاهـان و گشت جهان   بگفتند پیـشـش یکایـک مهان

یکـی نـامـور نـامـه افـکند بن   چو بشنید ازیشـان سپهبد سخن

بـرو آفـریـن از کهـان و مهان   چنین یـادگـاری شد انـدر جهان

There was a book [*nāmeh*] from ancient times
in which there was an abundance of stories.
It was <u>dispersed</u> into the hands of every *mōbad*.
Every wise one [of the *mōbads*] possessed a <u>portion</u> of it.
There was a *pahlavān*, born of the *dehqāns*,
brave, powerful, wise, and noble,
one who inquired into the earliest days.
He sought to retrieve all the past stories.
From every region an aged *mōbad*
he brought, who would <u>remember</u> this book [*nāmeh*].
He asked them about kings of the world
and about the famed and glorious heroes,
when and how they held the world in the beginning
that they should have passed it down to us in such a wretched state,
how, with a lucky star,
every day completed a heroic exploit for them.
The great ones, one by one, recited before him
the stories [*sokhanhā*] about kings and the turnings of the world.
When the lord heard their words from them

> he set the foundations for a renowned book [*nāmeh*].
> Thus it became his memorial in the world.
> The small and the great praise him.[20]

According to the story, this archetypal book had once been disinte-grated – only to become reintegrated many years later at the initiative of a wise Shah who commissioned his vizier to collect the fragments of the disintegrated book. The vizier proceeded to gather experts in poetry from all over the Persian Empire, and each one of these experts brought with him a fragment of the original book. Then, lining up the experts in order, the vizier invited each one of the experts to recite, in proper order, what was contained in each fragment. This way, the archetypal book was reintegrated, and it was this book that became the primal source of Ferdowsi's own Book of Kings. As I have argued in earlier work, "Ferdowsi's description of this genesis amounts to a myth-made stylization of oral poetry";[21] in this chapter I argue that this kind of stylization is a general feature of Iranian traditions writ large.

The medieval Persian narratives about a disintegrated and then rein-tegrated book can be traced back to earlier Iranian narratives. Already in the ancient Avestan tradition, a book could be seen as the foundation of performance. A case in point is a narrative that we find in the *Dēnkard*, which is a tenth-century Middle Persian compendium of Zoroastrian beliefs and customs (in Middle Persian, the word *Dēnkard* or *Dēnkart* means "Acts of Re-ligion"). In the *Dēnkard*, we find a story about the transmission of archetypal Avestan texts – texts that date back ultimately to the second millennium BCE. According to this story, three pivotal moments in the transmission happened in three successive eras of Iranian imperial kingship. The three eras are represented by three kings who stem from three successive Iranian dynasties, which are, (A) the Achaemenid, (B) the Parthian, and (C) the Sasa-nian.

Here I give the relevant text as translated by the noted Iranist Mary Boyce:

Item 3. From the *Dēnkard*, a tenth-century compendium of Zoroastrian beliefs and customs:

(A) Daray, son of Daray, commanded that two written copies of all Avesta and Zand, even as Zardusht [= Zoroaster] had received them from Ohrmazd [= Ahura Mazda], be preserved ... (B) Valakhsh the

---

20. *Shāhnāmeh*, I 21. ed. Bertels et al: 126–36. My own translation.

21. Olga M. Davidson, "Persian/Iranian Epic," in J. M. Foley, ed., *A Companion to Ancient Epic*, ed. (Oxford and Malden, MA: Blackwell, 2005), 268.

Ashkanian commanded that a memorandum be sent to the provinces (instructing them) to preserve, in the state in which they had come down in (each) province, whatever had survived in purity of the Avesta and Zand as well as every teaching derived from it which, scattered through the land of Iran by the havoc and disruption of Alexander, and by the pillage and plundering of the Macedonians, had remained authoritative, whether written or in oral transmission. (C) His Majesty Ardashir, King of kings, son of Pāpak, acting on the just judgement of Tansar, demanded that all those scattered teachings should be brought to the court. Tansār assumed command, and selected those that were trustworthy, and left the rest out of the canon.[22]

As I emphasize in the extract, by way of inserting the letters A B C, there is a spanning of three consecutive dynasties in this narrative. Here I offer a diachronic summary:

(earliest phase A) The Achaemenid dynasty is represented here by the king Darius III, who ruled the Persian Empire from 336 to 330 BCE. In the *Dēnkard*, Darius III is known simply as Daray son of Daray.

(later phase B) The Parthian dynasty is represented here by the king Vologases I, who ruled the Parthian Empire from about 51 to 78. In the *Dēnkard*, Vologases I is known simply as Valakhsh.

(still later phase C) The Sasanian dynasty is represented here by the king Ardashir I, founder and first ruler of the Sasanian Empire, whose kingship extends from 208 to 242 CE. In the *Dēnkard*, Ardashir I is known as Ardashir son of Pāpak.

Item 3 serves as proof that the medieval Persian narrative of Ferdowsi's *Shāhnāmeh* about a disintegrated and then reintegrated book can be traced back to earlier Iranian traditions. One particular detail in this passage needs to be emphasized, namely the reference to the scattering of the texts of the Avesta: To quote again from the translation of Boyce, these texts were "scattered through the land of Iran." In brief, then, the ancient Avestan tradition is seen in terms of a book that serves as the foundation of performance. So there is a deep prehistory to be found in the linkage of book and performance.

All three passages that we have considered here, Items 1, 2, and 3, can be interpreted as evidence for the existence of cultures "where written text

22. Mary Boyce, *Textual Sources for the Study of Zoroastrianism* (Manchester: Manchester University Press, 1984), 114.

and oral tradition coexist."[23] In such cultures, as Gregory Nagy argues, "the idea of a written text can even become a primary metaphor for the authority of recomposition-in-performance."[24] The consequences, as Nagy suggests, are enormous:

> The intrinsic applicability of *text* as metaphor for *recomposition-in-performance* helps explain a type of myth, attested in a wide variety of cultural contexts, where the evolution of a poetic tradition, moving slowly ahead in time until it reaches a relatively static phase, is reinterpreted by the myth as if it resulted from a single incident, pictured as the instantaneous recovery or even regeneration of a lost text, an archetype. In other words, myth can make its own "big bang" theory for the origins of epic, and it can even feature in its scenario the concept of writing.[25]

On the basis of the myths that I have adduced from Irish and Iranian cultures, then, we can say that both of these cultures show an active coexistence of oral and written traditions. But the question remains: are the myths that show this cultural parallelism cognate with each other? That is to say, are these myths inherited from a common cultural source? If there were no linguistic evidence to show that the Irish and Iranian languages were cognate, it could be argued that the parallelisms that we have seen may be simply a matter of coincidence, not common inheritance. But the fact is, these two languages are indeed cognate, as we know from the discipline of Indo-European linguistics, and this fact indicates that the myths we see being transmitted in these languages can likewise be cognate. Wherever we see striking parallelisms in detail between the Irish and the Iranian myths that we compare, the most likely explanation is that such parallelisms are the result of shared inheritance from the Indo-European language family to which Irish and Iranian both belong. Such is the case, I propose, with the shared mythological theme of the disintegrated and then reintegrated text.

23. G. Nagy, *Homeric Questions*, 70.

24. Ibid.

25. Ibid. This argumentation, together with the argumentation I present in my own work, as summarized in the reference I give in footnote 21, seems to be misunderstood by Julia Rubanovich, who quarrels with what she describes as the "oral poetics approach," dismissing as "circular" what can more justly be described as a comparative approach. See Julia Rubanovich, "The *Shāh-nāma* and Medieval Orality: Critical Remarks on the 'Oral Poetics' Approach and New Perspectives," *Middle Eastern Literature* 16:2, 217–26, esp. 218.

Part II

Literature

4

A Trout in the Milk

Vis and Ramin and Tristan and Isolde

Dick Davis

THE PERSIAN ROMANCE *Vis and Ramin*, written by the poet Fakhr al-Din Gorgāni between 1050 and 1055, is in many ways a uniquely fascinating text. It is the first significant Persian romance, and although it differs from its numerous successors in a number of ways, it was nevertheless the source of much of their rhetoric, and also of a number of specific motifs that maintained a central position within the genre as it was practiced in Persian in subsequent centuries. The work is also of interest for what might be called it internationalist implications. Elsewhere[1] I have argued that the rhetoric of *Vis and Ramin*, along with that of two virtually contemporary Persian romances (Ayyuqi's *Varqeh and Golshah* and Onsori's *Vameq and Ozra* – the latter surviving only in very fragmentary fashion) has strong similarities to the rhetoric of Hellenistic and late Roman literature, and that it can be seen as an almost text-book example of what was in Classical antiquity initially referred to as "the Asiatic style," which developed into what came to be called "the Jeweled style." I argued that these poems' rhetoric was probably a late flowering of a style that had been in existence in Western Asia and the Eastern Mediterranean since the time of the Parthians (and, not by coincidence I believe, *Vis and Ramin* is in origin a Parthian tale[2]), when Hellenistic and Asian/Persian culture were permeated with one another, and their literary techniques and motifs formed a spectrum that may have been very Greek at one end and very Persian at the other, but which was clearly, at the cultures' points of contact, a hybrid of both. However, in this chapter I wish to talk less about the poem's rhetorical origins than about its shadowy *Nachleben*,

1. Dick Davis, *Panthea's Children: Hellenistic Novels and Medieval Persian Romances* (New York: Bibliotheca Persica, 2002), passim, and in the introduction to the translation of Fakhraddin Gorgani's *Vis and Ramin* (London: Penguin Classics, 2009), xxi-xxiv.

2. See Vladimir Minorsky, "Vis u Ramin: A Parthian Romance," *Bulletin of the School of Oriental and African Studies* 11 (1943–46): 741–63; 12 (1947–1948): 20–35; 16 (1954): 91–92; "New Developments," 25 (1962): 275–86.

which again, I would contend, takes us beyond the confines of Persia and back into Europe.[3]

To the best of my knowledge the first suggestion of a connection between *Vis and Ramin* and the Tristan legend was made by the distinguished nineteenth-century Italian scholar of Persian literature, Italo Pizzi (1849–1920), in the 1890s. In 1911 Rudolph Zenker, in his article "Die Tristansage und das persische Epos von Wis und Ramin,"[4] concluded that *Vis and Ramin* was probably a major source of the Tristan legend. For a while, the notion hung about in a vague manner in circles interested in Persian medieval literature (at this time it found almost no traction among specialists in medieval European literature), but cold water was poured on the idea by Vladimir Minorsky, who was acknowledged to be the leading expert on *Vis and Ramin* in the 1940s and 1950s, and his perfunctory dismissal of the thesis that *Vis and Ramin* could have been a source for the Tristan legend seemed effectively to put the idea beyond consideration; Minorsky's immense, and well-deserved, scholarly reputation, together with his virtual "ownership" of *Vis and Ramin* in the 1940s and 1950s, meant that no scholar of Persian was especially eager to argue the point with him. Perhaps surprisingly, the cause was then taken up by a couple of specialists in European medieval literature (neither of whom could read Persian), briefly and cursorily by Denis de Rougemont, who referred in passing to the "Persian" quality of the Tristan tale (for Rougemont this "Persianness" was a distinct negative), and thoroughly and exhaustively by the French medievalist Pierre Gallais in his book *Genèse du roman occidental*.[5] Gallais, like Rougemont, remarks on the "un-French" quality of *Tristan* legend, and his book is, among other things, an enthusiastic defense of the argument that *Vis and Ramin* is its primary source.

Once the two tales are set side by side it is immediately obvious that they share a considerable number of motifs, and what is more, these motifs are not scattered randomly through the narratives but occur virtually in the same order to tell what is, with the exception of the narratives' conclusions, in essence the same tale. These motifs include: the hero is a minstrel who is a close relative of the king, and who falls in love with the heroine while escorting her to his king as the king's bride; the central role of the

3. I have found that, in general, European scholars can be quite keen on the idea that *Vis and Ramin*'s rhetoric could owe something to a hybrid Hellenism; they are inclined to be more skeptical toward the notion that the European tale could owe anything to *Vis and Ramin*; with Iranian scholars the reactions tend to be reversed.

4. Rudolf Zenker, "Die Tristansage und das persische Epos von Wis und Ramin," *Romanische Forschungen* 29 (1911): 322–369.

5. Pierre Gallais, *Genèse du roman occidental: essais sur Tristan et Iseut et son modèle persan* (Paris: Tête de feuilles, 1974).

heroine's servant/confidante, who is incidentally a practitioner of magic, as go-between, and, at one point, the substitution of this servant for the heroine in the king's bed; after the hero and heroine have declared their love for one another, the hero turns away from the heroine and persuades himself that he has fallen in love with another woman; the characterization of the women in question (Gol in *Vis*, Isolde of the White Hands in *Tristan*) is extremely similar in the two narratives; a threatened but averted trial or punishment of the adulterous lovers by fire; the lovers' escape to an "uncivilized" forested area, where they "fleet the time carelessly as they did in the golden world" like Shakespeare's courtiers in the forest of Arden;[6] the hero's disguising himself in an enveloping cloak/veil (Ramin as a woman, Tristan as a leper) in order to gain access to the heroine; the king (Mobad) in *Vis* being killed by a boar, while the castle of the king (Mark) in *Tristan* is despoiled by a boar (the moment is crucial to the plot *Vis*, it serves no purpose in the plot of *Tristan*). There are broader and more general similarities as well; both Mark and Mobad are sympathetically portrayed as betrayed older husbands (and kings), rather than as contemptible villains, and neither is treated as the conventional cuckold-as-figure-of-fun; both Tristan and Ramin are the putative inheritors of their kings' realms as there is no closer relative who would be the obvious heir (again, this is crucial to the plot of *Vis*, as Ramin survives Mobad and becomes king; it serves no special purpose in the plot of *Tristan*, as Tristan dies before Mark). Both poems contain spectacular leaps, of which much is made by the works' authors (effected by Tristan when he is cornered by his enemies, and by Vis in order to escape from the rooms where she has been imprisoned; the gender switch seems appropriate, as Vis is the central character of *Vis and Ramin* – compared to her Ramin is something of a cipher - while Tristan is far more central to *Tristan and Isolde* than Ramin is to *Vis and Ramin,* and since he is the male the plot's feats of derring-do are his rather than hers).

Even where there are differences between the narratives, details can indicate that they may be closer than a first impression might suggest. One such difference is the relationship of the hero to his king, who is also the husband of the heroine; Tristan is King Mark's nephew, while Ramin is King Mobad's younger brother. But Ramin's fraternal relationship to Mobad seems contradicted on a number of occasions when he is referred to as Mobad's son, and on more than one occasion he is called Mobad's brother *and* his son in the one statement. What is going on here? Which is he, brother or son? And how could he possibly be both? The answer lies in the marriage customs of pre-Islamic Iran, which not only countenanced but encouraged royal in-

6. *As You Like It*, 1.i.99.

cest. The Sasanian legal text, *The Book of a Thousand Judgments*,[7] includes a number of inheritance laws that deal with the offspring of what to us would be incestuous relationships, including father-daughter, brother-sister, and mother-son. That *Vis and Ramin* takes place in a world in which such marriages were seen as licit, and indeed normal, is confirmed by the fact that very close to its inception the narrative includes the celebration of a brother-sister marriage, and there is no suggestion whatsoever in the narrative that this is an untoward event. And so Ramin could be both Mobad's younger brother and his son if Mobad had married his own mother, which was possible according to Parthian marriage custom; the story doesn't tell us that he did so, and in fact some details in it seem to contradict this, but the quite numerous references to the fact that Ramin is Mobad's son as well as his brother suggest that at some stage in the story's evolution this had been the case. Such a dual relationship was obviously impossible in Europe, and if a tale that seemed to be saying the hero was both his king's sibling and his king's son turned up in Europe it seems plausible that this dual sibling-son relationship could have been rewritten as the hero being the king's sibling's son, which is Tristan's relationship with King Mark.

But there are two much more significant differences between *Tristan* and *Vis*, which seem to argue against a connection between the tales. The two things that everyone who has heard of the *Tristan* story knows about it are that the hero and heroine fall in love as the result of drinking a magic potion, and that the tale ends unhappily, with the lovers' deaths. Between them these two motifs more or less define the tale in the popular imagination, and neither of them are present in *Vis*. But, in the same way that the magic potion is handed to the lovers in *Tristan* by the heroine's confidante, the heroine's confidante in *Vis* is also a practitioner of magic, and though she does not make the lovers fall in love by means of a magic potion, she does facilitate their love by means of magic, in that she fashions a talisman that renders King Mobad impotent with Vis, so that Vis remains a virgin until Ramin sleeps with her, and he is her sole lover until the end of the tale. Now these two details that differentiate *Tristan* from *Vis* – the confidante's different use of magic in furthering her charge's love for the hero, and the fact that one tale ends with the lovers happily united in marriage while the other ends with them both dead – are both present in the poem

7. *Mādigān ī hazār dādistān. The Book of a Thousand Judgments*, (Introduction, transcription and translation of the Pahlavi text, notes glossary and indices by Anahit Perikhanian. Translated from Russian by Nina Garsorian (Costa Mesa: Mazda, 1997). This contains laws relating to brother-sister marriage (p. 237, section 105, 5–10; p. 281, A18, 7–12; p. 315, A36, 6–12), father-daughter marriage (p. 33, 3, 11–14; p. 121, 44, 13–14; p. 235, 104, 12–14) and mother-son marriage (p. 33, 4, 1–4).

Cligès by Chrétien de Troyes (who claims in the introduction to *Cligès* that he has already written a *Tristan*), a narrative which is usually seen as a variant of the *Tristan* story, and which was called by Gallais "a super-Tristan."[8] In *Cligès*, the nurse, like Vis's nurse, uses her magic powers to render the unwelcome husband of the hero's lover impotent with her, and in *Cligès*, as in *Vis*, the adulterous lovers end their lives happily as king and queen, after the fortuitous death of *Cligès*'s uncle, who is also both his king and his lover's husband. It seems clear that if the *Tristan* legend is indeed related to *Vis*, it is the story as it is recounted in *Cligès* that is the one that most closely corresponds to the Persian tale, and the more common European version, as it appears in Tristan, is the variant. Interestingly, and perhaps relevantly, *Cligès* is not set in Western Europe, as *Tristan* is, but in Thessaly and Constantinople, that is on the eastern edge of Christendom, the point at which it joins with the Levant and the lands of Islam, and in the same way that its geography is closer to that of *Vis*'s origin so its details are closer to the tale as it is recounted in *Vis*. The antithetical endings to *Tristan* and *Vis* can make them seem very far apart, and certainly the emotional tenor of the tales diverges radically as the stories end, a divergence that may be ascribed to the expectations of the different cultures that elaborated the tales. *Vis* comes ultimately from a culture that celebrated physical pleasure (the almost complete lack of sexual guilt in *Vis* makes extraordinary reading for a Christian audience, as it does for a modern Islamic audience too, which is clearly one reason why Gorgāni's poem has received only grudging respect in its home country), and Gorgāni's version was written during a period of nostalgia for Persian pre-Islamic civilization, when an imagined (and perhaps real) pre-Islamic *douceur de vivre* had a recognizable cachet within his culture. The tale of *Tristan* was elaborated within a Christian milieu, and the deaths of the hero and heroine imply that the values by which they lived have no ultimate validity in a Christian world, which cannot allow the lovers to be rewarded by success or happiness. It is this version of the tale that gained currency in Europe, and the *Cligès* version, which preserves the ending to the Persian story, became a dead-end within the European Christian context.

It is undeniable that there are important differences between *Vis and Ramin* and *Tristan and Isolde*, but given the many parallels between them, it seems fairly safe to say that if a tale had been found *anywhere* in Europe which displayed as many similarities to the *Tristan* legend, and which preceded that legend's first appearance by over a hundred years, there can be little doubt that a connection between the two would have been taken as *prima facie* obvious, to the point that few scholars would have thought it

8. Gallais, *Genèse*, 145.

worth their trouble to argue against the idea. If for example there were a pre-*Tristan* Celtic tale that contained as many parallels to *Tristan* as *Vis* does, I think we can assume that the case for a direct influence would be taken as closed. But of course there is nothing in Celtic literature, which is the usually assumed source of the *Tristan* story, which even remotely shows as many similarities to the tale of *Tristan and Isolde* as does the tale of *Vis and Ramin*. It is true that Celtic names that bear some similarity to those of the lovers have been found, and they may well have influenced the forms of the lovers' names in various versions of the *Tristan* story as it spread throughout Europe, but before Béroul's version appeared in France in the mid or late twelfth century, the people that these names designated were never associated together in the one tale, and there was no suggestion whatsoever that they were lovers. There is no evidence of a Tristan who was known as a lover in any Celtic story until well after the story of *Tristan and Isolde* was already circulating in Europe. Reviewing Gallais's book on *Vis* and the *Tristan* in *Medium Aevum*, C. E. Pickford, a recognized authority on the Tristan legend and not one to upset the scholarly consensus regarding its origins in a cavalier fashion, points out that "in Cornwall [Gallais] finds no prehistory of Tristan, nor in any other Celtic land" and goes on to state, "[t]he hypothesis of Celtic origin is examined, and, I feel quite rightly, subjected to vigorous scrutiny only to be rejected. Quoting Celticists such as Dr. Rachel Bromwich, Pierre Gallais shows that the thesis of the Celtic origin of the Tristan owes more to the eloquence of Gaston Paris than to the realities of Celtic literary history."[9] Of course dismissing the notion of a Celtic origin for *Tristan* does not mean that its source is necessarily the Persian tale of *Vis and Ramin*, but since there is no other story from any other culture that shows anywhere near as many similarities to *Tristan* as does *Vis and Ramin*, a connection between the two seems at the least plausible.

So far in this chapter I have felt that I am on fairly solid factual ground; the similarities between *Vis and Ramin* and *Tristan and Isolde* are as I have set them out; it is also true that in the two most significant moments in which the tales diverge from one another the "variant" of *Tristan*, Chrétien de Troyes's poem *Cligès*, reproduces the moments as they appear in *Vis and Ramin*, indicating that the Persian narrative, even in those places where *Tristan* apparently diverges from the Persian tale, had its counterpart in

---

9. C. E. Pickford, Review Pierre Gallais, *Genèse du Roman occidental: Essais sur Tristan et Iseut et son modèle persan*, *Medium Ævum* 46 (1977): 145. The French medievalist Gaston Paris (1839–1903) seems to have had Celts on the brain: at one point he ascribed the origins of Romanticism to Celtic, in this case specifically Breton, influence. See Isaiah Berlin, *The Roots of Romanticism* (Princeton: Princeton University Press, 1999), 16.

Europe during the period when the *Tristan* narrative was being elaborated in its various European vernacular embodiments. And in the conspicuous absence of any other candidate as the origin of the *Tristan* legend, it seems a reasonable supposition that there may well be a connection between the two tales. From this point on my suggestions are more speculative; I myself still find them persuasive, otherwise I would not be putting them forward, but I admit that the case for them as evidence of a connection between the tales can be considered more tentative than the parallels set out above.

I should like to consider first the names of the heroes and heroines of the two tales. Although Gorgāni usually refers to his heroine as "Vis" he occasionally calls her "Viseh"; it is clear that this is her real name and that "Vis" is its shortened, familiar form. Now if the tale of *Vis and Ramin* did in fact travel to the west, it would perforce have had to pass through an Arabic speaking country, and the names in the poems would probably have undergone some Arabicization in their pronunciation. The Perso/Arabic letters that spell "Viseh" could be pronounced in various ways in Arabic, but the most obvious way to pronounce them would be "Wisat" or "Wiset," depending on the local pronunciation of short vowels, which varies a great deal in Arabic dialects. The first version of the *Tristan* story to appear in Europe is that by Béroul, written at some time in the second half of the twelfth century; the name of Béroul's heroine is "Iseut" (the final "t" would of course have been pronounced in the twelfth century). From "Wisat" or "Wiset" to "Iseut" is phonetically a very short distance indeed. The dropping of the "w" sound as a word moves from one language or dialect to another is not rare (the comparison of ancient Greek dialects displays a well-known example of the phenomenon), and once the initial "w" is lost from "Wisat"/"Wiset" the name is virtually there. I think it quite likely that the Arabic pronunciation of "Viseh" ("Wiset"/"Wisat") is behind the name "Iseut."

To get from Ramin to Tristan is clearly not such a short phonetic journey as to get from Viseh/Wiset to Iseut. There is however something curious about the names of both heroes, in that in each case an author of the tale remarks on the meaning of the first syllable of his hero's name; further, he remarks on its meaning in the language of his source, not in the language in which he is at the moment writing his story, and he then uses this meaning to comment on the fate of his hero. To my knowledge this authorial drawing attention to the meaning of the first syllable of a hero's name, *and then using this meaning as a commentary on his hero's fate,* is unique for the period, in both Persian and European writing. A coincidence? Perhaps, but if so quite a startling one. Let us look for a moment at the meanings the authors highlight in the first syllables of their heroes' names. Gorgāni says that it is entirely appropriate that his hero is called Ramin, because in pre-conquest Persian "Ram" meant "contented," "satisfied" and after his long tribulations Ramin became a satisfied and contented man. Gottfried von Strassburg says that it is entirely appropriate that his hero is called Tristan, because in French "Triste" means "sad" and Tristan lived a sad life and came to a sad end. In each case the hero's name is seen as a commentary on the nature of his fate, and as the fate in question changes from a happy one to a sad one so the name of the hero changes from one whose first syllable means "contented" to one whose first syllable means "sad." This looks like a deliberate ploy, or even a private joke, on the part of whoever domesticated the tale to a European context and gave it a sad ending, particularly as the meanings of the relevant initial syllables are in each case explicitly emphasized, rather than being allowed simply to speak for themselves, as it were. When for a while, in some versions of the tale, Tristan disguises himself as a merchant, he reverses the syllables of his name and refers to himself as "Tantris." This suggests that his name is something malleable, involving world play and deliberate disguise, a trope that is consistent with the derivation of his name in the way that I have just suggested, since this too involves word play and a deliberate disguise.

Although the above suggestions as to possible connections between the names of the stories' heroes and heroines seem to me to be well within the bounds of the credible, I am aware that many might consider them to be rather far-fetched. I can only say that such readers are sure to find my concluding suggestions even more outré and unlikely, but once one allows for the possibility of a connection between *Vis and Ramin* and *Tristan and Isolde* they do not, I think, seem so improbable.

In *Vis and Ramin* the country of Iran is of course always referred to as just that, Iran, and the word occurs quite often in the course of the story. Now the word "Iran" was not a word that had reached Europe at this time; as far as I know, it does not exist in any medieval European text – the country is always referred to as Pers, or Persis or by some such similar word. So, a tale arrives in Europe set in "Iran." Where is this Iran, in which this exotic tale takes place? "What country, friends, is this"?[10] I do not think it is too much of a leap of the imagination to surmise that someone decided that "Iran" must be Erin, Eire, Ireland – it was the only country in Europe that had a name that sounded even remotely like "Iran." Once this decision had been made, if it was, a lot of the geographical details of the Tristan story fall into place.

From the perspective of France, where the story first appears in Europe, if one is going to get to Ireland one would expect to travel through some part of England, and the nearest way would be to go through Cornwall and

10. *Twelfth Night*, 1, ii, 1.

then across the Irish Sea north of Cornwall to the coast of southern Ireland. *Vis and Ramin* takes place in two areas that are culturally connected but geographically separated, by what is usually presented in the poem as more or less wasteland or desert, to be traversed as soon as possible. The two areas are Marv in what is now Turkmenistan, and Mah, now called Hamadan, in western Iran. Ireland and Cornwall could be assumed to have some cultural continuities, in that to a writer in twelfth-century France who was conscious of their existence both would be seen as countries somewhat beyond the borders of romance civilizations, that is they had an exoticism about them, as any version of *Vis and Ramin* that had reached Europe must certainly also have had, and it might well have been known that both the Cornish and the Irish spoke related versions of the same non-romance language, Gaelic – all this would give them the kind of geographical separation but cultural continuity within a generally exotic and non-romance setting that we find in *Vis and Ramin.*

There is though the awkward fact that Cornwall and Ireland are separated not by wasteland or by desert but by the sea, and indeed, as time went on, the sea became an important and integral part of the Tristan legend – in its romantic culmination in Wagner's opera the whole first act takes place on an ocean-going ship, and the last of the opera's three acts happens in sight of the sea, which is constantly scanned for the approaching ship which will bring Isolde to the dying Tristan. However, perhaps this fact of the sea instead of the desert separating the two main sites of the poem's action is not such a deal-breaker as it might at first appear to be.

Of interest here I would suggest is the Anglo-Saxon poem *Exodus*, which is a poetic retelling of the *Book of Exodus* from the Bible. The Anglo-Saxon *Exodus* is usually dated to the ninth century. What is interesting about it from the point of view of *Vis* is that it is a Western adaptation of a Near-Eastern tale, and that it consistently reinterprets unfamiliar Middle-Eastern features as familiar Western ones, as we might expect it to do. The particular feature that interests me here is that the Israelites' journey across the Sinai desert becomes, in the Anglo-Saxon *Exodus*, a protracted ocean voyage, with sea battles, and sea storms, and all the hazards of early medieval travel in ocean going ships. Anglo-Saxon culture was not familiar with deserts, but it was very familiar with the sea; when presented with a long difficult journey across something unfamiliar called a desert in their source text they substituted a long difficult journey of a kind they were familiar with, a sea voyage. The sea in the Anglo-Saxon *Exodus* stands in for the desert. If *Vis and Ramin* is in fact a source for the *Tristan* story, I suggest the same thing has happened here.

All the evidence adduced above for a connection between *Vis and Ramin* and *Tristan and Isolde* is, admittedly, circumstantial. But it is also I believe cogent and persuasive; how persuasive we can see if we ask ourselves, as I suggested above, whether there would be any doubt whatsoever of such a connection if any European tale that preceded *Tristan* shared as many details with the later tale. As Thoreau remarked, "Some circumstantial evidence is very strong, as when you find a trout in the milk."[11] What we have here, I would suggest, is a very obvious trout in the milk.

11. *The Writings of Henry David Thoreau, Journal*, vol. 2, *1850-September 15, 1851*, ed. Bradford Torrey (Boston and New York: Houghton Mifflin and Company, 1906), 94.

5

"From Hafiz"

Irish Orientalism, Persian Poetry, and W. B. Yeats

Oliver Scharbrodt

Introduction

THE PURPOSE OF THIS ARTICLE is to investigate the reception of and views on Persian mystical poetry within literary and intellectual circles in Ireland at the turn from the nineteenth to the twentieth century. The article thereby focusses on William Butler Yeats (1865–1939), the leading figure of the cultural and literary Irish Renaissance in this period. The initial source of inspiration for this article is Mansour Bonakdarian's historical survey of Iranian Studies in the twentieth-century United Kingdom – which included Ireland until 1922 – in which he refers to Hafiz, the fourteenth-century Persian poet, and his possible influence on Yeats's own mystical ideas.[1] This paper investigates the socio-cultural context in which Yeats was situated, the religious ideas circulated therein, and their expressions in his poetic and prosaic writings. While previous scholarship on his religious ideas has highlighted his interests in India and Hindu Vedantic philosophy in particular,[2] in this article, attention is given to his engagement with classical Persian poetry and its mystical expression, cognizant of the specific socio-cultural context in which this engagement occurred.

In the first part, light will be shed on the historical context and the socio-cultural milieu in which Yeats was placed by investigating his vantage points of engaging with Persian mystical poetry and everything "Oriental" more generally, namely his involvement in the Dublin Hermetic Society and

---

1. Mansour Bonakdarian, "Iranian Studies in the United Kingdom in the Twentieth Century," *Iranian Studies* 43:2 (2010): 274. See also Shamsul Islam, "The Influence of Eastern Philosophy on Yeats's Later Poetry," *Twentieth Century Literature* 19:4 (1971): 285–86.
2. On his religious ideas, see Margaret Mills Harper, "Yeats's Religion," *Yeats: An Annual of Critical and Textual Studies* 13 (1995): 48–71.

Theosophy in general. The second part will discuss the Orientalist reception of and fascination with Persian poetry in late Victorian Britain. Middle Eastern tropes and topics in Yeats's writings and possible influences by the mystical ideas of classical Persian poetry will be examined in the final part, exemplified by his engagement with a particular poem by Hafiz.

Irish Orientalism

Orientalism, since the publication of Edward Said's seminal book,[3] has been understood as "a discourse of domination, both a product of the European subjugation of the Middle East, and an instrument in this process."[4] According to Said, the "Orient" was essentialized and othered in order to justify European imperialism based on the notion of European cultural superiority as opposed to inferior "Oriental" cultures which are depicted as lacking agency, backward, passive, feminine, irrational and superstitious. Said's influential contribution to an understanding of the discourse of Orientalism and arguments against and forth have been well rehearsed in academic scholarship.[5]

However, as some of Said's critics have pointed out, another dimension of the Orientalist engagement with the "East," is not sufficiently recognized by Said and those who have followed suit. Richard G. Fox introduces the term "affirmative Orientalism,"[6] similar to Ronald Inden's coinage "romantic Orientalism,"[7] both of which are based on the dichotomizing nature of Orientalist discourse between "East" and "West" but affirm and revalue the cultural stereotypes inherent to Orientalism. The "Orient" remains the other of Europe but "the good other" whose sensuality and superstitious beliefs become the spiritual and mystical antidote to modern European scientific rationality, whose naturalness counters objectifying and exploitative scientific approaches to nature, and whose slavish adherence to tradition and backwardness is seen as an expression of its primordial cultural authenticity.[8] By affirming and also overturning the Orient-Occident dichotomy,

3. Edward W. Said, *Orientalism* (London: Penguin Books, 2003).

4. Fred Halliday, "Orientalism and Its Critics," *British Journal of Middle Eastern Studies* 20:2 (1993): 149.

5. For an overview of the debate see ibid. See also A. L. Macfie, *Orientalism: A Reader* (Edinburgh: Edinburgh University Press, 2000); idem, *Orientalism* (London: Longman, 2002).

6. Richard G. Fox, "East of Said," in Michael Spinkler, ed., *Edward Said: A Critical Reader* (Oxford: Blackwell, 1992), 152.

7. Ronald Inden, "Orientalist Constructions of India," *Modern Asian Studies* 20:3 (1986): 429–36. See also idem, *Imagining India* (Bloomington: Indiana University Press, 1990).

8. Fox, "East of Said," 151–52. See also Joseph Lennon, *Irish Orientalism: A Literary and Intellectual History* (Syracuse: Syracuse University Press, 2004), 310–11.

affirmative or romantic Orientalism is an expression of "an admiration for, and sometimes, a firm belief in the superiority of Eastern cultures."[9]

As Joseph Lennon illustrates in his seminal work on Orientalism in Ireland, there is a particular Irish dimension to the intellectual and literary engagement with the "East," different to that of late Victorian society in Britain. For figures such as Yeats affirmative Orientalism becomes a means to revive an ancient, pre-Christian Celtic spirituality and poetic imagination, inspired by Oriental tropes, as it is assumed that "the Oriental and the Celtic shared the same deep source – not modern, not industrial, but imaginative and sensual."[10] Yeats appropriated Orientalist narratives in order to culturally de-colonize Ireland and to forge a new "narrative of the nation"[11] or – to use the term of his lifelong friend George William Russell – a new "national being."[12] Yeats and other Irish revivalists engaged with the literature and philosophies of the "East" and established links with spiritual masters, literary figures and political activists whom they saw as authentic voices of Asia and as allies in the revival of a pre-modern, pre-colonial poetic and spiritual heritage common to Asia and Ireland. The identification of cultural resemblances between the Oriental and the Celtic as an expression of reversed or affirmative Orientalism pursues thereby anti-colonial objectives. Yeats searched for "something in Irish life so old that can no longer say this is Europe, that is Asia,"[13] while ultimately creating a cross-cultural anti-colonial fusion that was "*neither* European *nor* Asian; rather, it was *both* European *and* Asian."[14] Not much scholarship investigating Oriental tropes in Yeats's works has been produced. His fascination with Asia is either characterized as "unIrish"[15] or as superseded by his later interest in a Celtic literary revival. However, such a perspective, as Lennon suggests, ignores Yeats's lifelong fascination with the "Orient" and the resonances between notions of Celticism and Orientalism among Irish revivalists.[16]

9. Richard King, *Orientalism and Religion: Postcolonial Theory, India and "the Mystic East"* (London: Routledge, 2002), 92.

10. Lennon, *Irish Orientalism*, 248.

11. Homi Bhabha, "DissemiNation: Time, Narrative, and the Margins of the Modern Nation," in idem, *The Location of Culture* (London and New York: Routledge, 1994), 204. See also Lennon, *Irish Orientalism*, 248.

12. George Russell, *The National Being* (New York: Macmillan, 1930). See also Lennon, *Irish Orientalism*, 248

13. Lennon, *Irish Orientalism*, 250.

14. Ibid.

15. Roy F. Foster, *W. B. Yeats: A Life – Vol. 1: The Apprentice Mage, 1865-1914* (New York: Oxford University Press, 1997), 37. See also Lennon, *Irish Orientalism*, 251.

16. Lennon, *Irish Orientalism*, 262–65.

Yeats and the Theosophical Society

W. B. Yeats encountered Asian philosophies and religious thought through the mediation of Madame Blavatski's Theosophical Society. Theosophy provided him with a gateway to alternative worldviews following his own identity destabilization as a member of a socio-cultural class and community in Irish society that had been placed in a precarious position.[17] The Protestant Anglo-Irish elite in colonial Ireland had been a privileged minority among the Catholic majority and had experienced positive legal, political, and religious discrimination. The Church of Ireland as part of the Anglican Communion – despite a minority religion – was the established church of Ireland until 1871. The disestablishment of the Church of Ireland, the rise of Irish nationalism, the Catholic resurgence in late nineteenth-century Ireland, and the Home Rule Movement calling for greater autonomy of Ireland led to an identity crisis among the Anglo-Irish elite whose hyphenated identity label as both English and Irish was placed in a position of liminality at a time when Irishness began to be increasingly defined against Englishness. As a consequence, some intellectual representatives of the Protestant middle- and upper-class in Ireland such as Yeats and other Irish revivalists experimented with alternative lifestyles and philosophical and religious worldviews. This turn towards "Eastern thought," occultism and other alternative religious orientations resulted from "the Irish Protestant sense of displacement, their loss of social and psychological integration towards the end of the nineteenth century."[18]

The Theosophical Society was founded by the American Colonel Henry Steel Olcott (1832–1907) and the Russian aristocrat Madame Helena Blavatsky (1831–1891) in 1875. The Theosophical Society appears as a product of the various cultural, intellectual, and religious trends of the nineteenth century. As a result of the questioning of traditional Christianity in this period, Theosophy attacked both traditional forms of religion as well as a purely scientific worldview. In addition, the emergence of the Theosophical Society reflects the Orientalist encounter with religious and philosophical ideas of Asia, India in particular, which had been made accessible through various translations of religious texts and the works in the areas of comparative religion and anthropology which disseminated the mythological worlds of

17. On their involvement in Theosophy see Susan Johnston Graf, "Heterodox Religions in Ireland: Theosophy, the Hermetic Society, and the Castle of Heroes," *Irish Studies Review* 11:1 (2003): 51–59. For a general discussion of Yeats's religious and spiritual beliefs see Harper, "Yeats's Religion," 48–77.

18. Foster, *The Apprentice Mage*, 50.

different cultures and religions. Blavatsky, in her central book *Isis Unveiled* (1877), argues that all religions and philosophical systems share the same fundamental beliefs as they all originated from the same divine source. Furthermore, she purports the existence of a hidden spiritual elite, a secret Brotherhood, called the "Mahatmas," located in the Himalayas in Tibet to whom she had access when she visited Tibet and later via telepathy. The Mahatmas instructed her in a secret doctrine whose gradual revelation would propel the spiritual advance of humanity.[19] The major journal publication of the Theosophical Society, *Lucifer*, summarizes the "objects of the Theosophical Society" as follows:

1. To form the nucleus of a Universal Brotherhood of Humanity without distinction of race, sex, class, creed, or colour.

2. To promote the study of Āryan and other Eastern literatures, religions, and sciences, and demonstrate the importance of that study.

3. To investigate unexplained laws of nature and the psychical powers latent in man.[20]

The appeal of this movement lied in its explicitly syncretistic nature as it combined a fascination with Asian religions and philosophies with anti-clericalism and an opposition to atheism and scientific rationality, while at the same time confirming evolutionary and progressive notions of human and civilizational development.

Yeats, together with his friends George William Russell (A.E.) (1857–1935) and Charles Johnston (1867–1931), studied literature produced by the Theosophical Society in their youth and developed an interest in "Eastern philosophy" as a consequence. Together they formed the Hermetic Society of Dublin in June 1885[21] "to discuss the wonders of Eastern philosophy."[22] In his opening speech at the first meeting of the society, Yeats is critical of modern science and its truth claims, advocating a move "into the maze of eastern thought."[23] For Yeats and his associates, "Eastern thought" was discovered primarily through the prism of Hindu philosophy, as it is expressed

19. Richard Ellmann, *Yeats: The Man and the Masks* (London: Faber and Faber, 1961), 58–72. On the Theosophical Society see Bruce F. Campbell, *Ancient Wisdom Revived: A History of the Theosophical Movement* (Berkeley: University of California Press, 1980).

20. *Lucifer: Theosophical Monthly* 11:65, 15 January 1893.

21. See Nicholas Goodrick-Clarke, "3. The Dublin Hermetic Societies (1885–1939)," in Wouter J. Hanegraaff, ed., *Dictionary of Gnosis and Western Esotericism* (Leiden: Brill, 2006), 555–58.

22. Ellmann, *Yeats*, 42.

23. Yeats quoted in ibid., 43.

in the Advaita Vedanta interpretation of the Upanishads,[24] following the particular interest of the Theosophical Society in Hinduism. The visit of Mohini Chatterjee, an Indian missionary for the Theosophical Society to whom Yeats refers as a "Brahmin philosopher,"[25] triggered Yeats's life-long interest in and identification with Vedantic philosophy.[26]

Yeats's engagement with the Middle East and Iran more specifically needs to be seen in the context of his wider-reaching interests in the "East," including his engagement with Hindu Vedanta philosophy, Japanese Noh theater, and occultism and magic: "all these things were the background against which Yeats's intellect worked, and helped to shape his poetic

24. See Islam, "Influence of Eastern Philosophy," 284.

25. William Butler Yeats, *Reveries over Childhood and Youth* (London: MacMillan, 1916), 176.

26. See William Butler Yeats, "An Indian Monk," in idem, *Essays and Introductions* (London: Macmillan, 1961), 427–37. See also Harper, "Yeats's Religion," 62.

imagination."[27] The syncretistic nature of the Theosophical Society and its belief in the inherent unity of all religious and philosophical systems shaped also the outlook of the Irish Theosophers on "Eastern thought" and its relationship with other philosophical and religious traditions:

> From Lao-Tze in the far East to Plotinus, Boehme and other illuminati of the West; from ancient veda and Egyptian hymn to the Gnostic writings of the New Testament and the mystic rhapsodies of the Persian Sufis – the same great truth is nobly and glowingly presented.[28]

In addition this belief of a unity of various mystical traditions, Yeats's engagement with "Eastern" philosophies is often shaped by his own concerns. As Soheil Bushrui illustrates in relation to Yeats's references to Muslim philosophers, his depiction of them very often reflects his own specific occult interests. Yeats's awareness of philosophers like Ibn Sina (Avicenna) and al-Farabi emerges as early as 1896 and is expressed, for instance, in his poem *Rosa Alchemica* which depicts them not "as philosophers, but as magicians, while Arabia itself was the homeland of magic where alchemy has become one of the greatest sciences."[29] *Rosa Alchemica* refers to "Avicenna who was a drunkard and yet controlled numberless legions of spirits" and to "Alfarabi, who puts so many spirits into his lute that he could make men laugh, or weep, or fall in deadly trance as he would."[30] For Yeats, Ibn Sina and other Muslim philosophers were masters of "Eastern magic" reflecting his own aspirations to acquire magical powers through occult practices.[31]

Mir Awlad Ali, "a famous modern Persian poet" in Dublin?

Menachem Mansoor in his 1944 *The Story of Irish Orientalism* provides a brief overview of the history of Oriental Studies in Ireland. Among the figures he

---

27. Soheil B. Bushrui, "Yeats's Arabic Interests," in A. Norman Jeffares and K. G. W. Cross, eds., *In Excited Reverie: A Centenary Tribute to W. B. Yeats, 1865-1939* (London: Macmillan, 1965), 281.

28. *The Irish Theosophist* 4:1,15 January 1893, 11.

29. Bushrui, "Yeats's Arabic Interests," 281.

30. *Rosa Alchemica*, quoted in Bushrui, "Yeats's Arabic Interests," 281.

31. See Robert A. Gilbert, *The Golden Dawn Scrapbook: The Rise and Fall of a Magical Order* (York Beach, Maine: Samuel Weiser, 1997); George Mills Harper, *Yeats's Golden Dawn* (London: Macmillan, 1974); William T. Gorski, *Yeats and Alchemy* (Albany: State University of New Press, 1996).

introduces is Mir Awlad Ali, "a native of Persia"[32] and "famous Persian poet,"[33] who was professor of Arabic, Hindustani, and Persian at Trinity College Dublin and taught for the Indian Civil Service Examination. Likewise, Yeats, in his autobiographical recollections of the beginnings of the Dublin Hermetic Society, mentions a Trinity professor, "a Persian,"[34] who came to the meetings of the society "and talked of the magicians of the East":[35] "When he was a little boy, he had seen a vision in a pool of ink, a multitude of spirits singing in Arabic, 'Woe unto those that do not believe in us.'"[36]

MS 4896, p. 10. By permission of The Board of Trinity College Dublin

Mir Awlad Ali was not Persian but at least "Persianate," to borrow Marshall G. Hodgson's term that describes the spread of Persian language and literature outside of Iran in pre-modern Muslim Central and South Asia.[37] He

32. Menachem Mansoor, *The Story of Irish Orientalism* (Dublin: Hodges, Figgis & Co., 1944), 42.

33. Ibid.

34. Yeats, *Reveries*, 176.

35. Ibid.

36. Ibid.

37. See Marshall G. S. Hodgson, *The Venture of Islam: Conscience and History in a World Civilisation*, vol. 3 (Chicago: Chicago University Press, 1974), 46–52.

was a native of the Awadh state in North India, coming from a notable family from a village close to Lucknow. He worked for the Nawab of Awadh and accompanied him to Britain in his campaign to lobby for a royal stipend.[38] He was appointed as professor of Arabic at Trinity College Dublin in 1861 and later became professor of Hindustani and Persian.[39] He married into an English family and due to his exotic background and position as a Trinity professor became a Dublin socialite involved in various cultural and intellectual activities. As Dublin resident and living representative of the "East," he was invited to give various lectures on issues pertaining to Asia.[40] He was Persianate in the sense that as an aristocratic South Asian Muslim he had received training in and was able to compose Persian poetry. Within the Irish context, there are examples of him composing poetry in English imitating like other contemporaneous English authors the styles and genres of Persian poetry and including Middle Eastern poetical tropes.[41]

He was also a speaker and active supporter of the Irish language as member of the Society for the Preservation of the Irish Language from 1878 until his death in 1898. Playing a leading role in the Society, he was elected as a council member at its inception and often represented the Society at annual meetings of the Irish Teachers' Association.[42] He wrote a letter to the editor of *The Irish Times* in support of the Irish language in which he criticized that "it is despised and abandoned by some unnatural sons and daughters of Erin, and respected and studied by foreigners in France, Germany, and other parts of the civilised world."[43] Introducing the work of the Society for the Preservation of the Irish Language, he hopes that "this withering branch of the ancient tree of philology would ... fully revive and, deeply rooted in its native soil, protected from the hard frost and cutting blast of time, and clad in its emerald robe, will long continue ever fresh and ever green."[44]

Given his prominent position within the Anglo-Irish elite in Dublin and his Asian background, it is not surprising that Mir Awlad Ali became involved in the Dublin Hermetic Society. While his involvement in this society appears to be a reflection of the particular fascination with India of Yeats and

38. See *The Irish Times*, 20 July 1859, 3.

39. See Vivian Ibrahim, "The Mir of India in Ireland: Nationalism and Identity of an Early 'Muslim' Migrant," *Temenos: Nordic Journal of Comparative Religion* 46:2 (2010): 153–73.

40. See, for example, *The Irish Times*, 15 November 1878, 6.

41. See *The Irish Times*, 8 March 1883, 3.

42. Society for the Preservation of the Irish Language, *Annual Report for 1898* (Dublin: Society for the Preservation of the Irish Language, 1898), 28.

43. *The Irish Times*, 27 February 1877, 6.

44. Ibid.

his associates typical for other avant-garde circles in late Victorian society,[45] it is quite curious that his Indian background was not well-known and that he was identified as a Persian by both Yeats and others.

Awlad Ali's public lectures on religious issues also reflect concerns of the Dublin Hermetic Society and the wider Theosophical movement. In 1879, he gave a lecture on spiritualism and in which he refers to the increasing number of British and American associations with interests in spiritualism, emphasizing the universality of spiritualist beliefs to various religious traditions and cultures from Native Americans to the Chinese while discussing specifically "the belief of the Arabs in the existence of spiritual beings called genii."[46] An anonymous review of Mansoor's survey of Irish Orientalism provides indirect evidence that Awlad Ali also shared the syncretistic concerns of the Theosophical Society:

> And I have one small regret – not a complaint – that that picturesque figure of our youth Mir Aulad Ali is given so little space. It was our pleasant experience in those days when his turban adorned the streets of Dublin to hear him discuss the affinities of *Kismet* and Karman [sic], to whose ethical marriage he would have offered no impediment.[47]

The effort to identify different eschatological conceptions as manifestations of Hindu and Buddhist notions of *karma* is not untypical for the Theosophical Society, as an article in the journal *Lucifer* on Zoroastrian ethics which equates the belief in judgment at the *Chanvand* bridge with the law of *karma* illustrates.[48]

Given his expertise in Persian poetry, Awlad Ali gave a lecture on the fourteenth-century Persian poet Hafiz at Trinity College in 1881. He places him in the context of the Sufi tradition, referred to in *The Irish Times* report of the lecture as "Mohammadan Monks."[49] While Mir Awlad Ali admits that, as a student of Attar, Hafiz is closely associated with the Sufi tradition, he also says that Hafiz exhibits an ambivalent attitude towards its various manifestations, exposing in his poetry the hypocrisy and deceit of some Sufis. Mir Awlad Ali mentions in the lecture the initial opposition to Hafiz' burial because of his praise for wine, which should, however, be understood as "spiritual and mystical"[50] and "his intoxication... an allegory."[51] In the lec-

45. Foster, *The Apprentice Mage*, 47.
46. *The Irish Times*, 10 January 1879, 7.
47. H.F.N. (?), *The Dublin Magazine* 20:4 (October-December 1945), 60.
48. *Lucifer: Theosophical Monthly* 11:65 (15 January 1893), 399–407.
49. *The Irish Times*, 6 June 1881, 7.
50. Ibid.
51. Ibid.

ture he uses Herman Bicknell's[52] English translation of Hafiz's poetry and recounts the latter's visit to the poet's tomb in Shiraz: "In conclusion the professor chanted several most melodious odes of Hafiz exactly as they are chanted in the East."[53]

Mir Awlad Ali appears to be among the founding members of the Hermetic Society of Dublin[54] and regularly attended the meetings, as attested by Yeats as well. Given his background and education, it is quite possible that he introduced "Eastern magicians" like Ibn Sina and al-Farabi to Yeats as well as the Persian poet Hafiz in whom Yeats had a particular interest, providing a first-hand learned account of the "Orient" to the members of the Society.[55] Furthermore, there are certain intellectual and cultural synergies between Yeats and Awlad Ali. Both supported the revival of the Irish language and Gaelic culture as a part of a re-assertion of Irish cultural autonomy and were interested in spiritualism and mystical poetry. Both shared also a position of liminality as part of the colonial social elite. Awlad Ali stems from the ruling elite of British India and later associated with the Anglo-Irish establishment in Dublin, Yeats's social milieu. Awlad Ali as teacher for the Indian Civil Service Examination at Trinity College was also partly complicit in British colonialism. At the same time, both expressed strong anti-colonial attitudes. Despite Awlad Ali's position at Trinity, he made several controversial statements against British colonial policies in public,[56] while Yeats searched for ways to revive Gaelic culture against British colonialism.

Translating and Imitating Persian Poetry

A romanticizing encounter with Asian cultures is characteristic of Yeats's approach to "Oriental philosophies" and of the wider Orientalist appreciation of the philosophical and religious literatures of Asia in late Victorian society. While most of this fascination revolved around India and Indian religions due to important colonial ties and translations of Hindu scriptures such as the Upanishads and the Bhagavadgita,[57] the increasing amount of travel literature produced by Europeans who had visited the Middle East also yielded an interest in this region, further facilitated by translations of

52. See Herman Bicknell, *Háfiz of Shíráz: Selections from His Poems* (London: Trübner, 1875).
53. *The Irish Times*, 6 June 1881, 7.
54. Goodrick-Clarke, "Dublin Hermetic Societies," 555. Goodrick-Clarke refers to an "Alaud Alihad" as one of the early members of the Dublin Hermetic Society. Mir Awlad Ali is probably meant.
55. Lennon, *Irish Orientalism*, 192.
56. See, for example, *The Irish Times*, 15 November 1878, 6.
57. King, *Orientalism and Religion*, 118–24.

literary works from the Middle East.[58] Most prominent of these translations is Richard Francis Burton's (1821–1890) English rendering of *Alf Layla wa-Layla* as *Arabian Nights*, which introduced figures like Ali Baba and Aladdin to English literature.[59]

Similar translation activities made Persian poetry accessible and popular among an English-speaking readership. The publication of Edward FitzGerald's (1809–1883) English rendering of the *Ruba'iyat* by Omar Khayyam in 1859 is certainly the most noticeable example of this trend.[60] Omar Khayyam, an eleventh/twelfth century philosopher, mathematician and astronomer, born in Nishapur in North East Iran, was better known for his contributions to algebra than his poetry in the Muslim world. His quatrains were hardly known in the Persianate world before FitzGerald's translation which instigated an obsession with Omar Khayyam across the English-speaking world.[61] Numerous editions of his rendering were published, English imitations of Omar Khayyam's quatrains composed and societies founded to celebrate his life and poetry. An Omar Khayyam Club was established in London in 1892 for the purpose "that a Club be formed of admirers of the Astronomer-Poet on the basis of good fellowship as well as Oriental learning, with good fellowship as the predominant feature."[62] The existence of a similar club named after Omar Khayyam in Dublin is attested from 1897 onwards, holding regular meetings with "dinner as the chief item on the programme."[63]

The immense popularity of Omar Khayyam stems from the ethos of his quatrains which appear to echo the so-called "Victorian crisis of faith":[64]

> And if the Wine you drink, the Lip you press,

58. Bushrui, "Yeats's Arabic Interests," 289–93.

59. Burton was of Irish descent. His grandfather was a rector in Tuam, near Galway. See Mansoor, *Story of Irish Orientalism*, 38.

60. FitzGerald was of Irish parentage and a regular visitor to Ireland. See Mansoor, *Story of Irish Orientalism*, 39.

61. Mansoor – not without cultural stereotyping himself – attributes the success of FitzGerald's translation to his own Irish background and his consequent Irish poetic sensitivities needed for such a translation endeavor: "To the task of translating the Rubaiyat he [FitzGerald] brought the Celtic lyrical genius with its feeling for the underlying sadness of life, so that he succeeded in expressing the elusive mood of the Persian poet in melodious English verse." Mansoor, *Story of Irish Orientalism*, 12. See also *Encyclopaedia Iranica*, s.v. "Khayyam, Omar xi. Impact on Literature and Society in the West" (by Jos Biegstraaten).

62. [Charles Dana Burrage, ed.], *Twenty Years of the Omar Khayyám Club of North America* ([Boston]: Rosemary Press, 1921), 7.

63. *The Irish Times*, 17 July 1897, 6.

64. See Richard J. Helmstadter and Bernard Lightman, eds., *Victorian Faith in Crisis* (London: Macmillan, 1990); Elizabeth Jay, *Faith and Doubt in Victorian Britain* (London: Macmillan, 1986); Timothy Larsen, *Crisis of Doubt: Honest Faith in the Nineteenth Century* (Oxford: Oxford University Press, 2006).

> End in the Nothing all Things end in - Yes -
> Then fancy while Thou art, Thou art but what
> Thou shalt be - Nothing- Thou shalt not be less.[65]

An article in *The Irish Times* of 1899 connects the mania around Omar Khayyam on the British Isles with changes in the nature of religious beliefs in the late nineteenth century. While Omar Khayyam's poetry is often seen as espousing a materialistic and hedonistic ethos, it was more "the centrality of religious doubt"[66] and the skepticism toward "dogmatic certainty"[67] articulated in the quatrains that appealed to a certain segment of the intellectual elite for whom religion has lost its social, cultural and moral monopoly:

> There has taken place some recent change in the mood of the Anglo-Saxon race which enables a large number of people to understand and sympathise with the old rebel against the Orthodox Islamite Puritanism of the East, and that is probably the decay of religious beliefs noticeable of late years.[68]

Apart from the *Ruba'iyat* by Omar Khayyam, the mystical love poetry of the *Diwan-i Hafiz* likewise attracted the fascination of late Victorian society. Gertrude Bell's translation of Hafiz's *ghazals*[69] published in 1897 led to an increased interest in his poetry, while other translations - both in rhyme and in prose - had been available beforehand.[70] The Cork-born journalist, writer, nationalist politician and member of the Irish Parliamentary Party, Justin Huntly McCarthy (1859-1936), published his own translations of some of poems by Hafiz in prose, in addition to a translation of Omar Khayyam's quatrains.[71] In the introduction to his Hafiz translation, McCarthy refers to the oscillation in the reception and interpretation of his poetry between a literal understanding as erotic love poetry and an allegorical as symbolic for the mystical relationship with God, as espoused by other Sufi authors.

---

65. Edward FitzGerald, *Rubáiyát of Omar Khayyám* (Edinburgh and London: Foulis, 1905), no. XLVII.

66. Dick Davis, *The Rubaiyat of Omar Khayyam*, translated by Edward FitzGerald (London: Penguin, 1989), 9.

67. Ibid., 10.

68. *The Irish Times*, 17 June 1899, 6.

69. Ghazals are short love poems of a few verses. See Annemarie Schimmel, *A Two-Colored Brocade: The Imagery of Persian Poetry* (Chapel Hill: University of North Carolina Press, 1992), 22-23.

70. On English translations of Hafiz see Parvin Loloi, *Hâfiz, Master of Persian Poetry: A Critical Bibliography. English Translations Since the Eighteenth Century* (London: I. B. Tauris, 2004).

71. As Loloi establishes, McCarthy's Hafiz translation appears to be plagiarized from two other contemporaneous English translations with which his bears strong resemblances. See Loloi, *Master of Persian Poetry*, 377-80.

Alluding to a similar debate around the poetry of Omar Khayyam, McCarthy states:

> To some the head of Omar is circled with the halo of mysticism, while others see only the vine-leaves in his hair. You will decide for yourself, as you please, whether the Beloved is Spirit or very Flesh, whether the Wine is the Blood of the Grape or the Ichor of Doctrine.[72]

As the prominent example of FitzGerald's translation of Omar Khayyam's *Ruba'iyat* illustrates, a fine line exists between the translation and imitation of poetry. An original poem serves as a source of inspiration and is imitated when "the translator (if now he has lost the name) assumes liberty not only to vary from the words and sense, but to forsake them both as he sees occasion."[73] FitzGerald re-arranged and rendered Omar Khayyam's quatrains into Victorian English, thereby creating a sense of "universality"[74] of this poetry which appears "both familiar and distant; Victorian and English but at the same time medieval and Persian."[75] The success and popularity of FitzGerald's translation/imitation of Omar Khayyam – apart from appealing to the intellectual and spiritual climate of late Victorian society – results from the synergies existing between both figures in terms of their religious skepticism and sense of social and cultural alienation from their respective environments; FitzGerald abhorred the social conventions of Victorian society, while Omar Khayyam's philosophical beliefs set him at odds with the prevailing enforcement of a more dogmatic interpretation of Islam at his time.[76] In Omar Khayyam, "FitzGerald had found, or created, an alter-ego,"[77] a person from a distant place and time who mirrored his own attitudes and beliefs.

The style of Hafiz's *ghazals* was also imitated by English authors,[78] as, for instance, evident in *Hafiz in London* written by Justin Huntly McCarthy which is not a translation of Hafiz's poetry but McCarthy's own poems inspired by the Persian poet.[79] Although aware of the multiple interpretative layers of Hafiz's love poetry – as stated in the introduction to his own trans-

72. Justin Huntly McCarthy, *Ghazels from the Divan of Hafiz* (London: Nutt, 1893), vi–vii.

73. John Dryden quoted in Loloi, *Master of Persian Poetry*, 49.

74. Davis, *Rubaiyat*, 2.

75. Ibid.

76. Ibid., 10–19.

77. Ibid., 33.

78. For a discussion of Hafiz's influence on Romantic poets see Parvin Loloi, "Hafiz and the Language of Love in Nineteenth-Century English and American Poetry," in Leonard Lewisohn, ed., *Hafiz and the Religion of Love in Classical Persian Poetry* (London: I. B. Tauris, 2010), 79–294.

79. Justin Huntly McCarthy, *Hafiz in London* (London: Chatto & Windus, 1886).

HAFIZ IN LONDON

BY

JUSTIN HUNTLY M^CCARTHY, M.P.

اگر بزلف دراز تو دست ما نرسد
گناه بختت پریشان و دست کوته ماست

Londou
CHATTO & WINDUS, PICCADILLY
1886

[The right of translation is reserved]

lations from the *Diwan* - McCarthy in *Hafiz in London* under the impression of FitzGerald's *Ruba'iyat* gives preference for an Epicurean reading of Hafiz. The poem "Praise of Wine," taking a poem by Hafiz with a similar theme as role-model,[80] does not allow for any mystical interpretation but celebrates the consumption of wine as such:

> Once again the ruddy vintage storms the chambers of my brain,
> Steals my sense with its kisses, steals and yet shall steal again.
>
> But I do not blame the grape's blood for the vengeance it wreaks
> When it plants its purple standard on the stronghold of my cheeks.
>
> May Allah confer his blessings on the hands that pluck the grape,
> May their footsteps never fail who tread its clusters out of shape.
>
> Since the love of wine was written by Fate's finger on my brow,
> What is written once is written, and you cannot change it now ... [81]

80. Loloi, *Master of Persian Poetry*, 56–57.
81. McCarthy, *Hafiz in London*, 67–68. See also Loloi, *Master of Persian Poetry*, 56–57.

Quite similar to FitzGerald's appropriation of Omar Khayyam's poetry, "in his 'Hafiz' McCarthy has found an effective poetic mask for his own creative sensibility. In Hafiz McCarthy has discovered a philosophic and poetic stance – as much his own invention as objectively present in the Persian poet – which has enabled him to articulate his own view of his own times."[82]

The late Victorian encounter with Persian poetry, as the examples of translations/imitations of Omar Khayyam's and Hafiz's poetry suggest, illustrates the *modus operandi* of affirmative Orientalism in the appropriation of poetic, literary, or spiritual figures of the "East." They often serve as poetic personae or alter egos for the articulation of philosophical beliefs and socio-moral views of those who are inspired by their works and imitate and appropriate them. The "Orient" becomes a canvas onto which worldviews which potentially challenge or contradict established convictions are projected. It is through the poetic mask of the "Oriental Other" that such alternative views can be articulated. Yeats's own engagement with "Eastern thought" serves similar purposes as it provided an alternative spiritual and poetic landscape which appeared different to established forms of Christianity and challenged the dominant discourse of scientific rationality, while at the same time informing Yeats's own notions of revived or re-invented Celtic poetic and literary sensitivities: "He found in all of them remedies for modern ills; moreover, within them he discovered age-old parallels to what he saw as a vanishing Celtic Ireland."[83]

Yeats and Hafiz

Parvin Loloi in her survey and assessment of English writers and poets imitating the style of Hafiz's poetry arrives at the following judgment:

> It is disappointing that with some few honourable exceptions the meeting of English poets with Hâfiz, outside the act of translation itself, should have proved so unproductive...*No* comparable figure in English literature has undertaken an imaginative enterprise of such profundity and scope as Goethe's "meeting" with Hâfiz.[84]

One of these "honourable exceptions" among authors writing in English is the Irish writer W. B. Yeats. In November 1906, Yeats published a frag-

82. Loloi, *Master of Persian Poetry*, 58.

83. Lennon, *Irish Orientalism*, 247

84. Loloi, *Master of Persian Poetry*, 75. See Johann Wolfgang von Goethe, *West-östlicher Diwan* (Leipzig: Insel-Verlag, 1937). On Goethe's engagement with Hafiz see Ali Radjaie, *Das profan-mystische Ghasel des Hafis in Rückerts Übersetzungen und in Goethes Diwan* (Würzburg: Ergon Verlag, 1998).

ment derived from Hafiz in *The Gentleman's Magazine*, entitled "The Tresses of Hair":

> Hafiz cried to his beloved, "I made a bargain with that brown hair before the beginning of time, and it shall not be broken through unending time," and it may be Mistress Nature knows that we have lived many times, and that whatsoever changes and winds into itself belongs to us. She covers her eyes from us, but she lets us play with the tresses of her hair.[85]

Among his personal papers there is a handwritten note with these lines attributed to Hafiz: "From the unbeginning of eternity my heart made a bargain with your [?] to unending eternity it will not be broken."[86] They would re-appear slightly modified in different places later on. In the play *Diarmuid and Grania* it is Diarmuid who confesses his love to Grania before his death, exclaiming: "Life of my life, I knew you before I was born, I made a bargain with this brown hair before the beginning of time and it shall not be broken through unending time."[87] This line is also alluded to in Yeats's poem "His Bargain":

> Who talks of Plato's spindle;
> What set it whirling round?
> Eternity may dwindle,
> Time is unwound,
> Dan and Jerry Lout
> Change their loves about.
> However they may take it,
> Before the thread began
> I made, and may not break it
> When the last thread has run,
> A bargain with that hair
> And all the windings there.[88]

His life-long fascination with this line from Hafiz is also evident in its final appearance in Yeats's writings in a diary entry of 1930: "I made a bargain with that hair before the beginning of time."[89]

---

85. Re-printed in W. B. Yeats, *Early Essays*, ed. by George Bornstein and Richard J. Finneran (New York: Scribner 2004), 211.

86. National Library of Ireland, Yeats Papers, "From Hafiz" [NLI MS 30,049].

87. William Butler Yeats, *The Collected Works, Vol. 2: The Plays*, ed. by David R. Clark and Rosalind E. Clark (Basingstoke: Macmillan, 2001), 580.

88. William Butler Yeats, *Yeats's Poems*, ed. by A. Norman Jeffries (London: Macmillan, 1989), 378.

89. William Butler Yeats, *Explorations*, selected by Mrs. W. B. Yeats (London: Macmillan 1962), 300 quoted in Yeats, "The Tresses of Hair," note 1, in *Early Essays*, 445.

Yeats paraphrased a couplet from the *Divān-e Ḥāfez*:[90]

در ازل بست دلم با زلفت پیوند
تا ابد سر نکشد و از پیمانسر نرود

At the time when he published this line for the first time in 1906, a few translations of the *ghazal*, from which the couplet was taken, were available in English.[91] Sources for it were either Robinson's prose translation of 1875,[92] Clarke's translation published in 1891 or more likely Justin McCarthy's of 1893 which was produced in prose, similar to Yeats's rendering. Clarke translates this couplet as follows:

> In eternity without beginning, covenant with Thy tress-tip, my
>   heart established:
> Till eternity without end, it draweth not forth its head; and, from
>   the head of
> the covenant, ——— goeth not.[93]

McCarthy's prose translation is less poetic but more readable and closer to Yeats's version:

> From time without beginning, my heart made convenant [sic] with
> thy tresses: to time without end, my promise shall never be broken.[94]

This particular couplet by Hafiz and the entire *ghazal* as well as the available English translations of it illustrate the complexity and ambiguity of the *Divān-e Ḥāfez* in general around its literal romantic-erotic sense and its allegorical mystical interpretations.[95] The *ghazal* by Hafiz from which the line is taken develops the notion of a predestined love relationship. This love has been written onto the heart of the lover and will survive even after his death. This central statement on the nature of this love relationship is particularly emphasized in the couplet from the *ghazal* which Yeats appropriated. Apart from this literal meaning, an allegorical mystical interpretation addresses

---

90. This is based on the numbering of Mas'ud Farzād, *Jāme'-e Nosakh-e Ḥāfez* (Shiraz: Enteshārāt-e Dāneshgāh-e Pahlavī, Kānun-e Jahānī-ye Ḥāfeẓ-Shenāsi, 1968). See Loloi, *Master of Persian Poetry*, 81.

91. See Loloi, *Master of Persian Poetry*, 172

92. Samuel Robinson, *A Century of Ghazels, or a Hundred Odes, Selected and Translated from the Diwan of Hafiz* (Whitefish, MT: Kessinger Publishing, 2010 [reprint of 1875]).

93. H. Wilberforce Clarke, trans., *The Dīvān-i-Ḥāfiz* (Bethesda, MD: Ibex, 1998), 462.

94. McCarthy, *Ghazels*, 77.

95. On this debate see Carl W. Ernst, *The Shambhala Guide to Sufism* (Boston and London: Shambhala, 1997), 158–66.

salient mystico-theological doctrines about the relationship between God and humanity, usually described as that of two lovers in Sufi love poetry. The particular object of desire in the line, the Beloved's tress or lock (*zolf*), is a symbol frequently used in Hafiz's *ghazals*. In Sufi interpretations it signifies "the attraction of God's grace" and "the concealment of the divine essence."[96] The symbol of the tress articulates the notion that the divine essence as a whole is inaccessible and unfathomable for human beings with only a tress as a symbol of his flash-like "epiphany"[97] in reach. The Lover made a covenant (*bast ... payvand/paymān*) with the Beloved's tress. The term "covenant" has wider theological significance within the Biblical traditions and in the Qur'an. It describes the primordial covenant God made with humanity, as introduced in Qur'an 7:172, when God gathered the whole of humanity, all the "Children of Adam," before their creation and asked them: "Am I not your Lord (*alastu bi-rabbikum*)?," to which they replied in the affirmative. Sufi commentators refer to this event as the "day of 'am I not'" (*ruz-e alast*) which established the primordial and eternal love relationship between God and humanity,[98] even before the world had come into existence.[99] The pre-existence and eternity of this covenant is expressed in this *ghazal* through Arabic terms denoting two aspects of eternity: *azal* (eternity without beginning/pre-existence) and *abad* (eternity without end).

The idea of a predestined love relationship which survives the vicissitudes of time and even death is also articulated in Yeats's poem "His Bargain" and in the context in which the line is used in the play *Diarmuid and Grania*. Yeats was also aware of the more mystical meaning of this line which is evident in its initial publication in *The Gentleman's Magazine* in 1906. Following the quote from Hafiz, Yeats identifies "Mistress Nature" as the owner of the tresses with whom the lover had made "a bargain." Nature is seen as inaccessible – similar to Sufi notions of the divine – with only her locks being in reach to the lover to a limited extent. Yeats's further explication of the line also refers to the idea of reincarnation with Nature knowing the multiple lives of each human and being in control of the process as well. Seeing the divine in nature resembles the existential monism articulated in Vedanta

96. Clarke, *Dīvān*, 47, n4.

97. Leili Anvar, "The Radiance of Epiphany: The Vision of Beauty and Love in Hafiz's Poem of Pre-Eternity," in Lewisohn, ed., *Hafiz and the Religion of Love*, 126.

98. For a discussion of this theme in Hafiz's poetry see also Ali-Asghar Seyed-Gohrab, "The Erotic Spirit: Love, Man and Satan in Hafiz's Poetry," in Lewisohn, ed., *Hafiz and the Religion of Love*, 107–13.

99. For a discussion of Hafiz's references to the "day of covenant," see Anvar, "Radiance of Epiphany," 125–30.

philosophy as appropriated by the Theosophical Society which assumes the essential unity of the divine with the world and each individual soul.[100] Describing the divine and mystical in nature in terms of a love relationship resonates with Sufi interpretations of Hafiz's Persian love poetry as well.

The confluence of erotic human love and mystical divine love, which Sufi commentators attest to Hafiz's poetry and which some English translators likewise reiterate,[101] echoes Yeats's particular concern with a reconciliation of sexual and spiritual love and explains his attraction to this verse. Yeats and other Irish revivalists like A.E. shared a sense of dissatisfaction with the Christian separation of spirituality and sexuality, which the latter explicitly criticized in his essay "Religion and Love." Critical of the tradition of arranged marriages in Irish society in particular, A.E. attributes the unromantic and cold attitude towards sexuality to this tradition as well as to the Christian rejection of sexual love as inherently sinful. In contrast, A.E. argues, one should see the divine in women and the divine nature of sexual love: "In the free play of the beautiful and natural human relations lie the greatest possibilities of spiritual development."[102] As A.E. suggests here, romantic love and sexuality become means for enhancing one's spirituality. Yeats, in a similar vein, develops a connection between mystical and sexual love in the novel *A Vision*, identifying sexuality as the best symbol of the reconciliation of opposites: "One feels at moments as if one could with a touch convey a vision – that the mystic vision and sexual love use the same means – opposed yet parallel existences."[103]

Given Yeats's and A.E.'s Protestant background and socialization in a primarily Catholic environment in Ireland,[104] both drew inspiration from other sources in their efforts to create "an alliance between body and soul

100. This concept is not alien to Sufi thought either, as the notion of "unity of being" (*wahdat al-wujūd*), which is controversially debated among Sufi authors, illustrates. (See Abdul Haq Ansari, "Ibn 'Arabī: The Doctrine of *Wahdat al-Wujūd*," *Islamic Studies* 38:2 (1999): 149–92). Although Yeats's vantage point would have been Vedanta philosophy as appropriated by the Theosophical Society – clear, for instance, in his reference to reincarnation –, as a consequence of the belief of the inherent unity of all mystical systems he would have seen Hafiz as a proponent of similar ideas.

101. For instance, Clarke's Hafiz translation "professes to give the literal and the sufistic meanings" (Clarke, *Dīvān*, viii). See also Loloi, *Master of Persian Poetry*, 329–30.

102. George Russell, "Religion and Love," in *The Descent of the Gods: Comprising the Mystical Writings of G. W. Russell "A.E.",* ed. by Raghavan Iyer and Nandini Iyer (Gerrards Cross: Colin Smythe, 1988), 530.

103. Yeats quoted in Ellman, *Man and Masks*, 264.

104. For Yeats's critique of Christian views of sexuality and love see, for example, his "Supernatural Songs" (Yeats, *Poems*, 402–07). See discussion of Elizabeth Butler Cullingford, *Gender and History in Yeats's Love Poetry* (Cambridge: Cambridge University Press, 1993), 257–60.

our theology rejects."[105] The notion of affirmative Orientalism is also evident in their use of these various "Eastern" sources: the Christian Occident has lost its appreciation for romantic love and developed a cold and distanced attitudes towards human sexuality which needs to be redeemed by the sensuality of the Orient and its valorization as a symbol of and instrument for spiritual development and achieving mystical union with the divine.[106] Yeats's autobiographical novel, *The Speckled Bird*, articulates this idea of a revitalization of Christianity through Eastern influences when the novel's, hero, Michael, explains his plans to journey to the Middle East in order to reform Christianity and enrich it with emotionality and sexuality:[107]

> He was going to the East now to Arabia now to Persia, where he could find among the common people as soon as he had learnt their language some lost doctrine of reconciliation; the philosophical poets had made sexual love their principal symbol of divine love and he had seen somewhere in a list of untranslated Egyptian manuscripts that certain of them deal with love as polthugic [theurgic?] power... and surely he would find somewhere in the East, a doctrine that would reconcile religion with natural emotions, and at the same time explain these emotions. All the arts sprang from sexual love and there they could only come again, the garb of religion when that reconciliation had taken place.[108]

In the Persian poet Hafiz, Yeats found one of those "philosophical poets" that articulate the notion of divine love through the symbolism of romantic and erotic love.[109]

Conclusion

The encounter with Persian poetry in the context of affirmative or romantic Orientalism often involved the innovative re-creation of this poetry in translations/imitations onto which the translator/author projects his/her

105. W. B. Yeats, *Essays and Introductions* (London: Macmillan, 1961), 451. See also Culling-ford, *Gender and History*, 253.

106. See also Cullingford, *Gender and History*, 245–60. On engagement with Tantrism see Islam, "Influence of Eastern Philosophy," 286–89.

107. Islam, "Influence of Eastern Philosophy," 286.

108. William Butler Yeats, *The Speckled Bird: An Autobiographical Novel, with Variant Versions*, ed. by William H. O'Donnell (Basingstoke: Palgrave Macmillan, 2003), 80–81.

109. For a discussion of the mystical-cum-erotic imagery in Hafiz's poetry see Leonard Lewisohn, "The Mystical Milieu: Hafiz's Erotic Spirituality," in Lewisohn, ed., *Hafiz and the Religion of Love*, 31–73.

own beliefs and worldviews conceiving the respective Persian poet as his alter ego or soul-mate. Such a projection of the autobiographical self to the Oriental other is also characteristic of Yeats's intellectual and literary engagement with "Eastern" literatures and philosophies. Apart from assuming an inherent familiarity between ancient Ireland and Asia, Yeats also used Oriental role-models as "poetic masks" to articulate his own religious and spiritual ideas. Such an approach affirms Orientalist cultural stereotypes, construing the Orient as antithetical to Europe while celebrating its spiritual superiority.[110]

The manner in which Yeats and others engaged with the "East" also suggests that one cannot speak of any direct influence by specific Oriental figures, texts and ideas but rather of their selective appropriation to experiment with and develop new ideas. Yeats intended to create a new religious system that would be closer to pre-Christian Celtic spirituality. Similar to other Irish revivalists, it was the "Orient" that provided an inspiration to Yeats for such a re-creation of Celtic religion which was seen as closer to nature and more appreciative of sexuality. Yeats's and A.E.'s criticism of the Christian suppression of sexuality constructed the "East" as a counterweight in which sexuality and mysticism were not polar opposites but two expressions of the same reality. They could find support for such a view in Hafiz's Persian love poetry but also in Tantric philosophy or in the Krishna cult of Vaishnava Hinduism, to which Yeats's friend Rabindranath Tagore (1861–1941) was particularly affiliated.[111]

Yeats was part of a socio-cultural context in which the Orientalist engagement with Asia entailed among other things a particular fascination with Persian poetry, as the examples of Omar Khayyam and Hafiz illustrate. This chapter made a contribution to understanding this context by investigating Yeats's Orientalist engagement with Persian poetry, as part of his fascination and engagement with "Eastern thought" more generally. Despite his life-long interest in the "Orient" not much scholarship on Oriental tropes in his poetry and his engagement with "Eastern thought" has been produced and further research is needed to identify in particular Middle Eastern themes and motifs in Yeats's *œuvre*.[112]

110. Susan Bazargan, "W.B. Yeats: Autobiography and Colonialism," *Yeats: An Annual of Critical and Textual Studies* 13 (1995): 201–24.

111. See Cullingford, *Gender and History*, 252–57; Islam, "Influence of Eastern Philosophy": 286–89; Harper, "Yeats's Religion," 62. On the relationship between Yeats and Tagore see Lennon, *Irish Orientalism*, 265–81.

112. The exceptions are, for example, Lennon, *Irish Orientalism*, 247–89, and Bushrui, "Yeats's Arabic Interests," 280–314.

6

Joycean Modernism in a Nineteenth-Century Qur'an Commentary?

A Comparison of the Bab's *Qayyūm al-asmā'* with Joyce's *Ulysses*

Todd Lawson

We are the first generation in the West able to read the Koran, if we are able to read *Finnegans Wake*. ~ Norman O. Brown[1]

Introduction

NUMEROUS STRUCTURAL, THEMATIC, AND RECEPTION PARALLELS exist between two otherwise quite incommensurable literary works. The one is James Joyce's well-known, controversial and vastly influential *Ulysses*, generally considered the first major work of the modernist movement in European literature. The second, entitled *Qayyūm al-asmā'*,[2] is the virtually unknown, unpublished and unread yet highly distinctive and unusual commentary on the 12th sura of the Qur'an by the Iranian prophet Seyyed Ali Mohammad Shīrāzī (1819–50), better known to history as the Bab. By suggesting the existence of parallels and similarities between these two works it is not also suggested that there is any sort of connection between them or their authors, genetic, social, historical, or otherwise. But, both authors wrote at specific and intense moments of cultural crisis and change in their respective socio-historical situations. And each was profoundly and acutely aware of the particular centrality of the literary tradition in which they wrote and the literary weight of the sources and models for their respective compositions. In the case of Joyce and *Ulysses*, the weight and

---

1. "The Apocalypse of Islam," *Social Text* 8 (Winter 1983–1984): 155–71, 168.
2. "Sustainer of the Divine Names" There are two other titles for this extraordinary composition: *Commentary on the Chapter of Joseph* (Qur'an 12)/*Tafsīr sūrat Yūsuf* and *The Best of Stories/Aḥsan al-qaṣaṣ*. *Qayyūm al-asmā'* – though difficult to translate properly – is probably the most common. See Todd Lawson, *Gnostic Apocalypse in Islam: Qur'an, Exegesis, Messianism, and the Literary Origins of the Babi Religion* (London and New York: Routledge, 2011), 77.

authority of this literary history is represented by the Odyssey and Joyce's appropriation (and simultaneous celebration and critique) of the epic tradition, exemplified by the Odyssey. In the case of the Bab and his *Qayyūm al-asmā'*, the quite considerable and truly unique weight and authority of his tradition is represented by the Qur'an, on which this ostensibly exegetical work is modeled.[3] In actuality, with this composition, which is better thought of as being in the disguise of exegesis, the Bab is claiming the same authorial independence and originality exemplified by the Qur'an itself. The adoption of the similarly monumental and sacrosanct genre of scriptural exegesis (*tafsīr*) for this disguise is only a little less daring than the Qur'an imitation that it "hides." Our author, a merchant by profession and class, came from outside the typical learned class and was indeed unschooled in the Islamic sciences according to prevailing standards. He was also only 25 years old at the time of writing and would have thus been regarded as far too immature, even were he of the scholarly class, to attempt such a work. The grandiosity and brashness of presuming to compose a new Qur'an is analogous to Joyce's rewriting the epic in his *Ulysses*, but actually outstrips it in terms of outrageousness because of the Qur'an's unique place in Islamic religious scholarship and culture. In both authors their work is simultaneously a literary fiction paying homage to tradition and an authentic occasion for unprecedented – if not shocking – originality. This is the primary structural analogy: both the Odyssey and the Qur'an (and its traditional exegesis) occupy monumental and epic space in their respective cultural contexts, and both will appear to be deeply violated and disfigured by our authors. Such innovative, thoroughgoing and self-conscious imitation and improvisation on these venerable symbols and metonyms of culture had not been previously achieved or attempted to the degree we have in these two works.[4] (See below figures 1 & 2). In what follows, we will give some brief introduction to the generally well-known life and celebrated works of James Joyce, some necessarily more extended introduction to the much less well-known life and works of the Bab. After this, we will focus on a comparison of the two works at hand to illustrate formal and thematic similarities. This comparison will focus on a few major topics: (1) the formal structure of the two works and (2) the thematic concerns of the two works, such as (a) time, (b) polarities or oppositions and their resolution, (c) the relation between form

---

3. Todd Lawson, "Interpretation as Revelation: The Qur'an Commentary of Sayyid 'Alí Muhammad Shírází, the Báb," in Andrew Rippin, ed., *Approaches to the History of the Interpretation of the Qur'an* (Oxford: Oxford University Press, 1988), 223–253.

4. On epic as metonym for culture see Richard P. Martin, "Epic as Genre," in John Miles Foley, ed., *A Companion to Ancient Epic* (Malden, MA: Blackwell Publishing, 2005), 9–19.

and content, (d) the prominence of epiphany, manifestation, advent and apocalypse, (e) the theme of heroism, reading and identity.

James Joyce and His Work

James Joyce (1882–1940) was born in Dublin, acquired from the Jesuits a thorough education including the classics and theology, excelled as a scholar of modern languages at University, and at the young age of twenty-two left Ireland, more or less for good, in 1904. He is considered *the* father of literary modernism because of his two major books, *Ulysses* and *Finnegans Wake.* Both works represent radical innovations in the art of the novel and changed forever the way literary art was construed and practiced. The works were also highly controversial, attracting censorship, ban, derision, and condemnation on the grounds of obscenity and general structure and style of which the famous (or infamous) "stream of consciousness" (perfected by Joyce) was a major feature and which challenged the reader in ways no earlier work of literary art had done. Today, Joyce has been vindicated and recognized as a great literary genius. No less an authority than Northrop Frye deems his *Finnegans Wake* a uniquely powerful example of literary art in our time.[5] The library of Joyce scholarship is massive, with commentaries, concordances, dedicated journals, analyses, appreciations, imitations, criticism and *explications de texte* seemingly without number. During his life he struggled with poverty, ill-health and family crises and is distinguished by his heroic dedication to his art – which he never abandoned, even momentarily.[6] In the case of the author of the older Arabic work, there is really no reason to believe readers should have even the barest notion of who he was. In fact, one of the somewhat ironic facts that the present comparison records is that on the one hand, in the case of *Ulysses*, a daring literary experiment resulted in universal renown (and/or infamy), celebrity and veneration, highly productive literary influence and a continuous tradition of scholarship devoted to the study of Joyce and his works.[7]

5. "This is the only twentieth century book that I find myself living with, in the way that I live with *Tristram Shandy*, Burton's *Anatomy*, Dickens, and the greater poets. It is an inexhaustible word hoard of humor, wit, erudition, and symbolism; it never, for me, degenerates into a mere puzzle, but always has on every page something to astonish and delight." Northrop Frye, in *The American Scholar* 30:4 (Autumn 1961): 606. (My thanks to Robert Denham for this quotation.)

6. The standard biography is Richard Ellmann, *James Joyce* (New York: Oxford University Press, 1982).

7. It is very difficult to choose a single title for a comprehensive study of Joyce, his art and influence, however the interested reader will be handsomely repaid in the recent *James Joyce*

The Bab and His Work

The daring literary experiments of the Bab resulted in the opposite: obscurity, disregard, contumely, and ultimate imprisonment and death by firing squad.[8] The literary innovations of the text were not pursued or emulated by later authors because of such extra-literary and extra-artistic factors as the deeply embastioned cultural and religious attitudes toward the Qur'an as inimitable and final revelation. It will be of some useful interest to provide a very brief outline of this author's life and career before continuing further with the more purely literary comparison of the two works, *Ulysses* and the *Qayyūm al-asmā'*. "The Bab" is an Anglicization of the Arabic *al-bāb*, the usual word for "door" or "gate" in that language. In the present instance, it functions as a title with a very long history, especially in Shi'i Islamic religious literature. The general understanding is that the word designates one who represents the twelfth or hidden Imam of *Ithna-'ashari* (so-called Twelver) Shi'ism, even though it is clear that the word has frequently indicated statuses other than mere representative to suggest the Imam and the prophet himself. It is also true that in the Islamic philosophical tradition the intellect was frequently termed "the gate" [to knowledge].[9]

The Bab was born in Shiraz in 1819 into a family of merchants. His precocity and piety caused remark and anxiety amongst his family, and teachers were challenged by his intellect and originality. The time, according to Shi'i sacred history, was propitious and pregnant with eschatological event, it being 1,000 years since the disappearance of the long-awaited hidden Imam. In his early twenties, the Bab abandoned the life of a merchant to join the circle of a prominent millenarian teacher based in the holy shrine cities of Iraq. This teacher, Seyyed Kāzem Rashti (1793–1844), was a learned Persian mulla and mujtahid and successor to the Arab polymath, philosophical theologian, and mujtahid Shaykh Ahmad al-Ahsā'i (1753–1826). These

---

in Context edited by John McCourt, Cambridge University Press, 2009. Of course, there is no substitute for reading the major works of Joyce himself, beginning with the collection of short stories, *Dubliners* (1914), *The Portrait of the Artist as a Young Man* (1916), *Ulysses* (1922) and finally *Finnegans Wake* (1939). In what follows, reference to *Ulysses* will be indicated by *U*, standing for James Joyce, *Ulysses* (New York: Vintage Books, 1961), to *Finnegans Wake* by *FW*, standing for James Joyce, *Finnegans Wake* (London: Penguin Books, 1992).

8. The work may be thought to have had quite considerable influence from another angle, inasmuch as it was the first announcement of a powerful if short-lived messianic movement in Iran which ultimately led to the rise and world-wide expansion of the Baha'i Faith. But this is not literary influence as usually understood.

9. Todd Lawson, "The Terms Remembrance (*dhikr*) and Gate (*bab*) in the Bab's Commentary on the Sura of Joseph," in Moojan Momen, ed., *Studies in Honor of Hasan M. Balyúzí*, Studies in the Babí and Baha'í Religions, volume 5 (Los Angeles: Kalimat Press, 1989), 1–63.

two teachers had, on the brink of the Twelver Shi'i eschaton, attracted a large following especially of young seminarians, because of their creative and compelling interpretation of the standard topics of Shi'ism, including the idea of the return of the hidden Imam, the imminent resurrection and day of judgment (*qiyāma*), or rising of the Qā'im who, as Mahdi ("rightly guided one"), would lead an army of spiritual warriors against the forces of darkness at the end of time. This following, which burgeoned throughout Iran during the middle half of the nineteenth century came to be known as the *Shaykhiyya* – "the Shaykhis" – an eponymous reference to the above-mentioned Shaykh Ahmad al-Ahsā'i. The main thrust of the eschatological teaching of the first two masters of the Shaykhi School was that while the return of the hidden Imam is assured, the end of time and creation is not. Rather, what ends is a cycle of prophecy that will be replaced by a new cycle of fulfillment.[10] They furnished a vocabulary and method for thinking about and perhaps domesticating the potentially unruly and mysterious forces that were gathering at the time and would issue in profound social and historical change. In short, they provided a discourse for the emergence of a distinctive Qajar modernity from its traditional past.[11] There was also much about the form and content of the Shaykhi doctrine that appealed to an Iranian audience; not least, was the way in which the masters of the school combined the mystical with the rational in the interest of solving the many supra-rational problems confronting Shi'i religion. In addition, the prolific writings of the first two teachers are characterized by a strong literary and poetic aesthetic very much in keeping with the general élan of Islamicate scholarship in which style is as important as substance. In the case of the Shaykhis, their technical terminology, deriving from the broader Islamic philosophical and mystical tradition, is at times transmuted into a kind of poetry of metaphysics. Thus, one may also be justified in thinking of it as a literary movement as well as a theological movement in which theological connections and resonances have literary *value* and literary connections

10. A specifically Viconian cyclism eventually would be adopted by Joyce, not in *Ulysses*, but rather in his last work, *Finnegans Wake*. However, cyclism is not absent from *Ulysses*, as will be seen.

11. Abbas Amanat, *Resurrection and Renewal: The Making of the Babi Movement in Iran, 1844-1850* (Ithaca, NY: Cornell University Press, 1989); Mangol Bayat, *Mysticism and Dissent: Socioreligious Thought in Qajar Iran* (Syracuse: Syracuse University Press, 1982); Juan Ricardo Cole, *Modernity and the Millennium: The Genesis of the Baha'i Faith in the Nineteenth-Century Middle East* (New York: Columbia University Press, 1998); Denis MacEoin, "Orthodoxy and Heterodoxy in Nineteenth-Century Shi'ism: The Cases of Shaykhism and Babism," *Journal of the American Oriental Society* 110:2 (April 1, 1990): 323–329; Todd Lawson, "Orthodoxy and Heterodoxy in Twelver Shi'ism: Ahmad Al-Ahsā'í on Fayḍ Kashaní (the *Risalat al-'Ilmiyya*)," in Robert Gleave, ed., *Religion and Society in Qajar Iran* (London: RoutledgeCurzon, 2005), 127–54.

and resonances have theological *implications*. Such a movement and such a discourse was evidently irresistible for our author, Seyyed Ali Mohammad Shirāzi (1819–50), soon to become known as the Bab. And he, accordingly, abandoned his career as a merchant to study at the feet of Seyyed Kāzem Rashti. At the time of composition of the work at hand, his beloved teacher had died and his followers were left to search or wait for the realization of the Shiʻi eschaton: the return of the hidden Imam, the promulgation of the true Qurʼan, the establishment of justice throughout the world through the defeat of the forces of darkness and the establishment of the rule of the Mahdi. At the time, this doctrine had generated numerous interpretations and was teeming with a variety of possibilities including (1) the appearance of a general age of enlightenment, as distinct from (2) the actual triumph of an individual messianic figure, or to (3) a combination of both.[12]

Composition of the *Qayyūm al-Asmā'*

We have precise, if enchanting, details of how the Bab came to compose his revelatory exegesis, the *Qayyūm al-asmā'*. As these circumstances are inseparable from the resulting literary form of the work, it is important briefly to relate them. The actual composition began during a meeting with one of the senior students of the recently deceased Kāzem Rashti, the young and talented mulla, Hoseyn Boshru'i (1813–49). Upon the death of Rashti, he, together with a few companions, set out from Karbala in quest of the long-awaited advent: the manifestation of the hidden Imam and the beginning of the new cycle of fulfillment. Their search had taken them to Shiraz where Boshru'i encountered the young merchant, Ali Mohammad (the Bab), whom he had apparently known from his Karbala sojourn. The year was 1844CE (1260AH) and our author was 25 years old. He invited Mulla Hoseyn to his home and there, in discussions about how the hidden Imam was to be identified, the Bab is said to have suggested that he himself could be the promised one as he fulfilled many of the descriptions outlined in the traditions. Mulla Hoseyn, nonplussed by what he took as unwonted arrogance and perhaps thinking to quench the impudent and impertinent messianic pretensions of his host, remembered to himself that their teacher, Seyyed Kāzem Rashti, had added to the list of requirements and physical attributes that would identify the promised one another more purely literary requirement: the promised one would compose a commentary of the Qurʼan's Sura of Joseph. At this point, so the story goes, the Bab, apropos of apparently nothing, announced that it was now time for him to reveal the commentary on the Sura

---

12. Todd Lawson, *Exegesis as Mystical Experience* (Leiden: Brill, forthcoming), chapter 5.

of Joseph and then proceeded to write the first of the 111 chapters of this highly unusual work, the *Sūrat al-mulk*, the Chapter of Divine Dominion or Ownership.[13] So important is this literary event in the mind of the author, its date is fixed in Babī and Baha'i scripture: 22 May 1844, corresponding to the early evening of the Islamic date 5 Jumada I, 1260, almost exactly 1000 (lunar) years since the assumption of the Imamate by the "hidden" Twelfth Imam, Muhammad ibn al-Hasan al-Askari in the year 260AH/874CE. In addition, the actual astro-chronological moment for the beginning of the new cycle is fixed by the Bab, in a later work, at 2 hours and 11 minutes after sunset on that date.[14] Amanat is doubtless correct when he suggests that this unusual precision in timing the beginning of the long-awaited resurrection, the day of judgment, represents the moment when Mulla Hoseyn assented to the Bab's claims to be the return of the hidden Imam.[15]

The author of the completed commentary, which he tells us was composed over a forty-day period, eventually attracted a large and active messianic following, known to Iranian Religious history as the Babi religion. Announcing that with these new revelations the new cycle of fulfillment had been inaugurated and the *qiyāma*, the resurrection and day of judgment, were now in play, it was now necessary to recognize the Bab as the source and focus of all religious authority, the word for which in Islamic theological terminology is *walāya/wilāya* (Persian *valāyat/velāyat*). His mission would last nearly six years until he was executed in Tabriz for blasphemy and heresy on 6 July 1850. The remnants of his movement eventually formed the Baha'i religion in which followers saw the fulfillment of prophecies found in the remarkably voluminous writings of the Bab. These writings may be briefly summarized as an attempt to reorient and recast the sacerdotal and political hierarchical authority in the social imagination of Shi'i Iran in which the main elements were: the Prophet and the Imams (including Fātima, the daughter of Muhammad and wife of the first Imam Ali); the royal family,

13. Amanat, *Resurrection and Renewal*; Nabíl Zarandí. *The Dawn-Breakers: Nabíl's Narrative of the Early days of the Baha'í Revelation*. Translated by Shoghi Effendi (Wilmette, IL: Baha'í Pub. Trust, 1974); Denis MacEoin, *The Sources for Early Babí Doctrine and History: A Survey* (Leiden: Brill, 1992); Denis MacEoin, *The Messiah of Shiraz : Studies in Early and Middle Babism* (Boston: Brill, 2009); Juan R. I. Cole, *Modernity and the Millennium*; Juan R. I. Cole, "Individualism and the Spiritual Path in Shaykh Ahmad Al-Ahsa'i," *Occasional Papers in Shaykhi, Babi and Baha'i Studies* 1:4 (1997): http://www.h - net.org/~bahai/bhpapers/ahsaind.htm; Nader Saiedi, *Gate of the Heart: Understanding the Writings of the Bab* ([Waterloo, Ont.]: Wilfrid Laurier University Press and the Association for Baha'i Studies, 2008); Lawson, *Gnostic Apocalypse*.

14. The Bab, *Bayán-i Fársí*, vahid II, bab 7, 30–31: INBA62 (Tehran: Azali Publication, 1946). Reprinted, East Lansing, Mi.: H-Baha'i, 1999, 30–31. Cited in Amanat, *Resurrection and Renewal*, 170. See also Nabil Zarandi, *Dawn-Breakers*, 62–65.

15. Amanat, *Resurrection and Renewal*, 170.

the Qajars, their retainers and officials; the religious estate, comprising the classically educated religious classes, and others, unevenly divided between scripturalists and rationalists; and of course the general population of believers, the Shi'i community.[16]

An attempt to clarify lines of authority in a culture, it has been suggested, is also intimately related to the perennial problem of and quest for identity, which presents a single and powerful literary theme in world literature and one of the main themes of the epic genre as such.[17] The writings of the Bab may be thought an attempt to provide orientation in a highly turbulent period during which standard and traditional notions of identity, authority, and allegiance were in flux and were being debated in various quarters throughout Iranian society, from the very highest levels of courtly life, to the religious seminaries, to the bazaar and its environs. Another similar attempt may be discerned in the decisive developments at this time in understanding the "sacerdotal" office of universal authority for the Shi'i community, the *marja' al-taqlīd* (authoritative exemplar), closely related to what has come to be known after WWII as the office of Grand Ayatollah, a relatively recent religious innovation.[18] However much the literary activities of the Bab were fraught with profound and dramatic religious and theological implications, in the present somewhat experimental exploration, I am studying the Bab's writings from the point of view of artistic and literary considerations. Although it was thought important to provide some theological background as context, in what follows, I will, as much as possible, avoid theological and religious questions, even though there is an obvious deep connection between the artistic/aesthetic and the religious in Islamicate culture in general, Iranian Islamic culture more specifically, and the life and the work of the Bab himself as heir to these cultural realities and predispositions. In the case of the Bab the seamless interplay between the artistic/aesthetic and what might be thought the more purely "religious" dimensions of his life and ministry has been noted from the very

16. In his *Risalat al-sulūk*, the Bab delineates the levels of authority and application of religious truth and allegiance (God, the Prophet, the Imams and the Shi'a) and says that they are all dependent on each other. See Todd Lawson, "The Bab's Epistle on the Spiritual Journey towards God," in Moojan Momen, ed., *The Baha'i Faith and the World Religions: Papers Presented at the Irfan Colloquia* (Oxford: George Ronald, 2005), 231, 237, 241. For a discussion of these factors from a socio-historical perspective, see Amanat, *Resurrection and Renewal*.

17. Northrop Frye, *Words with Power: Being a Second Study of the Bible and Literature* (New York: Viking, 1990), 125.

18. On the various ways in which this quest for authentic identity were debated and contemplated, see Linda Walbridge (ed.), *Most Learned of the Shia: The Institution of the Marja' Taqlid* (New York and Oxford: Oxford University Press, 2001).

beginning.[19] It now remains to focus on the two texts that are the subject of this chapter.

Form and Sructure

The form and structure of both works suggests a veneration or sacralization of the past and a simultaneous desire to replace the old with the new. The following tables illustrate to some degree the way in which each work is structured by its author to represent a reworking of two culturally central texts, the Odyssey and the Qur'an. And because these structures are themselves so symbolically meaningful, their adoption has implications for thematic and narrative content.

Joyce himself made two different tables illustrating the close relationship between his *Ulysses* and the Odyssey.[20] The schema in Figure 1 was prepared in 1921 for his friend Stuart Gilbert and demonstrates how Joyce simultaneously took great liberties with and venerated the Odyssey, rearranged it and recast its stories and myths which in the original take place over a twenty year period (a generation), in order to fit it all within a single day in the life of Dublin: 16 June 1904.[21] Further, the events and narrative flow of Joyce's epic are, according to his schema, intricately coordinated with numerous other factors and elements. Thus, the first episode, not marked off in the actual published novel, may be identified with Telemachus, the name of Odysseus' son who searches for his father and awaits his return back home in Ithaca. There is in *Ulysses* a correspondence between this and the opening scene and the time of day. Joyce also assigns to this episode a particular color and science or art (theology) and literary tech-

19. For a recent comprehensive discussion of the Bab's artistic nature and aesthetic preoccupations see Moojan Momen, "Perfection and Refinement: Towards an Aesthetics of the Bab."

20. Nicholas A. Fargnoli, and Michael Patrick Gillespie, *Critical Companion to James Joyce: A Literary Reference to His Life and Works* (New York, NY: Facts On File, 2006), 392–93 for a reproduction from Hugh Kenner's finished composite of Joyce's two schemata for his friends and colleagues Linati and Gilbert.

21. This Joycean turn may be thought to have been anticipated by the ancient Arabian poetic tradition, which saw in the idea of "the day" – *al-yawm* (pl. *ayyām*) – a certain epic dignity and challenge as in "the days of the Arabs (*ayyām al-'arab*)," where the word connotes battle and the heroic resources required to survive the day through struggle for survival. The Qur'an's (and the Bible's) a "day with thy Lord is as a thousand years" would also seem to resonate: Qur'an 22:47; Psalms 90:4; 2 Peter 3:8. See Sebastian Günther, "Day, Times of," in *Encyclopaedia of the Qur'an*, edited by Jane Dammen McAuliffe, 1:499–504 (Leiden: Brill Academic Publishers, 2001) and Eugen Mittwoch, "Ayyām al-'Arab," *Encyclopaedia of Islam, Second Edition*. Edited by: P. Bearman, Th. Bianquis, C. E. Bosworth, E. van Donzel, W. P. Heinrichs. Brill Online, 2014. Reference. University of Toronto. 16 September 2014.

Title	Scene	Hour	Organ	Colour	Symbol	Art	Technic
Telemachus	The Tower	8am	-	White / gold	Heir	Theology	Narrative (young)
Nestor	The School	10am	-	Brown	Horse	History	Catechism (personal)
Proteus	The Strand	11am	-	Green	Tide	Philology	Monologue (male)
Calypso	The House	8am	Kidney	Orange	Nymph	Economics	Narrative (mature)
Lotus Eaters	The Bath	10am	Genitals	-	Eucharist	Botany / chemistry	Narcissism
Hades	The Graveyard	11am	Heart	White / black	Caretaker	Religion	Incubism
Aeolus	The Newspaper	12pm	Lungs	Red	Editor	Rhetoric	Enthymemic
Lestrygonians	The Lunch	1pm	Oesophagus	-	Constables	Architecture	Peristaltic
Scylla and Charybdis	The Library	2pm	Brain	-	Stratford / London	Literature	Dialectic
Wandering Rocks	The Streets	3pm	Blood	-	Citizens	Mechanics	Labyrinth
Sirens	The Concert Room	4pm	Ear	-	Barmaids	Music	Fuga per canonem
Cyclops	The Tavern	5pm	Muscle	-	Fenian	Politics	Gigantism
Nausicaa	The Rocks	8pm	Eye, nose	Grey / blue	Virgin	Painting	Tumescence / detumescence
Oxen of the Sun	The Hospital	10pm	Womb	White	Mothers	Medicine	Embryonic development
Circe	The Brothel	12am	Locomotor apparatus	-	Whore	Magic	Hallucination
Eumaeus	The Shelter	1am	Nerves	-	Sailors	Navigation	Narrative (old)
Ithaca	The House	2am	Skeleton	-	Comets	Science	Catechism (impersonal)
Penelope	The Bed	-	Flesh	-	Earth	-	Monologue (female)

Figure 1: Joyce's own diagram of the structural and thematic correspondences between *Ulysses* and the Odyssey (this example is from Wikipedia: http// en.wikipedia.org/wiki/Gilbert_schema_for Ulysses).

nique (narrative). Each of the following 17 sections of the novel is similarly structured. Thus the famous, if not notorious, Joycean stream of consciousness disguises an almost unbelievably and meticulously structured work of art. But apart from this, we may discern in this vast system of connections, correspondences, and resonances what might be thought – and surprisingly in this modernist literary experiment, a somewhat medieval certitude about the essential meaningfulness and interconnectedness of life, the kind of euphoric certitude that such totalizing devices as "The Great Chain of Being" or "The Diapason" bespeak.[22] In sum, Joyce takes great liberties with the Odyssey while at the same time remaining faithful to it. Such has been characterized as Joyce's "art of mediation," an art that seeks to negotiate the space between two apparently diametrically opposed elements, in this case the opposites are innovation and tradition.[23]

The interplay between tradition and the new is also the main focus of the Bab's work, whether from the point of view of structure or content. That we find a similar web of correspondences in the Bab's work is, perhaps, to be expected given the medieval ontological and mystical presuppositions of his tradition and his audience. So we see in his writing a vast grid of correspondences (even if a complete table illustrating them has yet to be made) in which climates, prophets, heavenly spheres, colors, hierarchical levels of Being, types of individuals and so on, provide both the flesh and the skeleton of his compositions.[24] For example, many of these compositions exploit to a very high degree the traditional *abjad* system of numerology, in which every word has a numerical value to be read and considered in a given context.[25] If we remain at the level of literature in comparing both compositions we see that they embody to a remarkable degree a great deal of exquisitely and intricately designed literary "hanging together," much of which has to do

22. Umberto Eco, *The Aesthetics of Chaosmos: The Middle Ages of James Joyce* (Cambridge, MA: Harvard University Press, 1989).

23. David Weir, *James Joyce and the Art of Mediation* (Ann Arbor: University of Michigan Press, 1996).

24. Vahid Rafati (translated by Omid Ghaemmaghami), "Colours in the Writings of the Báb," in Todd Lawson and Omid Ghaemmaghami, eds., *A Most Noble Pattern: Collected Essays on the Writings of the Báb, 'Alí Muḥammad Shírází (1819-1850)* (Oxford: George Ronald, 2012), 3-51. Lawson, *Gnostic Apocalypse*.

25. Here, we follow Frye's insight about the function of "numerology" in the Book of Revelation in such topoi as "the seventh seal" and the 144,000 companions of the Lamb of God, where we understand that the first function of such occult-esque passages in the Bible is, in fact, a literary one – one which helps the reader to experience coherence and cohesiveness in the text, to experience, in Frye's simple phrase, how the words "hang together." Northrop Frye, *The Great Code: Bible and Literature* (New York & London: Harcourt Brace Jovanovic, 1982), 60; Robert Denham, *Northrop Frye : Religious Visionary and Architect of the Spiritual World* (Charlottesville: University of Virginia Press, 2004), 227.

with the relationship of their respective works to their monumental and epic exemplars. In Joyce's case this model is the Odyssey. In the Bab's case, it is the Qur'an.[26]

The Sacramental Day

The Bab, like Joyce, goes to great lengths to innovate and improvise while also preserving and honoring the sanctity of tradition. In this, one could also refer to his as the "art of mediation." The central narrative at the core of the Bab's work, the Biblical story of Joseph son of Jacob, is the epic quest of a son for his father and a father for his son after separation. The structure of the work, which is divided into suras ("chapters") and āyas ("verses"), is explicitly patterned on the Qur'an, a feature Muslims would and did consider heretical.[27] At the same time, it is clear that the Bab is also concerned with a single day, that day outside time and space when all humanity – "God's children" – were gathered in God's presence. This is the day referred to at Q7:172 and known to the Islamic tradition as the day of the covenant. In mythic terms, it symbolizes for the Islamic tradition the birth of both consciousness and history.[28] In Qur'anic terms, it is the essential prelude for the creation of the world as told, for example, in the Biblical book of Genesis.[29] Evidence of the Bab's deep concern for this mythic event is woven into the very structure of the composition, through versification (explained below) and in innumerable explicit textual references. The covenant and its renewal is the central concern of the work because it supplies a sacred paradigm for the Josephian theme of separation and reunion through the cyclicism mentioned earlier. For the moment, suffice it to remark that the day of the covenant involves also another day, the day of judgment. According to the Qur'an, all of humanity was gathered in the presence of God on the day of the covenant at a time and place before actual creation so that they would have no excuse on the

26. Todd Lawson, "The Qur'an and Epic," *Journal of Qur'anic Studies* 16:1 (2014): 58–92.

27. The words *sūra* 'chapter', (Arabic plural, *suwar*) and *āya* 'verse' (Arabic plural *āyāt*) are only used for the Qur'an. Tradition forbids their use to describe the corresponding elements of any other work.

28. Todd Lawson, "Typological Figuration and the Meaning of 'Spiritual': The Qur'anic Story of Joseph," *Journal of the American Oriental Society* 132:2 (2012): 221–244. Todd Lawson, "Paradise in the Qur'an & the Music of Apocalypse," in Sebastian Günther and Todd Lawson, eds., *Roads to Paradise: Eschatology and Concepts of the Hereafter in Islam. Volume I: Foundations and the Formation of a Tradition. Reflections on the Hereafter in the Qur'an and Islamic Religious Thought,* vol. 1 (Leiden: Brill, 2015), 49–94.

29. Wadad al-Qadi, *The Primordial covenant and human history in the Qur'an.* The Margaret Weyerhaeuser Jewett Chair of Arabic Occasional Papers, edited by Ramzi Baalbaki (Beirut: American University of Beirut, 2006).

day of judgment for not having obeyed God and his prophets. It is clear that the *Qayyūm al-asmā'* is also a new rendition or performance of the day of the covenant.[30] When Mulla Hoseyn Boshru'i accepted the claims of the Bab, the momentousness of the act was enshrined in its exact time being recorded in the Bab's later book of laws, *Persian Bayan*. Such momentousness resides in its making present the drama of the original primordial covenant mentioned in the Qur'an (Q7:172). This was when God interrogated Adam and all of humanity with the question: "Am I not your Lord?" (*A lastu bi-rabbikum*) and to which Adam and all humanity immediately responded "Yes! Indeed! (*balā*)." Here the Bab, from the literary (metaphorical and spiritual) perspective is God – or more accurately the face of God (*wajh allāh*) and Mulla Hoseyn is Adam/Muhammad.[31] And to the degree that the work is concerned with the journey between affirmation of the covenant and judgment it may be thought to assume a circular form where the two ends of the composition are indicated in each other. This is of course one of the more prominent features of Joyce's *Finnegans Wake*: its end is its beginning and its beginning is its end, what Joyce calls "Doublends Jined"(FW20).[32] Such points to the multi-layered meaning of the title: revelation/awareness, resurrection (*Wake*), cyclical repetition (Man [*finn*] again), and the concomitant circular nature of history, the wake of human activity. Such continuity and stability as is represented in this totalizing design, whether of the *Qayyūm al-asmā'* or *Ulysses*, seems to offer solace and assurance for chaotic times, in the promise of a new day that is simultaneously and mysteriously ancient.

In the case of Joyce's day, we have a compression of thousands of days (the 20 years of the original Odyssey) into a single 24-hour period. In the case of the Bab's day, it is the opposite. Rather than a condensation of time, we have what might be thought, in musical terms, the melismatic cantillation over ages, generations, verses, words, and syllables of the original and originating power of that mysterious and momentous day (or moment) of the covenant represented by the word *balā* – Yes! Thus the considerable spiritual energy of the myth of the day of the covenant is joined with that of the day of resurrection. It is not only a powerful literary trope, it is, given the basic apocalyptic structure of the Qur'anic revelation, the central el-

30. Lawson, *Gnostic Apocalypse*, 6, 29, 36, 90–91.

31. The Bab explicitly fixes this day and time in the *Persian Bayan* (see Amanat, *Resurrection and Renewal*, 191–192).

32. On the Qur'anic resonances in this circularity see Aida Yared, "'In the Name of Annah': Islam and *Salam* in Joyce's *Finnegans Wake*," *James Joyce Quarterly*, ReOrienting Joyce, 35:2/3 (Winter-Spring 1998): 401–38 (408 & 410). It has also been argued that a similar structure is discernible in *Ulysses* in which the last letter –"s" – of the first word of the text is the last letter of the all important last word of the book: "yes".

ement of Islamic religious consciousness, which believers are called upon by the Qur'an continuously to remember or call to mind, the practice instituted in Sufism known as *dhikr* (Persian *zekr*).[33] Thus is the original (and originating) moment present in every other moment.[34] Indeed, one of the other important titles by which the Bab refers to himself in this work is precisely "*the* Remembrance" (*al-dhikr*) – embodiment or personification of the day of the covenant. Both the Bab and Joyce offer an implicit commentary on and radical interpretation of the idea of time and history in relation to the nature of consciousness. They demonstrate in their respective works the subjectivity, malleability, and shape-shifting quality of time and what the otherwise commonplace notion "day" can possibly mean. For both authors, the extraordinary "enchanted" quality of the epiphany is in contrast to the humdrum and "mundane" occasion of its occurrence.[35] Both the *Qayyūm al-asmā'* and *Ulysses* in some ways turn time into a literary trope, or, express concern with the unity and literary significance of time in interesting and innovative ways demonstrating that both authors seem intrigued by the recurrence of character types and cycles in the wake of which normal historical and chronological time becomes transmuted into something approaching sacrament.

Ulysses came at a time in the history of the English novel when traditional notions of literature and authorial vocation were in flux. The Babi movement also arose during a transition period in which the nature of orthodoxy and religious authority was being negotiated. In the first case we use the term modernism as signal and "symptom" of the change.[36] The Bab and his audience used the word *qiyāma*: resurrection and judgment (Persian: *rastākhiz*). The Bab takes even greater liberties with the Qur'an than Joyce did with the Odyssey in composing this new work, one that he explicitly

33. *Dh-K-R*, the triliteral root upon which the word remembrance is formed, occurs 292 times in the Qur'an. Of these, the majority of occurrences indicate the obligation and command to remember God and the day of the covenant. Remembrance is thus a major theme of the Qur'an (as it is in Plato). For the specifically mystical aspects of the institution of the covenant, see Gerhard Böwering, *The Mystical Vision of Existence in Classical Islam: The Qur'anic Hermeneutics of the Sufi Sahl At-Tustari (d. 283/896)* (Berlin: de Gruyter, 1980).

34. During the Iranian revolution and the protracted and tragic war between Iraq and Iran, the battle cry was frequently heard, in both Persian and Arabic: "Every day is the day of resurrection (*kullu yawm qiyāma*)" and "Every day is Ashura," the day on which the martyr-hero par excellence of Islam, Husain, the son of Ali, was massacred along with his family. It is a nationally sanctioned holy day in Iran and observed elsewhere throughout the Muslim world.

35. Morris Beja, "Epiphany and the Epiphanies," in Zack Bowen and James F. Carens, eds., *A Companion to Joyce Studies*, (Westport, CT: Greenwood Press, 1984), 707–25 (p. 719).

36. Jacques Aubert, "Lacan and the Joyce-Effect," *Joyce Studies in Italy* 1 New Series/14 Old Series (2013): 79–88.

presented as an emblem of the arrival of the resurrection: namely, the True Qur'an that had been in the safekeeping of the hidden Imam during his occultation.[37] Figure 2, below, gives some indication of the Bab's iconoclastic desire to compose a "new Qur'an". Note here the pervasive use of the uniquely Qur'anic literary device of the mysterious disconnected letters (*al-ḥurūf al-muqaṭṭaʿāt*) that appear in various combinations at the beginning of 29 of the 114 *suras* of the Qur'an.[38] As can be seen, in the Bab's composition the disconnected letters are used in all but four of his new *suras*, i.e., in almost all 111 of them.[39] We will return below to some of the other ways in which the Bab's work imitates the Qur'an and in some senses "out-Qur'ans" the actual Qur'an. Suffice it here to say, that the implications of such an unprecedented outrage were not lost on his contemporaries. Even during the Bab's lifetime, a combined Sunni and Shiʿi court of Islamic jurists was convened in Baghdad to deliberate on the legality of the provocative literary act. Their joint fatwa condemning the author of the *Qayyūm al-asmāʾ* for composing an imitation of the holy Qur'an demonstrates how a contemporary audience would be scandalized by such a daring and provocative literary event.[40] As is well known, Joyce's work was repeatedly challenged in the courts, most frequently for obscenity. While there is nothing that could be construed as obscenity in the Bab's compositions, the religious scandal his writings provoked was, in the context of this cross-cultural comparison, analogous in the intensity of the outrage it provoked.

Epic, Monomyth, and Epiphany

Both artists rethink and reconstrue their respective "monomyths" – a word coined by Joyce in *Finnegans Wake* as a near synonym for the epic telling of collective humanity's genealogical, historical, and mythic experience. Joyce wants us to understand the epic dignity and value of the mere quotidian: the grand interconnectedness of the ordinary. The Bab wants us to understand something similar, but in reverse, if you will. All time and history is a perpetual and continuous performance of a single day, the day of the covenant. In both Joyce and the Bab, the idea of the day acquires a distinctive sacra-

---

37. Lawson, *Gnostic Apocalypse*, 4.

38. See the recent discussion of their importance in the Sunni tradition in Martin Nguyen, "Exegesis of the ḥurūf al-muqaṭṭaʿa: Polyvalency in Sunni Traditions of Qur'anic Interpretation," *Journal of Qur'anic Studies* 14:2 (October 2012): 1–28.

39. It is possible that this figure will change once all the 15 or so known manuscripts of the work have been properly collated.

40. Moojan Momen, "The Trial of Mullá ʿAlí Bastámí: A Combined Sunní-Shíʿí Fatwá against the Báb," *Iran* 20 (January 1982): 113–43.

#	السورة	الحروف المقطعة
١	سورة الملك	
٢	سورة العلماء	آلم
٣	سورة الإيمان	طه
٤	سورة المدينة	آلمطه
٥	سورة يوسف	آلمع
٦	سورة الشهادة	آلمس
٧	سورة الزيارة	طس
٨	سورة السرّ	آلمص
٩	سورة العماء (i)	آلمن
١٠	سورة العماء (ii)	آلمغ
١١	سورة المسطّر	طمع
١٢	سورة العاشوراء	كمتن
١٣	سورة الفردوس	طهم
١٤	سورة القدس	آلمط
١٥	سورة المدينة	طهص
١٦	سورة العرش	آلمق
١٧	سورة الباب	آلمعرا
١٨	سورة الصراط	كهيعص
١٩	سورة السيناء	آلمرا
٢٠	سورة النور	آلمي
٢١	سورة البحر	آلميص
٢٢	سورة الماء	طظل
٢٣	سورة العصر	آلغم
٢٤	سورة القدر	آلمص
٢٥	سورة الخاتم	آلمعص
٢٦	سورة الحلّ	آلرا
٢٧	سورة الأنوار	آلمق
٢٨	سورة القارية	آلم
٢٩	سورة الحورية	كميع
٣٠	سورة التبليغ	آلمع
٣١	سورة العزّ	آلمح
٣٢	سورة الحيّ	كهيعص
٣٣	سورة النصر	آلمهص
٣٤	سورة الإشارة	خمرا
٣٥	سورة العبودية	آلر
٣٦	سورة العدل	طه
٣٧	سورة التعبير	فحمن
٣٨	سورة الفاطمة	طه
٣٩	سورة الشكر	آلمرا
٤٠	سورة الإنسان (i)	طله
٤١	سورة الكتاب	كهيعص
٤٢	سورة العهد	آلرا
٤٣	سورة الوحيد	آلمع
٤٤	سورة الرؤياء	طظرا
٤٥	سورة هو	كهيعص
٤٦	سورة المرآت	آلمع
٤٧	سورة الحجّة	المحضترا
٤٨	سورة النداء	الهل
٤٩	سورة الأحكام (i)	طه
٥٠	سورة الأحكام (ii)	النص
٥١	سورة المجد	طه
٥٢	سورة الفضل	
٥٣	سورة الصبر	كهم
٥٤	سورة العلام	آلمعص
٥٥	سورة الركن	كهيعص
٥٦	سورة الأمر	حمرا
٥٧	سورة الأكبر	حمرا
٥٨	سورة الحزن	الهل
٥٩	سورة الأفئدة	كهعص
٦٠	سورة الذكر (i)	طهعص
٦١	سورة الحسين	كهن
٦٢	سورة الأولياء	كهيل
٦٣	سورة الرحمة	طلن
٦٤	سورة المحمد	
٦٥	سورة الغيب	آلتق
٦٦	سورة الأحدية	المصر
٦٧	سورة الإنشاء	
٦٨	سورة الرعد	المصن
٦٩	سورة الرجع	كهيعص
٧٠	سورة القسط	آلتر
٧١	سورة القلم	آلمص
٧٢	سورة البحير	آلمع
٧٣	سورة الكهف	آلم
٧٤	سورة الخليل	
٧٥	سورة الشمس	آلترا
٧٦	سورة الورقة	حمرا
٧٧	سورة السلام	المعطس
٧٨	سورة الظهور	آلمعص
٧٩	سورة الكلمة	آلمط
٨٠	سورة الزوال	كهيعص
٨١	سورة الكاف	المتع
٨٢	سورة الأعظم	المح
٨٣	سورة الباء	المتف
٨٤	سورة الاسم	المترا
٨٥	سورة الحق	المطط
٨٦	سورة الطير	آلرا
٨٧	سورة النبأ	آلرا
٨٨	سورة الإبلاغ	المصنع
٨٩	سورة الإنسان (ii)	آلم
٩٠	سورة التثليث	المعنص
٩١	سورة التربيع	آلرا
٩٢	سورة المجل	المعنص
٩٣	سورة النحل	كهمع
٩٤	سورة الإشهار	المترا
٩٥		طلع
٩٦	سورة القتال (i)	المعنص
٩٧	سورة القتال (ii)	المعنس
٩٨	سورة الجهاد (i)	المتعق
٩٩	سورة الجهاد (ii)	المترا
١٠٠	سورة الجهاد (iii)	المعطل
١٠١	سورة القتال (iii)	آلم
١٠٢	سورة القتال (iv)	كهيعص
١٠٣	سورة الحج	المتع
١٠٤	سورة الحدود	طله
١٠٥	سورة الأحكام (iii)	المعزا
١٠٦	سورة الجمعة	آلمعنص
١٠٧	سورة النكاح	آلمح
١٠٨	سورة الذكر (ii)	علي
١٠٩	سورة العبد	محمد
١١٠	سورة السابقين	المطع
١١١	سورة المؤمنين	آلم

Figure 2: A provisional Table of Contents for the Bab's *Qayyūm al-asmā'* the *Tafsīr sūrat Yūsuf*. The first column shows the sura (chapter) number, the second the title of the sura and the third shows the mysterious disconnected letters chosen to head the sura. I am grateful to Dr. Omid Ghaemmaghami for assistance in preparing this table.

mental value: the day looms as a central integer and quantum of experience, revelation/epiphany and being.

The epic, whether Homeric or Qur'anic, seeks, among other things, to demonstrate or imitate the interconnectedness and therefore meaningfulness of experience, consciousness, and history. Such interconnectedness may be thought a given of the Bab's religious perspective. Joyce, forging a new understanding of the existential and psychological realm, has Stephen contemplate "the ineluctable modality of the visible," the realm in which Stephen is called upon to read "the signatures of all things."[41] The implication is, of course, that there is much else besides the visible and the sensible to which this visible is somehow connected, even if it is only connection itself. And, we know that much more than connection itself is indicated namely, the great unseen and unknown inner world of the psyche or soul to which access is gained precisely through the epiphany and which would remain incompletely known without it.[42] Such an attitude towards the natural, visible world has a great deal in common with the Bab's logocentric universe where the true believer is really a true reader who has been charged with reading and contemplating the "signs of God" that have, according to Islamic teaching, been placed in the Qur'an, the physical universe and the souls of human beings:

> We shall show them Our signs in the horizons and in themselves, till it is clear to them that it is the truth. (Q41:53)

Creation, whether divine or artistic, has profound literary implications. The Bab wishes to emphasize the interconnectedness of being-as-such (*wujūd*) symbolized by the central notion of spiritual and worldly authority that circulates through these three distinct "modalities": the readable Book, the visible Cosmos and the invisible Soul. *Walāya*, the word for this authority, has a special charisma as the all-important Qur'anic divine attribute which stands for religious (and, for that matter, "secular") authority, allegiance, guardianship, friendship, intimacy, sanctity, love, and being. The Prophet Muhammad and the Imams were bearers of this divine quality and as such are the sources of all authority in the cosmos (which was, in fact, created for them), whether construed as secular and political or spiritual and religious. The Bab as representative of the hidden Imam would also be a bearer of this authority. Ultimately, *walāya* may be understood as a metaphor for consciousness itself: that through which all things are connected and thus endowed with or acquire meaning. Recall that it is really *walāya*,

41. James Joyce, *Ulysses* (New York: Vintage Books, 1961), 37.
42. Weir, *Mediation*, 39.

God's guardianship, that is set in play on the mythic day of the covenant described at Q7:172. As "divine friendship," the notion is preeminently participatory and renders even the most ordinary thing or event holy or sacred through a distinctly islamicate version of holy communion.[43]

Coincidentia Oppositorum

Both Joyce and the Bab may be thought, therefore, to explore the possibilities of what is sometimes referred to these days as an enchanted reality. Nowhere is concern for such enchantment more palpable than in the way both authors contemplate and demonstrate the essential fundamental unity or resolution of oppositions – the *coincidentia oppositorum* of the Scholastics, including the alchemists.[44] This ancient philosophical theme has enjoyed a similar life in both Christian European and Islamic Middle Eastern thought where it is frequently encountered in writers of a more mystical orientation. More than any other conceit or trope, it speaks of the paradoxical nature of reality and calls into question such manmade notions as "good" and "evil," "justice" and "tyranny." This is the apperception behind Blake's "Fearful Symmetry." As a frequent feature of paradox, the *coincidentia oppositorum* has, as it were, one foot in the realm of philosophy and theology and one foot in poetics and the art of literature. There is an ongoing debate in Joyce Studies, as to which preponderates in his thought and work. One argument suggests that he took the idea from Bruno's theological work and adapted it to a more or less purely literary usage.[45] Others suggest that Joyce's interest in and use of the *coincidentia oppositorum* goes deeper than this, that it indicates a faith that true knowledge rises above such "logical entanglements" as result from a slavish devotion to the epistemic value of such notions as saved and damned, heaven and hell, up and down, here and there, past and present, day and night and so on. Joyce's interest in the "figure" has been studied with regard to the final chapter of *Ulysses,* the Penelope episode.[46]

43. On the prominence of the topic in the Bab's writings, see Lawson, *Gnostic Apocalypse,* passim; on *walaya* see Hermann Landolt, "Walayah," *Encyclopedia of Religion.* 2nd edition, Lindsay Jones, ed. (Detroit: MacMillan Reference USA, 2005), vol. 14, 9656–62.

44. On *coincidentia oppositorum* see the major study by C. G. Jung, *Mysterium Coniunctionis: An Inquiry into the Separation and Synthesis of Psychic Opposites in Alchemy* (Princeton, NJ: Princeton University Press, 1977).

45. Northrop Frye, "Cycle and Apocalypse in Finnegans Wake," in Robert Denham, ed., *Myth and Metaphor: Selected Essays, 1974-1988* (Charlottesville: University Press of Virginia, 1990), 371.

46. Joseph C. Voelker, "'Nature It Is': The Influence of Giordano Bruno on James Joyce's Molly Bloom," *James Joyce Quarterly* 14:1 (October 1, 1976): 39–48; Roland McHugh, *The Sigla of Finnegans Wake* (London: Edward Arnold, 1976), 27–31.

"Penelope" begins and ends with the word "yes," emblematic of the circularity of lived experience, the circle being a representation of the resolution of polarities. The resolution of opposites is also evident in the character Molly Bloom whose heroic response "yes" to the otherwise unjustifiable and perhaps unbearable contradictions and defeats offered by life is the goal to which the entire novel has been traveling on its epic journey. For Joyce, the greatest man in literature was Odysseus whom he had encountered for the first time as a schoolboy through Charles Lamb's retelling of the story.[47] Lamb highlights how Odysseus was saved from Circe by the intervention of the god Hermes/Mercury, who gave him the ugly and black-rooted plant with the beautiful white flower (and the instructions how to use it) called *moly* as a magical protection. The entire passage deserves to be quoted:

> But neither [Mercury's] words nor his coming from heaven could stop the daring foot of Ulysses, whom compassion for the misfortune of his friends had rendered careless of danger: which when the god perceived, he had pity to see valor so misplaced, and gave him the flower of the herb *moly*, which is sovereign against enchantments. The moly is a small unsightly root, its virtues but little known and in low estimation; the dull shepherd treads on it every day with his clouted shoes; but it bears a small white flower, which is medicinal against charms, blights, mildews, and damps. "Take this in thy hand," said Mercury, "and with it boldly enter her [Circe's] gates; when she shall strike thee with her rod, thinking to change thee, as she has changed thy friends, boldly rush in upon her with thy sword, and extort from her the dreadful oath of the gods, that she will use no enchantments against thee; then force her to restore thy abused companions." He gave Ulysses the little white flower, and, instructing him how to use it, vanished.[48]

In a recent study of duality in the Odyssey (having nothing directly to do with Joyce or Joyce studies) it has been suggested that the magical power of the *moly* comes from none other than its joining the opposites of mortal and divine, ease and difficulty, black and white, root and flower in its

47. Charles Lamb, *The Adventures of Ulysses, Edited with Notes for School* (Boston: Ginn & Company, 1886). According to Joyce himself, from this time on he was preoccupied with the Odyssey; Richard Ellmann, "The Backgrounds of Ulysses," *The Kenyon Review* 16:3 (1 July 1954), 341. See also Richard Ellman, *James Joyce*, new and rev. ed. (New York: Oxford University Press, 1982), 46; Zack R. Bowen, and James F. Carens, eds. *A Companion to Joyce Studies* (Westport, CT: Greenwood Press, 1984), 43: Joyce advised several people who complained of the obscurity of *Ulysses* to read Lamb's *Adventures* for guidance and clues to the text.

48. Lamb, *The Adventures of Ulysses*, 18.

very biological and botanical structure. It was this structure and composi-tion that rendered it a "saving device" for Odysseus.[49] In short, the magical plant, the *moly*, is a *coincidentia oppositorum*. Molly Bloom is also a *coincidentia oppositorum* and may also be thought to embody a kind of salvific function. She is: Madonna and whore, mother and daughter, good and evil, beautiful and ugly, joyful and sad, tender and scold, dismissive and loving, jealous and faithful; she "saves" (gives meaning to) the epic of *Ulysses* with her affirma-tive engagement with life.[50]

Joyce's interest in the *coincidentia oppositorum* as something of a foun-dation for his personal religious and spiritual vision was, as is well known, deeply influenced by his great admiration for the fifteenth-century "her-etic" Giordano Bruno (1548–1600). It is from the "trope" or "device" of the coincidence of opposites that the much-studied Joycean epiphany emerges out of the "ineluctable modality of the visible (at least that if no more)" (U37). This background is useful for coming to terms with Joyce's highly personal relationship with the numinous, as distinct from his relationship with the Catholic church.[51] It also provides a firm basis upon which to pro-ceed with the comparison of the two otherwise literally incomparable works examined in this essay. This basis is none other than the ontological pre-suppositions from which and because of which the *coincidentia oppositorum* and its expressive power emerges as both literary trope and philosophical axiom. The coincidence of opposites speaks to the possibility of a noetic experience with creation (viz: epiphany) as the "device" through which God's presence as imminent in matter is encountered or at least witted. It bespeaks an adamantly non-dualistic view in which "flesh" is no longer the enemy of "spirit" but one half of a syzygy that comprehends both and rises above "logical entanglements"– precisely, Blake's "fearful symmetry." And the description of Joyce's epiphanic experience resonates beautifully and harmoniously with the Islamic apophatic mysticism that was the central pillar of the Bab's religious universe in which Absolute Being and Reality were frequently considered synonyms, if not "improvements," for the word

49. Chet A. Van Duzer, *Duality and Structure in the Iliad and Odyssey* (New York: Peter Lang, 1996), 4–6.

50. James Van Dyck Card, "'Contradicting': The Word for Joyce's 'Penelope'," *James Joyce Quarterly* 11:1 (October 1, 1973): 17–26, 20–21. See the impressive litany of opposites in James Van Dyck Card, *An Anatomy of "Penelope"* (Rutherford: Fairleigh Dickinson University Press; London: Associated University Presses, 1984), 50–52 and 66–67. It should be remarked, in pass-ing, that Card makes no substantial mention of Voelker's insights in this book and seems to have no interest at all in the Brunonian substrate of Joyce's writing. Neither Voelker nor Card observe that Molly, whose birth name was Marion Tweedy, may be thought to take her "he-roic" or "magical" name from the magical plant known in the Odyssey as the *moly*.

51. Gert Lernout, *Help My Unbelief: James Joyce and Religion* (New York: Continuum, 2010).

"Allah" or "God" vis-à-vis the type of "entity" those words were meant to indicate.[52] Pointing out that Bruno himself was deeply influenced by the pre-modern "father of the *coincidentia oppositorum*," Nicholas of Cusa (1401–1464), Voelker quotes from one of Joyce's favorite books about his martyr hero on the topic of Being:

> Knowledge is posterior both in time and in value to Being, or Reality, of which it is at best a copy or sign, hence Reality can never be wholly comprehended by it. Every human assertion is at best a "conjecture," a hypothesis or approach to truth, but never the absolute truth itself. Only in the Divine spirit are thought and reality one; the divine thought is at the same time creative, human only reflective, imitative, thus the Ultimate Being is and must remain incomprehensible.[53]

At U782 Molly says "well who was the first person in the universe before there was anybody that made it all who ah that they dont know neither do I so there you are" – in perfect demonstration of Brunonian apophaticism. Molly is also singled out as expressing most perfectly the metaphysical and poetic implications of this same Brunonian existential monism and its influence on the young Joyce, who, in a 1903 review of the then new book on Bruno by Lewis McIntyre, wrote:

> As an independent observer, Bruno ... deserves high honour. More than Bacon or Descartes must he be considered the father of what is called modern philosophy. His system by turns rationalistic and mystic, theistic and pantheistic is everywhere impressed with his noble mind and critical intellect ... In his attempt to reconcile the matter and form of the Scholastics ... Bruno has hardly put forward an hypothesis, which is a curious anticipation of Spinoza ... It is not Spinoza, it is Bruno, that is the god-intoxicated man. Inwards from the material universe, which, however, did not seem to him, as to the Neoplatonists the kingdom of the soul's malady, or as to the Christians a place of probation, but rather his opportunity for spiritual activity, he passes, and from heroic enthusiasm to enthusiasm to unite himself with God.[54]

Inhabited or possessed by God, the literal translation of the word "enthusiasm," is the sense one has of Molly in the closing pages of *Ulysses*. The "Penelope" episode represents a crescendo of the meeting of contraries and

---

52. Lawson, *Gnostic Apocalypse*, 75–92.

53. J. Lewis McIntyre, *Giordano Bruno* (London: Macmillan, 1903), 142–43.

54. James Joyce, *Critical Writings of James Joyce*, edited by Ellsworth Mason and Richard Ellmann (New York: Viking Press, 1959 [hereafter CW]), 133–34.

contradictions in the person of Molly, who was, as it happens, born on the Feast of the Virgin, 8 September.[55] The following underlines what might be thought, for want of a better term, the "sacramental value" of the *coincidenta oppositorum* in *Ulysses*[56] and its apotheosis in Penelope and the character of Molly who therefore emerges as something of simultaneous (living) martyr saint to and high priestess of Joyce's powerful spiritual or mystico-poetic vision:[57]

> God of heaven theres nothing like nature the wild mountains then
> the sea and the waves rushing then the beautiful country with the
> fields of oats and wheat and all kinds of things and all the fine cattle
> going about that would do your heart good to see rivers and lakes and
> flowers all sorts of shapes and smells and colours springing up even
> out of the ditches primroses and violets nature it is as for them saying
> theres no God I wouldnt give a snap of my two fingers for all their
> learning why dont they go and create something I often asked him
> atheists or whatever they call themselves (U 781–782)

This passage is revealing on another level. It provides yet another entree into the comparison between Joyce and the Bab. In Bruno, as in the Qur'an and the Islamic philosophical tradition, nature is not the opposite of the divine but a vehicle for its expression and encounter. To one familiar with the Qur'an, a decidedly non-dualistic book,[58] it is impossible to read the above lines without thinking of such verses as:

> Hast thou not seen how that God sends down out of heaven water, and
> therewith We bring forth fruits of diverse hues? And in the mountains
> are streaks white and red, of diverse hues, and pitchy black; men too,
> and beasts and cattle – diverse are their hues. Even so only those of

55. James Van Dyck Card, "Contradicting: The Word for Joyce's 'Penelope'," *James Joyce Quarterly* 11:1 (October 1, 1973): 17–26, 21. Incidentally, Card points out that the roses mentioned in this passage "Id love to have the whole place swimming in roses" (U782, and elsewhere in *Ulysses*) may allude to the ecstatic religious vision in Dante symbolized by the multifoliate rose. See William York Tindall, *The Literary Symbol* (New York: Columbia University Press, 1955), 199–202 and William York Tindall, *A Reader's Guide to James Joyce* (New York: Noonday Press, 1959), 91–92. Joyce himself had quite early on expressed his interest in the "history of religious ecstasies." CW, 134.

56. The existence, function and form of the *coincidentia oppositortum* thus explicated by Voelker, it is clear that the figure occurs not only in Penelope with Molly, but on almost every page of the novel. Gian Balsamo, *Joyce's Messianism: Dante, Negative Existence, and the Messianic Self* (Columbia: University of South Carolina Press, 2004).

57. On the poetry in this passage see Card, *Anatomy*, 80.

58. Fazlur Rahman, *Major Themes of the Qur'an* (Minneapolis, MN: Bibliotheca Islamica, 1980), 12.

His servants fear God who have knowledge; surely God is All-mighty, All-forgiving. (Q35:27–28; see also, for example Q67:19; Q24:43; Q24:45; Q13:2–4; Q13:13; Q16:48; Q16:68–69)

Such exemplifies a cardinal presupposition of Islam, universally applicable regardless of which Islamic community we are studying, Sunni, Shi'i, Sufi, traditional or modern. This is the theory (or "doctrine") of signs, briefly detailed above, in which everything other than God is in fact a sign or portent, precisely "epiphany" of God. This applies to the verses of the Qur'an, the material universe including nature and its constituents, or to the ideas, thoughts and feelings that compose the interior of the individual. Thus the Qur'an and eventually, but not exclusively, the mystical philosophers of Islam, such as Ibn al-'Arabi (1165–1240) anticipate the theology of Eckhart (1260–1328), Cusanus (1401–1464), and Bruno and such modern spirits as Berdayev (1874–1948).[59]

The Bab was fully at home in and indeed celebrated this deeply mystical and religious existentialism. In addition to the centrality of Q7:172 in the Bab's composition, the above verse (Q41:53), much beloved by the Islamic tradition as a whole, is quoted or alluded to literally hundreds of times in the *Qayyūm al-asmā'* as well as in other of his works.[60] The two authors, Joyce and the Bab, may have much more in common than initially suspected.[61]

Chaosmic Epic and Reader as Hero

All this seems to suggest that Joyce knew the Qur'an, and of course this is true, as Atherton, McHugh, and Yared have convincingly demonstrated.[62]

59. Todd Lawson, "Duality, Opposition and Typology in the Qur'an: The Apocalyptic Substrate," *Journal of Qur'anic Studies* 10:2 (2008): 23–49. It should be remarked that the question of Bruno's indebtedness here to Cusanus has recently been questioned: Leo Catana, "The Coincidence of Opposites: Cusanian and Non-Cusanian Interpretations," *Bruniana & Campanelliana* 17:2 (2011): 381–400.

60. Lawson, *Gnostic Apocalypse*, passim.

61. Another evidence of Joyce's exposure to the Qur'an may be read in Molly's rhetorical question "why dont they go and create something I often asked him atheists or whatever they call themselves" (U782) which is also remarkably similar to the so-called challenge verses in the Qur'an. These are five passages which have been read traditionally as a response to the skeptics and cavilers who doubted Muhammad's mission. One will suffice: And if you are in doubt concerning that We have sent down on Our servant, then bring a sura like it, and call your witnesses, apart from God, if you are truthful. And if you do not – and you will not – then fear the Fire, whose fuel is men and stones, prepared for unbelievers. (Q2:23–24)

62. James S. Atherton, *The Books at the Wake: A Study of Literary Allusions in James Joyce's Finnegans Wake* (Mamaroneck, NY: P. P. Appel, 1974); Roland McHugh, "Mohammad in Notebook VI.B.31," *A Wake Newslitter: Studies in James Joyce's Finnegans Wake* n.s. 16:4 (August 1979):

Whether or not this specific passage is the direct result of such knowledge is not possible to confirm at this time. However, the idea that joining, reconciling or resolving the nearly infinite instances of opposition and duality encountered during mundane lived experience in the sublunary realm provides the modality or occasion for epiphany is one held both by Joyce, as has been demonstrated, and by the Bab, especially in the work at hand, the *Qayyūm al-asmā'*.[63]

Ulysses emerges as a critique, an interpretation and a typological re-presentation-cum-appropriation of the traditional epic. It is also a representation and critique or commentary on social reality. It is massive, creative, inventive, very rich and difficult to read. The modern world is in Joyce's word "chaosmic."[64] Neither purely chaos nor cosmos, it is both together and it represents serious problems for the thinking and feeling individual who would like to make sense of it all. The task of making sense of it all, in the case of *Ulysses* is most definitely left to the reader in much the same way the aware individual must reconcile the oppositions and contradictions of lived experience to perceive the truth of their revelatory message. The relationship between the reader and the text here is a microcosmic example of the relationship between the individual and the world. Apart from the epic tasks of the main characters in *Ulysses* (Leopold Bloom, Stephen Dedalus, and Mol-

---

51–58; Yared, "In the Name of Annah"; Idem, "Introducing Islam in Finnegans Wake: The Story of Mohammed in VI.B.45," *Genetic Joyce Studies* 1 (Spring 2001). It would appear to be no accident, given the interest in Islam and the Qur'an evident in in his Newslitter article mentioned above that McHugh in *The Sigla*, had devoted an entire chapter to the topic of the *coincidentia oppositorum*. In addition, there are a number of studies dealing generally with Joyce and the Middle East and/or the Saidian theory of "orientalism" in the special edition of the *James Joyce Quarterly*, ReOrienting Joyce, mentioned above. In addition to the excellent article there by Yared, see also those by Bouazza, Bowen, Ehrlich, Harris, Kershner, King, and Shloss. Another related publication is Suheil Bushrui, and Bernard Benstock, eds. *James Joyce, an International Perspective: Centenary Essays in Honour of the Late Sir Desmonde Cochrane*. Irish Literary Studies 10 (Gerrards Cross, Buckinghamshire: Totowa, NJ: C. Smythe ; Barnes and Noble Books, 1982). See here, especially, the article by Bushrui, "Joyce in the Arab World," 232–37. (The possibility that Dante also transmitted Islamic and Qur'anic influence to Joyce has not been noted.) See the interesting comment, available online, in a blurb for Firoozeh Dumas' "Funny in Farsi" which discusses the censorship issues surrounding her best-selling memoir in Iran. She says: "A translation of James Joyce's *Ulysses* has been with censor's office for seventeen years!" http://www.randomhouse.com/highschool/RHI_magazine/pdf3/Dumas.pdf

63. Todd Lawson, "*Coincidentia Oppositorum* in the Qayyúm Al-asmá': The Terms 'Point' (*nuqta*), 'Pole' (*qutb*), 'Center' (*markaz*) and the Khutbat al-Tatanjiya," *Occasional Papers in Shaykhi, Babi and Baha'i Studies* 5, no. 1 (2001): http://www.h – net.org/~bahai/bhpapers/vol5/tatanj/tatanj.htm.

64. Eco, *Chaosmos*; see also Michael Patrick Gillespie, *The Aesthetics of Chaos: Nonlinear Thinking and Contemporary Literary Criticism* (Gainesville, FL: University Press of Florida, 2003).

ly Bloom), the work is also an epic that the reader accomplishes through the heroic process of reading and understanding.[65] In the nineteenth century, the "outside" third-person narrator was in complete control of everything that went on in the novel. Even if the novel was problematic and difficult and chaotic, the narrator saved us at the end by being in control and solving the problems, answering the questions. Joyce, Virginia Woolf, T. S. Eliot and their "progeny" say it is not like this any more (if it ever was). And this is a hallmark of modernity and many works of literary modernism.[66] In the end, Joyce, through *Ulysses*, specifically through the voice of Molly Bloom, affirms a hopeful and life-affirming response to the chaotic "nightmare" of history[67] and modern life with her famous series of twelve yesses that end the novel and which transforms the chaos into not cosmos but "chaosmos."[68]

There is also an epic at the center of the Bab's composition, the Qur'an.[69] This is the story of God's relationship to humanity from the beginning on the day of the covenant, to the end, on the day of judgment. The Bab's composition is based on the Sura of Joseph, the Qur'anic model of narrative continuity and coherence as a result of which it is frequently known by its other name: The Best of Stories (*ahsan al-qisas*) a self-descriptive epithet found at Q12:2. Indeed, that sura 12, the Sura of Joseph, may be thought the narrative core of the Qur'an because it sets out the terms of the paradigmatic Qur'anic "monomyth" in clear and consecutive detail. By choosing the Sura of Joseph, the Bab demonstrates that he is alive to the special place of this sura in the Qur'an as the best and most complete iteration of the distinctively Islamic monomyth and as simultaneous emblem of the entire

65. Frye, *Cycle*, 366, discussing *Finnegans Wake*.

66. Woolf's *Mrs Dalloway* (1925) and, to some extent *To the Lighthouse* (1927) follows the example of Joyce's meditation on the "wonders" of the epic quality of a single day in *Ulysses*. But both may be thought anticipated in the search for the epic in the otherwise drear diurnal by Baudelaire, who famously observed in 1845: "[T]he heroism of modern life surrounds and presses upon us ... There is no lack of subjects, nor of colours, to make epics. The painter, the true painter for whom we are looking will be he who can snatch its epic quality from the life of today and can make us see and understand, with brush and pencil, how great and poetic we are in our cravats and our patent-leather boots. Next year let us hope that the true seekers may grant us the extraordinary delight of celebrating the advent of the new." Charles Baudelaire, "The Salon of 1845," in *The Art of Paris* (Oxford: Phaidon Press, 1965), 31–32.

67. "History, Stephen said, is a nightmare from which I would like to awake." (U34)

68. Not only are these rarely remarked twelve yesses prominent in the closing lines of *Ulysses*, but if we scan the pages carefully, reading with the ear, we find other yesses hiding in the foliage of the vocabulary. Quite apart from the fact that the title of the book itself, *Ulysses* is composed of Ul + ysses (= yesses), such words in the final lines as "yellow houses" "Jessamine" "cactuses" "kissed" "eyes" "breasts" all echo the sound of the affirmative English adverb.

69. Lawson, "The Qur'an and Epic."

Qur'an, divine revelation.[70] It is not without significance that the story of Joseph, like *Ulysses*, entails a quest of a father for a son and a son for a father.

Ulysses is a retelling of or commentary on the Odyssey. It is an imposition of the Odyssean template on the events and character of modern life in Dublin, and so is simultaneously very old and completely new. In Islamic terms, Joyce confuses or disturbs an easy understanding of the difference between revelation (*tanzīl*) and interpretation (*ta'wīl*).[71] In both *Ulysses* and the *Qayyūm al-asmā'*, differences and relationships and reversals between content and form are privileged and explored. In the case of the Bab's composition, his commentary proceeds without the use of the typical and universally employed technical exegetical connectives such as "this means" (*ya'ni*) or "the intention of the text here is" (*al-murād*), devices used frequently in his earlier *tafsir* and also used in some of his later work. Rather, here the commentary is the composition and the composition is the commentary. Another aspect of *Ulysses* that is most suggestive of comparison with the *Qayyūm al-asmā'* is the way it highlights and problematizes the relationship between text ("father") and commentary ("son"). Their "re-union" in the *Qayyūm al-asmā'* is indicated in the device of paraphrase offering an excellent comparative example of the way in which form and content exchange roles in this work.

This finds a parallel in those episodes in the first half of *Ulysses* in which the character, say Bloom, *is* the episode (as in Lestrygonians) through the replacement of a typical nineteenth-century-type narrator with Joyce's original and newly-crafted technique of stream of consciousness and "interior monlogue." We do not read *about* Bloom, we *read* Bloom directly. The Circe episode, in the latter half of the novel, is written as a play precisely because everything in the brothel is speaking, everything has a tongue. "Everything" is connecting itself as speaking itself into existence. Again, a Qur'anic resonance may be seen in the fact that its main topic there is precisely revelation, discourse, and communication: form and content are a perfect generative unity.[72] This Qur'anic "conceit" is continued and intensified in the Bab's *Qayyūm al-asmā'*. In *Ulysses* the form becomes content in the

70. Lawson, "Typological Figuration."

71. In English literature perhaps the most instructive and entertaining example of this Joycean insight is elaborated in Nabokov's *Pale Fire*. It is interesting therefore that Nabokov himself seems to have disdained Joyce's last work *Finnegans Wake*. On this see Maria Kager, "The Bilingual Imagination of Joyce and Nabokov," paper presented at the 18th Trieste Joyce School, June 29- July 5, 2014.

72. Daniel Madigan, *The Qur'ân's Self-Image: Writing and Authority in Islam's Scripture* (Woodstock, Oxfordshire: Princeton University Press, 2001).

Oxen of the Sun which functions also as a chrestomathy of English prose styles in forty sections (the number of weeks for human gestation), or in the chapter Aeolus in which the advertising and newspaper layout is the content. Both works embody a resounding and unambiguous – if quite *avant la lettre* – demonstration of McLuhan's "the medium is the message."[73]

By its structure, the Bab's composition has much in common with the literary rupture represented by Joyce's *Ulysses*. The *Tafsīr sūrat Yūsuf* (another name by which the *Qayyūm al-asmā'* is known) is, as we saw, the work through which he proclaimed his messianic mission. In this title we see, perhaps, some Joycean mischief with the word *tafsīr*, a technical term meaning "scriptural commentary," and always indicating the long tradition of Muslim scholasticism that produced it.[74] In reality, this work has virtually nothing in common with that tradition and is as much unlike a standard work of *tafsir* as it could possibly be. It is, however, a reconfiguration of the Qur'an and a rewriting of the Qur'an, in the same way that Joyce's *Ulysses* is a creative reconfiguration of the Odyssey. That Joyce did not have to resort to such a disguise for his work and could proclaim openly that it was an imitation of the Odyssey says something about the differences in the respective cultural settings and the differences between the two texts, the Odyssey and the Qur'an and their respective functions.

The word *al-Qayyūm* comes from the Qur'an (Q2:255; 3:2; 20:111) where it always appears as a divine attribute in tandem with *al-hayy,* "the everliving." It is frequently translated as "self-subsisting." Its choice as part of the title of this work is related to its numerological (*abjad*) value,[75] a gematric iteration of the name Yusuf: both Qayyūm and Yūsuf have the same numeric value (156) and are therefore read as equivalent in the deep "unseen" structure of the language. Additionally, the word *Qayyūm* is derived from same Arabic root as the key messianic terms *qā'im* (resurrector) and *qiyāma* (resurrection/judgment). Thus the figure of Joseph is understood and presented in a messianic and eschatological mood. The prominence of the word, which tends to elude a "crisp" translation, especially in the title of

73. Marshall McLuhan, *Understanding Media: The Extensions of Man* (New York: McGraw Hill, 1964), 7–21.

74. *Tafsīr* expresses the authority of tradition in Islam the same way the word *midrash* does in Judaism.

75. *Abjad* refers to the system by which each Arabic letter has a numerical value. This is a common – and ancient – phenomenon in the alphabets of many Middle Eastern languages, perhaps related to the need for a computational system in a trade-oriented culture. The numerical value of words is part of their esoteric meaning in much mystical and theological writing throughout the history of Islamic letters.

the work *Qayyūm al-asmā'*, is explained by its connotative function as symbol of the resurrection and day of judgment through articulating the same sounds of the words *qā'im* and *qiyāma* and bearing the central semantic value of the triliteral Arabic root Q-W-M.

In the *Qayyūm al-asmā'*, there are a hundred and eleven chapters designated by the author "suras."[76] Each *sura* is composed of verses designated by their author as *āyāt*, usually translated as "divine signs." A wordier though accurate translation is: "miraculous portents" of God's transcendent oneness. They are miraculous in the first place because the prophet Mohammad, through whom they were spoken, was an unschooled merchant[77] and because any description of God is, according to the Qur'an, paradoxically-cum-miraculously fraught because of "His" utter unknowability (Q112). The word *āya*/sign reflects something of the idea in the New Testament's "signs and wonders" (John 4:48; Romans 15:9) without the negativity implied in the John passage. Here it is the author, Ali Mohammad Shirāzi, who uses the term *tafsīr* in the opening words of the first sura. But the composition is in reality taking the form of a "new" Qur'an or more accurately, from the mythopoeic point of view, it is the "true" Qur'an that had until now been in hiding with the hidden Imam.

> God has ordained the coming forth [from concealment] of this book
> in explanation (*fī tafsīr*) of the Greatest of Stories directly from
> Muḥammad bin al-Ḥasan bin Alī bin Muḥammad bin Alī bin Mūsā
> b. Ja'far b. Muḥammad b. Alī bin al-Ḥasan b. Alī b. Abī Ṭālib upon
> his servant [i.e. the Bab: Sayyid Alī Moḥammad] a conclusive and
> eloquent proof of God from the Remembrance before all the worlds.
> (QA3, *sūrat al-mulk*, 9)

76. Inexplicably, this is the same number of suras mentioned in *Finnegans Wake*. Atherton, *Books at the Wake*, 203 (see however some inconsistency in Atherton on this subject at 45 and 172). The proper number of Qur'anic suras is 114. There is no reason to believe that Joyce had any knowledge of even the existence of the Bab's writings although he did have knowledge of the Qur'an and Islamic history and was also in some ways consciously trying to "rewrite" the Qur'an. (See Yared above in note 64). Atherton's view (p. 203) is that Joyce's 111 is a veiled condemnation of or expression of "hostility towards" the Qur'an because it is also an allusion to a condemnatory sura (#111) of the Qur'an in which the arch villain of early Islamic history, Abu Lahab, is roundly condemned to hell. I do not agree that Joyce was hostile to the Qur'an.

77. On Muhammad's so-called "illiteracy" see Sebastian Günther, "Muhammad, the Illiterate Prophet: An Islamic Creed in the Qur'an and Qur'anic Exegesis," *Journal of Qur'anic Studies* 4:1 (2002): 1–26. On the parallels between the life of the Prophet Muhammad and the biography of the Bab, see Stephen Lambden, "An Episode in the Childhood of the Bab," in Peter Smith, ed., In *Iran, Studies in Babí and Baha'í History* volume 3 (Los Angeles: Kalimát Press, 1986), 1–31.

Each *āya* of the Qur'an's *Sūrat Yūsuf,* which has 111 verses, becomes the lemma for each of the *suras* in this work, the topic-heading under which the commentary is generated. The first chapter of the Bab's composition, as mentioned earlier, is entitled the *Sūrat al-mulk.* After this first element of a given sura, comes the *basmala* - that is the ubiquitous Islamic short prayer and invocation: *In the Name of God, the Merciful the Compassionate,* a formula that heads all but one of the Qur'an's 114 suras and which is also used throughout Islamic social and learned culture on countless other occasions, literary, liturgical and social as blessing or prayer. After the *basmala* comes, in the spirit of the "occasions of revelation" genre of Qur'anic sciences,[78] and in imitation of Qur'ans which typically list the number of verses at the head of each sura, the following statement: "this was revealed in Shiraz in forty-two verses" as part of the title section of each sura.

As in *Ulysses,* so in the *Qayyūm al-asmā',* there is a pervading sense of affirmation, assent, acceptance, and commitment. The number forty-two, the total number of verses for each sura, the Bab himself points out, is the numerical equivalent of the word *bala* "Yea verily" which is, as mentioned earlier, the answer of humanity to the question posed by God on the day of the covenant, the day of *alast.* This "Yea verily" – which in the Qur'anic chronotope represents the beginning of consciousness and history – finds an unexpected yet powerful resonance in Molly Bloom's future directed affirmation in Penelope, ending the entire novel with "yes I will I will Yes." And just as chaos and cosmos are combined in Joyce's modernist literary masterpiece, by making each of his new 111 suras 42 verses in length lends a heretofore-unimaginable regularity to the idea of "Qur'an." But, as we saw, the number 42 is not accidental, even if the number 111 in *Finnegans Wake* is, encoding how form becomes content in this remarkable work by the Bab. It may be thought that this primordial "yes" flows through the "veins" of the entire work, all 4,442 verses, as the Bab himself explicitly says.[79] Casting new verses, braiding direct quotations from the Qur'an with his own words and words and phrases from Hadith in a seamless new verse, the author regulates it all with the familiar – and here unvarying – Qur'anic rhymed prose, *saj'.* There can be wide variation in the length of the individual verse in the Bab's composition, just as there is in the original Qur'an, from the short-

---

78. On this topic see Andrew Rippin, "Occasions of Revelation," in *Encyclopaedia of the Qur'an,* edited by Jane Dammen McAuliffe, vol. 3 (Leiden: Brill Academic Publishers, 2003), 69–73.

79. See below the translation from the *Qayyūm al-asmā':* "the Letter 'B' that circulates in the water of the two groups of letters." "Two groups of letters" is a poetic way of referring to all language. The letter 'B' is, among other things, the first letter of the word *'balā':* Yes!!.

est, e.g. a set of disconnected letters, to the longest (the 15 lines of verse 8 of the *Sūrat al-ʿabd*, (QA108: 225–6). The Bab combines commentary with text, audience with performance, revelation with interpretation. In terms of European literary history, such may certainly be considered a modernist gesture.

Following this first section of a given sura, comes the citation of the Qur'anic verse from the *Sūrat Yūsuf* that is to be the object of commentary – the lemma – for the particular chapter. Then come, for all but four suras, the disconnected letters (some Qur'anic, some new). After the disconnected letters, comes the third section of the commentary. It is difficult to characterize this third section satisfactorily because it can be so different from sura to sura and sometimes highly variegated within each sura. In many of the suras, this third section represents a further level of paraphrase, gloss and commentary. For example, the Bab's composition from suras 80 to 91,[80] in addition to offering a commentary for the Qur'anic verses 12:79 to 12:91 (as would be expected following the structural logic of the work) also presents a running paraphrase of a long series of verses in Qur'anic order that takes into account the bulk of the actual Qur'an from suras 10 through 16. The final or fourth section or division is the return to the actual verse from the *Sūrat Yūsuf* under which the new sura has been written. Here the authorial creativity assumes the character of pure paraphrase. The verse itself is recast to reflect the concerns of the author. These concerns are largely to do with the appearance of the hidden Imam and the inauguration of the return, the *qiyāma* and the day of judgment all in one literary moment. In comparison with *Ulysses*, this final section may be thought a similarly life affirming response to the challenges and "nightmare" of history – in short, an awakening, a revelation. In order to illustrate what might otherwise be difficult to visualize, reproduced here is a translation of the opening of chapter 109 of the Bab's *Qayyūm al-asmāʾ*, the Sura of the Servant. Here the Qur'anic form will be quite apparent in the opening invocation, the mention of the number of verses and the place of revelation, and perhaps most importantly, the close relationship between commentary and text in which it is very difficult to discern at times where the Qur'anic material ends and the Bab's so-called commentary begins. In order to illustrate this aspect of the work I have employed the typographical expediency of showing the verbatim Qur'anic passages and words in small capitals.

80. QA *suwar al-zawal, al-kaf, al-aʿzam, al-baʾ, al-ism, al-ḥaqq, al-tayr, al-nabaʾ, al-iblāgh, al-insān* (ii) and *al-tathlith*.

The Sura of the Servant[81]

Forty-two verses, revealed in Shiraz

IN THE NAME OF GOD THE MERCIFUL THE COMPASSIONATE

NOR DID WE SEND BEFORE THEE [AS MESSENGERS] ANY BUT MEN WHOM
WE DID INSPIRE – [MEN] LIVING IN HUMAN HABITATIONS. DO THEY NOT
TRAVEL THROUGH THE EARTH, AND SEE WHAT WAS THE END OF THOSE
BEFORE THEM? BUT THE HOME OF THE HEREAFTER IS BEST, FOR THOSE
WHO DO RIGHT. WILL YE NOT THEN UNDERSTAND? (QUR'AN 12:109)

Verse 1

Mím Ha Mím Dal [= "Muḥammad" when connected in script]

Verse 2

O People of the THRONE! Listen to the CALL of your Lord, THE
MERCIFUL, He who THERE IS NO GOD EXCEPT HIM from the tongue of
the REMEMBRANCE, this YOUTH son of the Sublime (*al-'alí*, also the first
name of the Bab: 'Alí), the 'Arab to whom [God has] in the MOTHER
BOOK testified.

Verse 3

Then LISTEN to WHAT IS BEING REVEALED TO YOU FROM YOUR LORD:
VERILY VERILY I AM GOD, OF WHOM THERE IS NO GOD BUT HIM.
NOTHING IS LIKE UNTO HIM while He is God, Lofty (*'alí*) Great.

Verse 4

O People of the Earth! HEARKEN to the CALL of the BIRDS upon the
TREES leafy and perfumed with the CAMPHOR of Manifestation
describing this YOUNG MAN descended from the Arabs, from
MOHAMMAD, from 'Alí, from Fatima, from Mekka, from Medina, from
Batha', from 'Iraq with what the MERCIFUL HAS MANIFESTED upon
their leaves, namely that he is THE SUBLIME (*al-'ala*) and he is God,
MIGHTY, PRAISED.

---

81. This is very slightly adapted from Todd Lawson, "The Súrat al-'Abd of the Qayyúm al-
asmá' (Chapter 109): A Provisional Translation and Commentary," in Todd Lawson and Omid
Ghaemmaghami, eds., *A Most Noble Pattern: Collected Essays on the Writings of the Bab, 'Alí Muhammad Shírází (1819–1850)* (Oxford: George Ronald, 2012), 116–45. This excerpt with footnotes and
other indications removed from the original, is from pp. 127–28.

Verse 5

This YOUTH most white in colour and most beautiful of eye, even
of eyebrow, limbs well formed like gold freshly cast from the two
springs, soft of shoulder like pure malleable silver in two cups,
sublimely awesome in appearance, like the awe-inspiring appearances
of the Elders, and outspreading his MERCY as the two Husayns spread
mercy over the land, the center of the sky (i.e. the sun) has not
seen the like of the justice of the two justices, and in grace like the
two Lights joined in the two names from the most lofty of the two
beloveds and the ISTHMUS between the two causes in the SECRET of
al-Tatanjayn, the abider like the upright *Alif (al-alif al-qā'im)* between
the two scrolls at the center of the two worlds, THE JUDGE, BY THE
PERMISSION OF GOD in the two later births (the SECRET of the two
'Alawīs and the splendour of the two Fatimīs and an ancient fruit
from the BLESSED TREE encrimsoned by the FIRE of the Two Clouds
and a group of those of the sacred veils pulsating with the shim-
mering light, the abider around the FIRE in the TWO SEAS the glory
of heaven unto the causes of the two earths and a handful of the clay
of the earth over the people of the two – these two GARDENS of DARK
GREEN FOLIAGE over the point of the TWO WESTS and those SECRET
two names in the creation of the TWO EASTS born in the two Harams
and the one looking towards the two Qiblas beyond the two Ka'bas,
the one who prays over the incandescent THRONE twice a possessor
of the two causes and the Pure Water in the two gulfs, the speaker
in the two stations and the knower of the two Imams, the Letter "B"
that circulates in the water of the two groups of letters and the Point
Abiding over the DOOR of the Two Alifs revolving around God in the
two cycles and the one made to speak on the authority of God in the
two cycles, the SERVANT OF GOD and the REMEMBRANCE of His PROOF.
This YOUNG MAN CALLED, because his grandfather is ABRAHAM, THE
SPIRIT in the forerunners and he is the Gate, after the two later gates.
And PRAISE BE TO GOD THE LORD OF ALL THE WORLDS. And he is God,
indeed the one who comprehends everything concerning ALL OF THE
WORLDS.

Such literary activity, in the guise of exegesis, may be understood partly
as excavating or carving out of the mass and chaos of revelation a here-
tofore-inconceivable regularity in which the pre-existing irregular and the
frequently non sequitur narratological aspect of Qur'anic suras become as
formally structured as sonnets. In the context of the return of the hidden
Imam with the true Qur'an, this could suggest that the irregularity of the
Uthmanic codex – the basis for all published Qur'ans – was a result of textual

violence on the part of the breakers of the covenant (*al-nāqiḍīn*). Whatever the implications of this new orderly Qur'an text might be, it is clear that the resulting composition mirrors the confidence of the author in claiming the authority to do such an otherwise unimaginable and heretical thing: to rearrange and re-write the Qur'an. It may be that Joyce's design, to collapse the 20-year long story of Odysseus into the confines of a single day in the life of Dublin bespeaks a similar desire to exercise control over the "nightmare of history" of which Stephen Dedalus so famously spoke (U34). Thus the name of the first sura written by the Bab: *mulk*, or [divine] ownership, may be read as his ownership and mastery of the Holy Qur'an, reorganizing it, making it regular, in a sense making it "rational," while at the same time announcing and declaiming through a torrential storm of language with "expectation on the verge of being fulfilled" inside it, anticipating a kind of Joycean "chaosmos." It should be recalled, as well, that the composition can be seen as a melding together of innumerable fragments of scripture making the resulting composition simultaneously old and new – another *coincidentia oppositorum*.

Such a storm is experienced in *Ulysses* but is even more manifest and intense in *Finnegans Wake*: a riot of language, which eventually emerges as quite deliberately and meticulously orchestrated – and this to a nearly unbelievable degree.[82] Eventually emerges, that is, after the heroic effort of the reader has succeeded in discerning the art and craft sometimes otherwise obscured by these two remarkable compositions, *Ulysses* and the *Qayyūm al-asmā'*, in which the epic adventure of language in extending the resources and significance of language itself is central.

We do not need to emphasize how shocking and scandalous – unthinkable even – such an imitation of the Qur'an was and is. But such extreme scandal – though in a different "key" – also relates to the literary act of Joyce 75 years later, when he takes ownership of and participates quite fully in the sacred aura and dignity of the epic tradition, and appropriates its authority for himself in refiguring it according to contemporary Irish life in all its "chaosmic" plenitude, from the sublime preoccupations of Stephen, to the fatherly and husbandly quest and the attendant peripeties of Bloom and the ultimate salvific affirmation of Molly. The life is told in the – at that time –

82. There are numerous works of scholarship devoted to decoding the otherwise extremely daunting *Finnegans Wake* and revealing its intricate logic and structure, we mention here only four, beginning with the oldest: Joseph Campbell and Henry Morton Robinson, *A Skeleton Key to Finnegans Wake: Unlocking James Joyce's Masterwork* (Novato, CA: New World Library, 2005 [first published 1944]); Adaline Glasheen, *A Census of Finnegans Wake: An Index of the Characters and Their Roles* (London: Faber and Faber, 1957); Clive Hart, *A Concordance to Finnegan's Wake* (Minneapolis: University of Minnesota Press, 1963); Atherton, *The Books at the Wake*; John Bishop, *Joyce's Book of the Dark*, Finnegans Wake (Madison, WI: University of Wisconsin Press, 1986).

scandalous graphic depiction of sexual and other intimate bodily acts and functions, in the roiling, sometimes tawdry and racist encounters in Dublin pub life, in the private tenderness that occurs between various characters. There is also pointed criticism of the hypocrisies and paralysis Joyce saw in Roman Catholicism. He makes the Odyssey his own in order to express his own particular artistic vision a vision that entails a significant Brunonian "mystical" noetic. The Bab does the same thing with the Qur'an. He says this is mine. And, I am demonstrating how I am taking ownership of it now. And, I am reorganizing it. Rewriting it according to the exigencies of the moment. Thus the Bab also interrogated, disturbed and problematized the relationship between revelation (*tanzīl*) and its interpretation (*ta'wīl*), in the life affirming hope to awaken from the nightmare of history marked most dramatically at his time by the mutual and frequently quite virulent heart-breaking enmity among various Muslim communal identities all of which traced their genesis to the gospel of divine unity originally preached by Mohammad. As a son of Shi'i Islam the Bab's awareness of such disunity was particularly exquisite.

When the *Qayyūm al-asmā'* was first brought to the attention of "Orientalism" in the nineteenth century, people said it is meaningless; the man was insane; there is no sense to this; "it is an unintelligible rhapsody"; the grammar is bad.[83] This response is of course very similar to the kind of thing that was said about *Ulysses* when it inaugurated literary modernism in 1922. However, neither the *Qayyūm al-asmā'* nor *Ulysses* is nonsense. Both are very clearly and intricately structured, even if the warp and woof of this structure is frequently overwhelmed by torrential linguistic virtuosity. It is worth noting that by the time the Bab was writing, Shi'i philosophy had established an interesting discourse in which the hidden Imam could be identified with an individual internal spiritual or existential reality, in addition to the expected advent of history, as in the Protestant transposition of the Return of Jesus to the inner realm of the individual soul. The Bab reorganized the words and verses of the Qur'an to apply specifically to the appearance of the hidden Imam and his own role as the gate of the hidden Imam. Thus, the hidden Imam serves in some ways as a poetic reference for the "new" individual as such, in addition to being a ever-living symbol of radical historical change, which seeks to resolve the problems tradition poses to the current moment in Iranian society. This would seem to be clearly indicated in the Bab's much recited short prayer, called in English "The Remover of Difficulties."[84]

83. Lawson, *Gnostic Apocalypse*, 46–47, 82.

84. The Arabic original is found in *Muntakhābāt āyāt az āthār Ḥaḍrat Nuqtah-yi Ūlā* (Chandigarh: Carmel Publishers, 2007), 156. For an English translation, see *Selections from the Writings of the Bab* (Haifa: Bahá'í World Centre 1976), 217.

> Is there any remover of difficulties save God? Say: Praised be God, He
> is God. All are his servants and all abide by His bidding.[85]

An equally accurate translation, and one which acquires a certain imme-
diacy in the exceptional context of the Shi'i "millennium" or *qiyāma* (during
which time the Bab composed his various works), would alter the translation of the last five words (which in Arabic are *wa kullun bi-amrihi qā'imun*) to
"and each is a *qā'im* in God's cause." In Twelver Shi'ism, the *qā'im* is typically
held to be the hidden or Twelfth Imam who had, until the time of his divine-
ly ordained return, been in occultation (*ghayba*). So, in another rendering of
the original Arabic prayer a "modern" notion of the individual emerges: "Is
there any remover of oppression apart from God? Say: All praise be to God!
He is God. All others are His servants and are to arise (*qā'im*) in obedience to
His holy cause (*amrihi*)." This indicates also that the time for waiting for a
savior is over. In the new cycle, the cycle of fulfillment, maturity and resurrection, all members of the human race are potentially *qā'ims*, arisers in the
cause of God. Naturally, it is also quite within the bounds of accepted usage
to understand both meanings as complementary to each other.

Here, we see another point of comparison with Joyce and the Bab and
another feature of the epic dimension of both *Ulysses* and the *Qayyūm al-
asmā'* (and of course of the Qur'an itself): in some ways the most salient
aspect of their epic qualities becomes apparent in the epic struggle of the
reader himself to "complete" the journey. The individual becomes singled
out as the center of narrative gravity and comprehension. Understanding
is heroic. The reader is an autonomous, creative-cum-heroic participant
without whom the composition would not exist. Revelation is cast in the
language of the recipient:

> And We have sent no Messenger save with the tongue of his
> people, that he might make all clear to them; then God leads astray
> whomsoever He will, and He guides whomsoever He will; and He is
> the All-mighty, the All-wise. (Q14: 4: *wa mā arsalnā min rusul illā bi-lisān
> qawmihi*)

Related to the idea of "reader as hero" is the quest for identity, emblematized
in the search of son for father in both works. It is the grand "monomythic"
theme of literature as such.[86] This theme emerges in both *Ulysses* and the

---

85. *Bahá'í Prayers: A Selection of Prayers Revealed by Bahá'u'lláh, The Báb, and 'Abdu'l-Bahá*, Wilmette, IL: Bahá'í Publishing Trust, 1982), 106.

86. On reader as hero: Northrop Frye, *Anatomy of Criticism* (Princeton: Princeton University
Press, 1973), 323–324; on losing and regaining identity as the central concern of the "monomyth"; Northrop Frye, *The Educated Imagination* (Bloomington: Indiana University Press, 1964),
55.

Qayyūm al-asmā' through revelation, recognition (anagnorisis) or epiphany (*zuhūr, kashf*), the Greek word for which is of course apocalypse. Both *Ulysses* and the *Qayyūm al-asmā'* are dealing in revelation. For *Ulysses*, this is intensely encountered in Penelope. For the *Qayyūm al-asmā'* the intensity of the encounter is maintained at a remarkable level throughout the entire work. Revelation, for the Bab, springs from the *coincidentia oppositorum*, which employs all created phenomena in order to demonstrate that there is something beyond logic and sense perception that shines through the "clash" of apparent oppositions. And in both the Bab and Joyce this is demonstrated over and over again through the epic adventure of language in which the *coincidentia oppositorum* has a simultaneous poetic or literary function and a philosophical or mystical function.[87]

The literary fiction, that the book was given to the Bab by the hidden Imam, asserts of course an important "religious" credential, namely that he is the "official" representative of the hidden Imam and so the focus and locus of all the power in the universe (viz. *al-walāya al-mutlaqa*). But the actual work establishes an even more important "literary" credential. Certainly the earliest followers of the Bab made much of his verbal artistry and prodigious literary abilities as a proof of his claims to be in touch with the hidden Imam. Without the hidden Imam there is, of course, no Twelver Shi'ism; without the idea of the absence or the discussion about the hidden Imam's representative, there is also no Twelver Shi'ism. But, there are certain clues throughout the text that the Bab himself is actually this same hidden Imam, clues that *he himself is the one from whom he himself received the book.*[88] What might be thought clear and unambiguous indication of this is found in the titles of the hundred-and-eighth and hundred-and-ninth *suras*. The disconnected letters for these two chapters, *Sūrat al-dhikr* (QA108) and *Sūrat al-'abd* (QA 109), are respectively A-L-Y (*'ayn-lam-yā*) and M-H-M-D (*mīm-hā-mīm-dal*). Neither set of disconnected letters occurs in the Qur'an and must be thought original – as disconnected letters – with the Bab (as are many other sets of disconnected letters in this work). Further, each set when looked at as *not* disconnected but as spelling a word are seen to be the names Ali and Mohammad. These are the names, in reverse order, of (according to Shi'i Islam) the first two bearers of divine authority in Islam: Ali ibn Abi Tālib (d.661) cousin and son-in-law of the Prophet Muhammad (d. 632). That these are

87. "The juxtaposition of opposites, however, is thematic at least as much as it is structural ...," Card, *Anatomy*, 52.

88. Lawson, *Gnostic*, 117. A similarly self-reflexive process is studied in Omid Ghaemmaghami, "The Báb's journey to the Kaaba," in Todd Lawson and Omid Ghaemmaghami, eds., *A Most Noble Pattern*, 175–95.

also the names of the author of the *Qayyūm al-asmā'* is obviously no accident, making the point that history is cyclical and is repeating itself in the revelation of the Bab. They are inserted here in an artistic, nearly playful, manner to underscore that he is indeed responsible for this text as its author. (See Figure 3 below.) The name of the author Ali Mohammad [viz: Shirāzi - the Bab] is thus camouflaged in these not too mysterious, "disconnected" letters, which are clearly not disconnected at all.[89] And, most importantly, with this assertion of authorship, the Bab complicates and challenge a traditional understanding of divine revelation.

The *Qayyūm al-asmā'* is the very embodiment of high seriousness and earnestness. No irony, no comedy or humor. These "disconnected letters" are striking evidence of authorial presence and an artistic gesture that combines the Bab's inborn temperament and preoccupations with his unconventional, even iconoclastic, religious ideas. These concerns are channeled through a traditionally pietistic religious modality: the Qur'an and its exegesis (*tafsīr*). The Qur'an is the raw material out of which issues this work, just as the *Odyssey* is the raw material out of which *Ulysses* emerges as Joyce's expression of his own unorthodoxy. Both are works that by their very nature ask questions about the relationship between tradition and change, narrative and authorial creativity, and the role of the reader. In the Bab's composition, the relationship between revelation and interpretation is privileged. This may be thought emblematic of the basic presupposition of a distinctively Shi'i hermeneutic in which the angel of revelation is also the angel of interpretation.[90]

This is of course where it parts company to some degree with *Ulysses*. *Ulysses* is not terribly religious in the traditional "institutional" sense of that word, although Joyce was himself saturated in Roman Catholicism, and much of his language and much of his point of view was formed by his early education and his conflicts coming up against Catholicism in the "modern world." It is indisputable that he rejected Catholicism. But, we have seen how Joyce's "religious faculty" was attracted to and stimulated by the mystical philosophy of thinkers like Bruno. It is not accurate to call *Ulysses* secular precisely because of its epic structure and élan, its seriousness, which may be thought highlighted and accentuated by the fluent, obbligato-like leitmotif of humor and its revelatory observation of the hallowed interconnectedness of all

---

89. While I am unaware of the any of the sets of actual Qur'anic disconnected letters being identified as proper names, the reverse is certainly true. Sets of these mysterious letters have frequently been given as proper names in Islamic societies, e.g., Ta Ha (from Sura 20) and Ya Sin (from Sura 36).

90. Corbin, *En Islam iranien: aspects spirituels et philosophiques* (Paris: Éditions Gallimard, 1971), vol. 3, 292–300.

Opening lines of *sūrat al-dhikr* (QA 108, pp. 223-225).

٢٢٣

اللّه العلي يذكاك سورة الذكر ٱثنتان واربعون ايات ذلك الكتاب شيئا
لبــــــــم اللّه الرحمن الرحيم ه مثل هذه سبيلي ادعوا الى اللّه على بصيرة
انا ومن اتّبعني وسبحان اللّه وما انا من المشركين ه على ه هو اللّه الذي لا اله الا هو ربّ
والسماء وهو اللّه كان عليّا عظيمًا ه هو الذي تنزل الاسرار في اسطر من لا الواهو بالحقّ

Opening lines of *sūrat al-'abd* (QA 109, pp. 225-229).

المآ مشهودًاه وسبحان اللّه الحقّ الذي لا اله الا هو وهو اللّه كان بكلّ شيء مدبرًا
وهو اللّه مكّ سورة العبد لبــــــــم اللّه الرحمن الرحيم ٱثنتان واربعون من العالمين شيّا
وما ارسلنا من قبلك الا رجالًا نوحا اليهم من اهل القرى اعلم سيروا في الارض فينظر واكيف كا
عاقبة الذين من قبلهم ولدار الاخرة خير للذين اتقوا افلا تعقلون ه محمّد ه يا افضل
العرب استمعوا اذا ه وربّكم الرحمن الذي لا اله الا هو من لسان الذكر هذا الفتى ابن العلي العربي

Figure 3: The Bab's signature masquerading as disconnected letters:

things. *Ulysses* has the gravitas of scriptural purpose and the solemnity and
nobility of the epic. Just as the Qur'an is concerned with a universal human
experience – an epic which it casts in terms of *dīn* – sacred responsibility
or "religion," *Ulysses* locates sacred responsibility in Bloom's search for a
son (Rudy), Stephen's search for a father, and Molly's exuberant and somehow also highly devout affirmation of life. We can never imagine the Bab
saying anything like Joyce's: "How I hate God and death! How I like Nora."[91]
However, in the opening chapter of his work, the *Sūrat al-mulk*, the sura of
dominion, he says with similar vehemence and commitment that all power,

91. James Joyce, from a letter to Nora dated about 1 September 1904, in Richard Ellmann,
ed., *Selected Letters of James Joyce* (New York: Viking Press, 1975), 27.

explicitly that of the Shah and that of the ulema, has now been returned to its rightful place: the hidden Imam (i.e. himself). And though the Bab's *balā* "Yes indeed!" is a different affirmation than Molly's series of 12 yesses that end the book, both adverbial affirmatives assent to the power of life to endure, abide, flourish in order to provide the "modality" out of which more life can be created and renewed. Earlier, it was suggested that the word *qiyāma* may in some ways reflect and indicate Qajar modernist energies. Another word, much used in the Bab's writings and by later Baha'i writers, is *badī'*, which may be translated as "wondrously new." It is wondrous because it indicates a quality that is simultaneously new and eternal or ancient. It is the word used, for example to indicate the new calendar constructed by the Bab and followed by Baha'īs. This same tension uniting the old and the new is clearly present in *Ulysses*.

Thus does literary modernism, in the cloak of Iranian religiosity, anticipate by 70 years or so, a much more well-known and -recognized epochal literary shift whose emblem is James Joyce's *Ulysses*.[92] Whether this has relevance for theorizing about the relationship between such literary creativity and the more purely historical problem of the relationship between the modern and whatever its opposite might be, is a question that will have to be postponed. But for the moment, we can perhaps allow ourselves a little latitude to ask in closing whether we might not be somewhat justified in thinking of *Ulysses* as a case of Qajar literary modernism in a twentieth-century European masterpiece? Indeed, all of the Bab's literary works were condemned and demonized by the broader culture as heretical. Thousands of the Bab's followers were in fact slaughtered by the Shah's forces, at the behest of the clerical estate. Those who might otherwise have been attracted to and inspired by the literary achievements of the Bab had much more at stake than "mere" literary success or failure. But the comparison of the two works is suggestive on the level of literature precisely because of the structural and thematic parallels, the similarities between the two texts as scandalous, outrageous and "difficult," the respective authors' sense

---

92. The present exploration is not the first time the unique œuvre of the Bab has been likened to modernist European literary developments. Years ago, in conference presentation Denis MacEoin, prolific scholar of the Babi and Baha'i phenomena, said: "As a matter of fact, his Arabic was never as bad as his Muslim critics have suggested. There is something enticingly Dadaist about his defiance of linguistic tradition and his explosion of Arabic roots past all ordinary meaning." ("Deconstructing and Reconstructing the Shari'a: The Babi And Baha'i Solutions to the Problem of Immutability" British Society for Middle East Studies Conference 1997.) That presentation has recently been published in a collection of articles. See Denis MacEoin, *The Messiah of Shiraz : Studies in Early and Middle Babism* (Boston: Brill, 2009), 645–57, reference here is to p. 652.

of themselves as revolutionizing their own particular literary cultures and their singular and heroic dedication to their respective visions. From the point of view of the centrality of rupture, scandal and shock and the signal that something new was happening embodied by both works, there is much to commend the comparison and it is difficult to ignore their obvious similarities.

Postscriptum

Successive versions of this chapter were presented on four occasions: *Iranian Studies Seminar Series*, Foundation for Iranian Studies & Toronto Initiative for Iranian Studies (Department of Near and Middle Eastern Cultures and Civilizations, University of Toronto), 2 November 2012; *The Qur'an and its Exegesis in Modern Iran* (Institute of Ismaili Studies, London, UK), 2–4 September 2013; *Literature and Writing in Qajar Iran*, 14th International Qajar Studies Association Conference (Otto-Friedrich Universität, Lehrstuhl für Iranistik, Bamberg, Germany) 30–31 May 2014; *Bábí-Bahá'í and Religious Studies Academic Seminar* (Newcastle-upon-Tyne UK, Bahá'í Centre), 25–27 July 2014. I am grateful to the organizers of these events (respectively: Professors Mohamad Tavakoli-Targhi; Alessandro Cancian; Manoutchehr M. Eskandari-Qajar, Houchang E. Chehabi and Roxane Haag-Higuchi; and finally, Stephen M. Lambden and Sholeh Quinn) for their kind and generous hospitality and to the various conference participants for stimulating discussion. I am also very grateful to Professor John McCourt, and his fellow organizers and the participants of the *18th Trieste Joyce School* (29 June – 5 July 2014 Trieste, Italy) where I gathered much information and inspiration for the final form of this chapter. My sincere thanks go also to Jeffrey Einboden, Gary Fuhrman and Mustafa Shah who kindly read an earlier draft and made several valuable comments and suggestions.

7

Sharing Poetic Sensitivity and Misery

Encounters of Iranians with the Irish in Travel Writings and Fiction

M. R. Ghanoonparvar

I N MY SEARCH FOR THE PORTRAYAL OF THE WEST and Westerners in Persian literature for a book that was published nearly two decades ago, given the international political situation at the time, I found that the Persian terms *farang* (Europe) and *farangi* (European) and even *gharb* (West) and *gharbi* (Westerner) had negative connotations and do not universally refer to all the countries of Europe and the New World, but rather to specific parts and peoples of these regions.[1] Often excluded from these terms were Spain, sometimes even Italy, and generally speaking, Eastern Europe. Another intriguing exception from being considered as a part of Western Europe that I found in my search was Ireland and the Irish. The overall focus of that book, of course, was twentieth- century literature, and more specifically prose fiction. But I also looked at nineteenth-century travel accounts by Iranians who visited the West. Interestingly, the few examples of the Iranian writers' portrayal of the Irish, in contrast to the French and English, for instance, are generally sympathetic and friendly. This can be seen even in Mirzā Abu Tāleb Khān's *Masir-e Tālebi* [The Tālebi Route], the travel account of an Indian-born son of Iranian parents.[2] In the late eighteenth century, Mirzā Abu Tāleb, who had worked for the East India Company in his youth, on the provocation of English officials, becomes involved in a dispute with a rajah and kills him. Fearing the consequences, he flees from India and embarks on a journey to London. The route of his journey to London, however, is through South Africa and then Ireland. In Dublin, where he spends some time, he provides us in great detail with his first impressions of Europe and Europeans. Having had previous knowledge of the English, he compares them with the Irish and writes that the Irish are "free of the immodera-

---

1. M. R. Ghanoonparvar, *In a Persian Mirror: Images of the West and Westerners in Iranian Fiction* (Austin: University of Texas Press, 1993).

2. Mirzā Abu Tāleb Khān, *Masir-e Tālebi yā Safarnāma-ye Mirzā Abu Tāleb Khān*, 2nd ed., ed. Hoseyn Khadiv Jam (Tehran: Sherkat-e sahāmi-ye ketābhā-ye jibi, 1973).

tion of the English and the excessive piety and fanaticism of the Scots in following Christian religious laws; they are moderate."[3] Even more sympathetically, he then adds that the Irish "are distinguished from the English and the Scots for their courage, bravery, spending, hospitality, kindness to strangers, friendliness, and kindheartedness. Although they lack the astute, firm wisdom of the English, they are superior to them in intelligence and quickness of wit."[4] About the Irish, he further observes, "[b]ecause of their carefree nature, spending a great deal, and devoting time to friends, the Irish have few wealthy people among them."[5]

Despite all these general observations about the English and the Irish, it is not clear how Abu Tāleb reached these conclusions, since he readily admits at this point that he does not understand or speak English and he has to resort to sign language to communicate with his Irish landlady and her children. Nevertheless, to support his claim, he is eloquent in praise of his hosts and their willingness to help him and provide him with everything that he needs. Interestingly, he also comments on the excessive drinking of the Irish and, stating that he had heard from the British that they get drunk at the dinner table and kill each other, he says that during his stay he did not see any impolite behavior or inhumane action on the part of the Irish.

The expression of similar sentiments can also be seen in other nineteenth-century travel memoirs. For example, Hājj Sayyāh who traveled extensively in Europe and elsewhere in his travel account describes the Irish people as "kinder and more artistic than the English."[6] In contrast to the overtly sympathetic views of Mirzā Abu Tāleb Khān and the more thoughtful observations of Hājj Sayyāh are those of Abolhasan Khān Ilchi, who was sent by Fath Ali Shah Qajar as the Iranian ambassador to the English court in 1808. Although quite impressed by the English, in his brief remarks about the Irish he is yet somewhat sympathetic, describing the Irish people as "bold and brave." He further pontificates that regarding the Irish, there is "nothing in between; they are either extremely good or extremely bad" and that they are "very good looking," as well.[7]

    3. Ibid., 8.
    4. Ibid.
    5. Ibid., 81.
    6. Ali Dehbashi, ed. *Safarnāma-ye Hājj Sayyāh beh Farang* (Tehran: Nashr-e Nāsher, 1984), 510. A translation of this work by the granddaughter of Hājj Sayyāh, Mehrbanoo Nasser Deyhim was published in English as *An Iranian in Nineteenth Century Europe: The Travel Diaries of Haj Sayyah, 1859-1877* (Bethesda, MD: IBEX Publishers, 1998). Interestingly, the sentence I have quoted and in which Sayyāh compares the Irish and the English is left out in the translation, perhaps in deference to the late eminent British scholar of Persian who wrote the foreword to the translation.
    7. Hasan Morsalvand, ed. *Heyratnāma: Safarnāma-ye Abolhasan Khān Ilchi beh Landan* [Trav-

The pronouncedly sympathetic attitude toward the Irish is also quite evident in Simin Dāneshvar's popular novel, *Savushun*, which was published in the late 1960s, nearly two centuries after Abu Talāb's travel account and more than a century after the travel diaries of Sayyāh and Ilchi.[8] The story of *Savushun* takes place in the city of Shiraz during the Allied occupation of the country in World War II and revolves around the lives of a prominent family in the city and the reactions of the family members to the occupation forces, mainly the British. Although Dāneshvar tells the story mainly from the perspective of its protagonist, Zari, she also provides us with the attitude of other characters in the novel regarding the Western occupiers. The unsympathetic tone regarding the British is set from the first pages of the novel, with the introduction of Zinger, a long-term British resident of the city who used to sell sewing machines and who is suspected of having been a British spy, because he has put on a British army uniform. Zari's unsympathetic attitude toward the British triggers negative recollections of her British teachers from her childhood when she attended an English school.

In contrast to the portrayal of the British in *Savushun*, Dāneshvar presents us with a much more sympathetic picture of an Irishman by the name of MacMahon, who is serving in Shiraz as a war correspondent. A poet, MacMahon is an old friend of Zari's British-educated husband, Yusef, from his student days. Like Yusef, who is an idealistic uncompromising intellectual with perhaps xenophobic ideas and who defies the presence of the foreign forces in his country, MacMahon also resents the British rule over his own country. The political misery that these two characters share, however, is articulated beyond the fact that both nations are victims of the British. Using poetry as his weapon of choice to fight the British, in a drunken stupor one night, MacMahon poetically establishes the link between himself as an Irishman and his Iranian friend and his wife, Yusef and Zari, "We are kin, aren't we, Iran and Ireland? Both are the land of Aryans. You are the ancestors and we the descendants! Oh, our old, old ancestors. Give us solace. Give us solace!"[9] He then compares the Iranian and the Irish struggles for independence:

> Oh Ireland, oh land of Aryan descendants, I have composed a poem about a tree that must grow in your soil. This tree is called the Tree of Independence. This tree must be irrigated with blood, not water. Water will dry it up. Yes, Yusef, you were right. If independence is

el Diary of Abolhasan Khan Ilchi to London] (Tehran: Mo'assesah-ye Khadamāt-e Farhangi-ye Rasā, 1985), 232.

8. Simin Dāneshvar, *Savushun*, 9th ed. (Tehran: Khvārazmi, 1978).

9. Simin Daneshvar, *Savushun: A Novel About Modern Iran*, trans. M.R. Ghanoonparvar (Washington, D.C.: Mage Publishers, 1990), 28–29. All quotations from this novel are from this translation.

good for me, it is good for you too. And the story you told me was very useful to me. You told me about the tree in your legends, whose leaves when dried and applied to the eyes like *kohl*, can make one invisible and capable of doing anything. I wish there were one of these trees in Ireland and one in your city.[10]

Through the character of MacMahon as a poet and a drunk, Dāneshvar presents us with a somewhat stereotypical portrayal of the Irish; nonetheless, this portrayal is supposed to incite sympathy in her Iranian reader. In fact, Dāneshvar devotes one chapter of the novel to a sort of fantastical story that MacMahon has written and published, which he initially intended for children, but turns out to be a celestial parable about human freedom. Here is how MacMahon's story begins:

> The old Chariot Keeper gathered his white flowing beard, a memento of millions and millions of years, and dusted the Golden Chariot of the Sun with it. Then he reached for the Golden Key that hung on his belt and headed eastward. Yes, it was time now. The Sun, tired and weary, was returning from its journey. He opened the Gate to the East with his key. The Sun was late, and when it arrived, it was covered with dust and it yawned. The Chariot Keeper brushed off the dust of the journey, which had settled on the head and face of the Sun, with his massive white beard and polished its rays. The Sun mounted the Chariot to begin its journey in the sky. But it did not leave immediately, and the Chariot Keeper waited. The Sun said, "The Master has sent you a message, that is why I was delayed."[11]

The Master's message to the old Chariot Keeper is that he must clean out the Celestial storage room, take the stars of his subjects out of the cupboard, and send them to the people on Earth, because he wants everyone to become the owner of his own star. Although skeptical about the order, because he does not approve of the Master's creatures on Earth, the old Chariot Keeper mobilizes the cherubs and dispatches them to Earth. After four long celestial days and nights, the cherubs eventually return, but not all of them. A large number of them find Earth and its people very interesting, and decide to stay. As for the reaction of the people receiving their own stars of destiny, the cherubs report that the children had a very good time playing with them, the old people said that it was too late already, and most of the young and the middle aged did not even understand the purpose. The exception was one group of the latter, who said that they had never believed in fate and destiny.

10. Ibid., 30.
11. Ibid., 289.

When MacMahon is finished reading his story, Yusef offers him a glass of wine and comments: "You know, now that I have heard your story again ... it occurs to me that the subject that interests you is what you repeat in your poems, too. You're trying to atone for the sins of others."[12]

The narrator of Dāneshvar's novel is not Zari, and never appears as a character in the story, but rather than being a detached observer, she seems to be involved in the story she tells, in the joys and sorrows of her protagonist. Perhaps it is this involvement and the attachment of the narrator that is transmitted to the readers; and along with it, the Iranian readers also share in the misery and poetic sensitivity the author seems to suggest that the Iranians and the Irish also share. Indeed, in contrast to all other foreigners in the city, including the Indian soldiers who are British subjects and are also portrayed in a negative light and regarded as unwanted strangers, MacMahon is treated by Zari, Yusef, and their two little daughters not as a foreigner and stranger, but as a member of the family. Perhaps in a way in this novel – which is somewhat autobiographical and was written after the author and her husband, like many other Iranians and particularly the young intellectuals, experienced the events of the 1950s, namely the British-instigated American-executed ousting of the nationalist government of Mohammad Mosaddeq, the popular prime minister who nationalized Iranian oil, events that caused not only disillusionment but intensified anti-British and anti-American sentiments in the country – Dāneshvar has made an effort to exonerate herself, and even more so, her husband, from being xenophobic and anti-Western by including the Irish as a part of the greater Iranian family.

While nineteenth-century Iranians' encounters with the West and Westerners, including the Irish, presented in travel literature reveal a sense of curiosity mingled with wonder and even fantasy about the relatively unknown "Other" and twentieth-century encounters fictionalized by Iranian writers were often imbued with a sense of fear and apprehension of Western hegemonic powers, in the twenty-first century such encounters are more realistic and practical as the distances between the Iranian "Self" and the Western "Other" decrease, both in terms of communication and culture. Events in late twentieth-century Iran, including the Islamic Revolution and eight years of the devastating Iran-Iraq war, caused the displacement and eventual permanent emmigration of a large number of Iranians, especially to Europe and the United States. Among the most recent representations of the aforementioned encounters and the Iranian portrayal of the Irish and the relationship between Iranians and the Irish in the twenty-first century

12. Ibid., 298.

are two novels by Marsha Mehran, *Pomegranate Soup*[13] and *Rosewater and Soda Bread*.[14] Unlike Abu Tāleb, Hājj Sayyāh, and Abolhasan Khān Ilchi, whose stays in Ireland were temporary, and in contrast to the relatively brief encounter between the Iranians and an Irishman in Dāneshvar's novel, the intermingling of the Iranians and the Irish in Mehran's novels is permanent. Three Iranian sisters who have escaped the turmoil of the Islamic Revolution and some of its dangerous consequences arrive in the fictional village of Ballinacroagh, in County Mayo, Ireland, after having spent some time in England. The oldest sister, Marjan, is a great cook; and with the help of her siblings, she sets up the Babylon Café, serving Iranian food. The newcomers, however, face both friendliness and antagonism from the town's people. Some are delighted with the exotic, aromatic food that the sisters serve, while others resent the intrusion of the strangers in their town and in their lives. By the time we get to the second novel, the sisters have become permanent inhabitants and part of the Irish landscape. Ireland and the Irish have also transformed them, to the extent that the middle sister, Bahar, who had previously been married to an abusive revolutionary back in Iran, chooses to convert to Catholicism and become a nun, while the youngest, Layla, is undergoing the experiences of a rather typical teenager in her new homeland. And Marjan struggles, among other things, with whether or not to respond positively to the romantic approaches of an English writer who had spent some time in Iran and who tries to win her by reciting to her the poetry of Rumi. Interestingly, in Mehran's novels, it is not the Iranians and the Irish who share poetic sensitivity and misery, but the sisters, particularly Marjan, with an Italian widow who had immigrated to Ireland with her husband many years earlier. A most sympathetic character, Estelle Delmonico provides the novel with its love, romance, and poetry. The novelist herself seems to have such empathy for the character that at the end of the second novel, she inserts an imaginary interview between herself and her fictional creation, the Italian widow. The interview seems to enable the novelist to present her Iranian Self and the Italian Other as two kindred spirits, each constantly affirming what the other says. But still, the place Mehran has chosen as the locale of her novels, a small Irish village, shows her own empathy with the Irish. She says to Estelle in the interview that she "knew that Marjan and the girls [the fictional characters of her own creation] would be just fine here in this little Irish village."[15]

While Estelle and the Iranian sisters share empathy, perhaps as outsid-

---

13. Marsha Mehran, *Pomegranate Soup* (New York: Random House, 2005).
14. Marsha Mehran, *Rosewater and Soda Bread* (New York: Random House, 2008).
15. Ibid., 289.

ers who have intruded, as it were, on this small sleepy Irish village, gradually the sisters develop other close relationships, not with other foreigners and outsiders, but with the local people. The strange and foreign but at the same time mysteriously and sensuously appealing aromas of exotic spices like saffron, cinnamon, and cardamom that waft through the little town's main street from the Babylon Café soon attract, among others, a jolly, easy-going local priest, Father Mahoney, who cannot resist the food the sisters serve. With few exceptions, the magic of Marjan's recipes and her cooking talent gradually win over most of the town's inhabitants. The Iranian sisters had fled their homeland and sought a safe haven as their permanent home; and by the end of the second novel, they have found and settled in the home they sought. The old homeland remains with them in their perpetually haunting memories, but they have also brought the culinary gift of the old homeland to their new home. Literally and symbolically, food is the substance of life. Pointedly, Mehran highlights each chapter of her lyrically toned novels that take place in a traditional Irish setting with Persian recipes, perhaps signifying the infusion of the people of two cultures, Irish and Iranian, which MacMahon in Simin Dāneshvar's novel described as "kin," an infusion that perhaps reflects, in some way, Mehran's own life and marriage to an Irishman. Marsha Mehran describes her own Irish ties as follows:

> By the age of nineteen, my familial wanderlust had become personal. Feeling hemmed in on such a distant continent, I left Australia for the bright lights of New York City with only two hundred dollars in my pocket. I took on a variety of bizarre jobs in Manhattan – a Broadway poster girl, personal assistant on film sets, hostess in a restaurant owned by Russian mobsters, and the odd, humiliating waitressing gig – while I pursued my newest venture: writing. Manhattan was also where I met my future husband. He was Irish and worked as a bartender in Ryan's Irish Pub on Second Avenue, and, according to my father, was an Iranian once-removed. "Ireland," my father joked, when I notified him on my impending nuptials, "Ireland is really Iran-Land." Mad, perhaps, but my father's joviality was heartening. My husband Christopher and I spent the next two years in Ireland, living in a small cottage in the West that boasted an awesome view of Croagh Patrick, the country's holiest mountain. I came to love the smell of peat fires, the spirited fiddle sesiuns, and the cracking humor of the Irish, all of which inspired my first novel, *Pomegranate Soup*. There was something fatalistic about my marrying an Irishman, I felt. As though my Celtic schooling had somehow pre-destined such a meeting.
>
> My husband and I now divide our time between Ireland and

Brooklyn, where my next novel is set. I often muse on the strange, circuitous journey my young life has taken: the melding of Persian, South American, American, Australian and Irish cultures. Ultimately I am a mixture of all of these. All I know is that my soul is Persian, and I write and dream in English. Linguistically, the Celtic language, like Farsi, derives from the Indo-European family of tongues. Eire, the Irish word for Ireland, is named after the Gaelic goddess Eriu – not far off Arya, meaning noble, from which Iran, "realm of the Aryas," takes its direction. But all these are semantics, as they say. After a childhood of traveling and rootlessness, I have finally found a home.[16]

Marsha Mehran's intuitive feeling that there was something fatalistic about her marrying an Irishman seems to have been even more prophetic. After being uprooted from Iran along with her family in the wake of the Islamic Revolution, and in her quest to find a permanent new home, traveling to and living on various continents before, during, and after her marriage to her Irish husband, she became an Irish citizen and went back to a small town in Ireland in early 2014. To write her new novel, she intended to live in the solitude of the Irish countryside, perhaps unaware before her untimely death only a couple of months later that she had chosen Ireland as her eternal home.[17]

16. http://www.parstimes.com/books/marsha_mehran_background.pdf
17. For details about the last months of Mehran's life see Cahal Milmo, "The Mystery of Marsha Mehran – The Best-selling Young Novelist Who Died a Recluse in a Rubbish-Strewn Cottage in Mayo," *Irish Independent*, 1 January 2015, accessed January 25, 2015.

Part III

Travelogues

8

An Indo-Persian in Ireland, anno 1799

Mirzā Abu Tāleb Khān

Translated by H. E. Chehabi[1]

TRAVELOGUES (in Persian: *safarnāmeh*) were one of the main sources of knowledge about Europe for Iranians in the nineteenth century.[2] Through these accounts of the lands and people of *Farangestān*, as Europe was most often referred to, Iranians became aware of the cultural differences between them and the Europeans, especially those occasioned by the social transformations that resulted from the industrial revolution. Although these travel writers did not admire everything they saw and experienced in Europe, they did contribute to spreading awareness among the educated elite that Iranians had fallen behind Europe in overall development.[3]

The Persian language was then still widely known outside Iran,[4] especially in India, where for many literati, whether of Iranian origin or not, it was the language of choice for writing. Iran and India were still connected by a dense network of social, economic, and cultural networks, and so Persian texts produced in India circulated widely among Iranians, Afghans, and Central Asians.[5] This included travelogues.[6]

1. I should like to thank Sunil Sharma, who helped me navigate the shoals of Indo-Persian prose.

2. William L. Hanaway, "Persian Travel Narratives: Notes Toward the Definition of a Nineteenth-Century Genre," in Elton L. Daniel, *Society and Culture in Qajar Iran: Studies in Honor of Hafez Farmayan* (Costa Mesa, CA: Mazda, 2002), 249–268; and Naghmeh Sohrabi, *Taken for Wonder: Nineteenth-Century Accounts from Iran to Europe* (New York: Oxford University Press, 2012).

3. Monica M. Ringer, "The Quest for the Secret of Strength in Iranian Nineteenth-Century Travel Literature: Rethinking Tradition in the *Safarnameh*," in Nikki Keddie and Rudi Matthee, eds., *Iran and the Surrounding World 1501-2001: Interactions in Culture and Cultural Politics* (Seattle: University of Washington Press, 2002), 146–161.

4. Bert G. Fragner, *Die Persophonie: Regionalität, Identität und Sprachkontakt in der Geschichte Asiens* (Berlin: Das Arabische Buch, 1999).

5. Brian Spooner and William L. Hanaway, "Introduction: Persian as *Koine*: Written Persian in World-Historical Perspective," in Brian Spooner and William L. Hanaway, eds., *Literacy in the Persianate World: Writing and the Social Order* (Philadelphia: University of Pennsylvania Museum of Archaeology and Anthropology, 2012), 1–68.

6. Roberta Micallef and Sunil Sharma, eds., *On the Wonders of Land & Sea: Persianate Travel Writing* (Boston: Ilex Foundation, 2013).

The author of the first Persian-language account of Ireland, Mirzā Abu Tāleb Landani Esfahāni, was born in 1753, the son of an Iranian who had immigrated from Isfahan to Lucknow, capital of the Mughal successor state of Awadh (Oudh).[7] As a young man he was educated by distinguished scholars, most of whom were fellow immigrants from Iran. Abu Tāleb first embarked on an administrative career in Awadh, but later moved to Calcutta, where he wrote a number of works and edited the divan of Hafiz. He left Calcutta on 7 February 1799 in the company of his friend Captain David Richardson of the East India Company's Bengal army, intending to set up a government-sponsored Persian language training institute under his own supervision in England. He remained in Europe for over two years, and returned by land until Basra, where he took a boat to Bombay. Arriving in India in August 1803, he died in Lucknow in 1806.[8]

The British Orientalist Charles Stewart[9] published an English translation of this text shortly after it was written.[10] However, it is often inaccurate and omits passages that might have shocked the sensibilities of contemporary readers, such as the section on the advantages of European women's tight clothes. For this reason, a fresh translation of relevant pages of the Persian original is offered here.[11] The changes that Stewart made in the text would themselves make an interesting research topic, but my aim here is merely to make available Mirzā Abu Tāleb's own experiences in Ireland. At the risk of making our traveler sound naïve and child-like, I prefer to convey his sense of wonder by erring on the literal side in my translation.

Abu Tāleb Khān's ship was bound for London, but unfavorable winds and the naval war then raging between Britain and France made entry into

7. For this immigration see *Encyclopaedia Iranica*, s.v. India vii. Relations: The Afsharid and Zand Periods (by Mansour Bonakdarian).

8. *Encyclopaedia Iranica*, s.v. Abū Ṭāleb Khan Landanī (by M. Baqir); *Encyclopaedia of Islam, Three*, s.v. Abū Ṭālib Tabrīzī (by Sunil Sharma). For more elaborate analyses of Abu Tāleb Khān and his writings see M. R. Ghanoonparvar, *In a Persian Mirror: Images of the West and Westerners in Iranian Fiction* (Austin: University of Texas Press, 1993), 12–18; Gulfishan Khan, *Indian Muslim Perceptions of the West During the Eighteenth Century* (Karachi: Oxford University Press, 1998), 95–100; Michael H. Fisher, *Counterflows to Colonialism: Indian Travellers and Settlers in Britain 1600-1857* (Delhi: Permanent Black, 2004), 104–109.

9. Charles Stewart (1764–1837) served in the Bengal Army from 1781 until 1808. He was assistant-professor of Persian at Fort William College, Calcutta from 1800 until 1806. From 1807 until 1827 he was professor of Arabic, Persian, and Hindustani at East India College, Haileybury.

10. Charles Stewart, trans., *The Travel of Mirza Abu Taleb Khan in Asia, Africa, and Europe during the years 1799, 1800, 1801, 1802* (London: Hurtst, Rees, and Orme, 1810). This was followed by French, German, Dutch, and Urdu translations,

11. [Mirzā Abu Tāleb Khān Esfahāni], *Masir-e Tālebi, yā safarnāmeh-ye Mirzā Abu Tāleb Khān*, ed. Hoseyn Khadiv Jam (Tehran: Sherkat-e sahāmi-ye ketābhā-ye jibi, 1973), 55–96.

the English Channel impossible, so the captain took the ship into the Irish Sea. After a few days he decided to land in Cork.

Text

On 29 Jumadi II [1214] (28 November 1799) the outskirts of the town of Cove came into view. [We saw] a range of hills that seemed cultivated. Soon we entered the mouth of the Cove between two forts that have been erected to prevent enemy ships from entering the harbor. At a small distance, we saw a big slab of stone, like a small island, in the middle of the bay, which divided it into two [channels]. On that rock they have built a fort. We then arrived opposite the town of Cove[12] and dropped anchor.

Here we found fifty ships of different sizes, three of which were men-of-war.[13] The bay resembles a round basin, sixteen miles in circumference. On its eastern shore the crescent-shaped town is situated. On each side [of the town] is a fort. On one side of the bay, a large river resembling the Ganges extends inland and passes by the city of Cork. The circular form of this extensive sheet of water, the verdure of the hills, and the forts on the one hand, and the number of elegant houses and gardens on the other, together with the many large ships lying securely in the harbor, are so impressive and pleasant that it is difficult to imagine anything more grand. Without any doubt, there is no city like this one in the entire world, except perhaps Genoa, which has a circular bay but no forts, or Istanbul, whose bay is so large that it is not comparable in beauty to the one at Cork.

In the [late afternoon] we visited the town. It was not animated and did not contain any impressive buildings, because it is merely an anchoring place for ships. On high and low locations they have built narrow lanes and houses. The breadth of the main part of the town is half a mile, the rest consists of small houses built on the slopes. If the sea advances 30 yards nothing would remain of the town. In the shops there was an abundance of inexpensive apples, pears, and grapes; also a variety of dried fruits. Having done some sight-seeing, we went to the post-office, to dispatch our letters. The mistress of the house was a sweet-tempered woman. She insisted that we stay for dinner and hosted us, assisted by her sons and daughters. At table we had fish, milk, butter, beef, and potatoes and other vegetables, all of them better than anything I had hitherto had in my life. The mentioned ingredients are of very good quality here, so much so that they are exported

12. The town was known as Queenstown between 1850 and the late 1920s, when it was renamed Cobh, a gaelicization of Cove.

13. The author transliterates this term as *manvār*.

on ships to London. In the evening, when we were about to return to our ship, we wished to pay for our dinner, as is customary in this country where accepting payment is not frowned upon, but our hostess did not let us. She strongly advised us to visit the city of Cork, which is twelve miles away. She furnished us with three horses and ordered her son, a sweet-looking youth of eighteen years of age who was as amiable as she, to accompany us, and then she hired a few more horses for our friends. Even more astonishing was the fact that this lady had borne twenty-one children, eighteen of whom were then living, all of them obedient and most of them present in the house; notwithstanding which she had not the appearance of old age, and did not appear older than thirty.

On the 30th [of Jumadi II/29 November] we rode on our horses toward the city of Cork. After traveling about three miles, we came to the bank of the river [Lee], in which we found about fifty ships at anchor. Thanks to our good horses and our very competent sailors we quickly crossed over on a ferry. We reached Cork around noon, and put up at the city's best hotel, which had man and woman servants, pleasant rooms, and precious beds. Along the twelve-mile distance we had traveled, [we saw] gardens, country houses, and green cultivated fields, and the countryside showed signs of habitation. After a short time we went out to see the town. It being the rainy season, the streets were dirty and muddy, and we did not enjoy ourselves. As far as we could tell, the buildings were all four stories high and built of brick and mortar, with doors of equal height and windows all glazed. The houses were large, their exteriors and interiors beautifully fitted; the wooden parts were in many different colors. The shops were filled with all kinds of products, especially neatly arranged fruit, the whole exuding great urbanity. But as this city has been established for the purposes of commerce and has been constructed on the slopes of hills so as to facilitate conveying goods to the houses of the merchants, it is divided in two by hills and lacks grandeur. You do not see it until you reach its edge. Its streets never dry between the beginning of winter and spring. They have dug a dirty canal in the middle of the city and lined it with stone and cement; in it there are many ships, mostly for repair. Its water is black and putrid. Over this canal they have constructed numerous heavy bridges, which can be opened and shut at one end to allow ships to enter and exit ...

We had a very delicious dinner at the hotel and ate a lot of fruit, and then the day came to an end. Since Captain Clarke expected a change of wind, we did not stay there and returned on our horses by the same road we had come and slept on board our ship.

In Cork I learned that Lord Cornwallis,[14] who was the King of England's governor of this island, was in Dublin, which is four to five days from Cork by mail coach. The rebellion started by the people of Ireland against their king a few years ago has now been quelled, after much bloodshed, by the said lord with prudence and courage.[15] The freshness of the weather and the ready availability of transportation convinced me to abandon the ship and proceed towards London by land. From the outset of my journey I had intended to come to this island after my visit to England so as to pay my respects to his lordship; now that by some unforeseen circumstances I had come to Ireland, I might as well do at the outset what I had planned to do last. It seemed that the stay at Cove would be long on account of unfavorable winds, and the newspapers had reported that two ships had been lost in the English Channel. Captain Richardson agreed that this course of action would be best and decided to accompany me with his children ... On 2 Rajab [30 November] we left superfluous things and the servants on board the ship and returned to Cork with a few necessary clothes. We crossed the river on a small open boat and took lodgings at the same hotel. We spent two days in Cork.

On one of the days, Captain Baker, whom I had met during the Ghulām Muhammad Rohila war at Rohilkhand[16] and who was one of Captain Richardson's friends, came to visit us. He invited us to his house, situated four miles outside the city on the seashore, where he gave us a sumptuous reception. I very much enjoyed the sight of the garden and the buildings, which had separate rooms for different purposes, such as a kitchen, a room for washing the dishes, and another for putting the chinaware. The wheels of the kitchen turned the kebab skewers and ground the meat and the onions like a clockwork. In Cove at the aforementioned post-office, I had seen a spit for roasting meat turned by a dog which was put into a hollow wheel which he turned, anxious as he was to escape it. The dog had been thus employed in the kitchen for fifteen years. In the room for chinaware they had installed a faucet for warm water with a basin underneath it where dishes could be washed with little effort. In that same room shelves had been built with holes in them on which various pieces of china were put after washing.

14. Charles Cornwallis, 1st Marquess Cornwallis (31 December 1738 – 5 October 1805), was one of the main British generals in the American war of independence. He was governor general and commander in chief in India from 1786 to 1794, and Lord Lieutenant of Ireland and Commander in Chief of Ireland from 1798 to 1801.

15. A reference to the Irish Rebellion of 1798, also known as the United Irishmen Rebellion, which was an uprising against British rule in Ireland and lasted from May to September 1798.

16. Nawab Ghulam Muhammad Khan Bahadur (1763 – 1828) was briefly Nawab of Rampur from 1793 to 1794. Deemed a danger to the region's stability, he was deposed by troops of the East India Company and of the ruler of Awadh in 1794.

Captain Baker had divided the grounds of this estate into different parts for wheat, fruits and vegetables, and grazing, which provided the milk, butter, and meat for his kitchen. Other than clothes and wine he had no need for anything from outside. He has only twelve servants and bought the estate for 20,000 rupees. Spending little, he lives better than the English grandees of India could live on 100,000 rupees a year. Among the inhabitants of his house are his two nieces, one of whom is unrivalled for her wit and repartee, the other for her beauty. The latter is courted by many young men in Cork, but she is so difficult to please and so haughty that so far she has not accepted any of them. [verse]

At the dinner table this delicate woman and some other women from the neighborhood did their utmost to show me hospitality. I was all eyes for these beautiful huri-like women. [verse]

After dinner that nymph made tea for us, and asked if it was sweet enough. I replied that a tea prepared by so sweet a creature could never lack in sweetness – if anything it would be too sweet. The company liked what I said and laughed.

Another person in this household was a certain Din Mohammad, a native of Murshidabad in Bengal.[17] Captain Baker's brother had brought him up from childhood and brought him to Cork, where he sent him to school to learn to read and write English. At the school he became acquainted with a pretty girl; the daughter of respectable parents, and eloped with her. After getting married in a different town, they returned to Cork. They had several fine children; and he has written a book containing an account of his life and the customs of India, which he has published in Ireland.[18]

On 4 Rajab [2 December] we boarded a mail coach to go to Dublin; the fare was three guineas per person, corresponding to thirty rupees. As this carriage conveyed official letters, and the roads were not quite secure yet, we were escorted by three dragoons, who were regularly relieved whenever we stopped to change horses. For the above reason we would also stop after a third of the night [had passed]. On this road we found ample supplies of everything we needed. At each stop, Captain Richardson's ill-tempered

17. Formerly Dean Mahomet (1759–1851), he served in one of the Bengal army's European regiments before emigrating to Ireland in 1784. He converted to Anglicanism and eloped with an Anglo-Irish woman in 1783. He attempted several business ventures, but is most known for his bath houses and shampooing (Indian therapeutic massage) and his Indian restaurant, the Hindostanee Coffee House, in Portman Square. In 1793–94 he wrote *The Travels of Dean Mahomet* and published a treatise entitled *Shampooing, or; Benefits resulting from the use of Indian medicated vapour bath* (1822) and thus became the first Indian to publish in Britain (Note by Charles Stewart).

18. See also Michael H. Fischer, *The First Indian Author in English: Dean Mahomed (1959–1851) in India, Ireland, and England* (Delhi: Oxford University Press, 1996).

daughter, whose nanny had remained in Cork, was competently looked after by 2–3 nannies.

We breakfasted the first day at a small newly-built town, called Fermoy, and dined and slept at Clonmell. Upon hearing the sound of the coachman's horn, the people of the inns had everything prepared, so that there was never the smallest delay: comfortable beds and lovely bed-mates were waiting for us everywhere. However, we could not eat or sleep without worry, since if a traveler appears only one minute after the coach's horn has been blown, he will not find it. His luggage will have left together with his companions, while he has to wait one day for the next coach. And if that coach is full, he has to wait yet another day.

On the 5th [3 December] we breakfasted at Kilkenny. This city is one of the famous and love-inspiring places of this island; its beauty and pleasantness are celebrated by poets. I was so delighted with that town that I did not sit down to breakfast, but, having put a piece of bread in my pocket, took a walk. On one side [of the town] there is a river on the opposite shore of which gardens and orchards without enclosures can be found, beautiful like paradise. [At one point] the river [feeds] a waterfall so beautiful that all sadness is erased from one's heart. The purity of the air and the joyfulness of this place are such that one has an impulse to start dancing. On that day a drizzle was in the air. On the roadside grew a tree with delicate leaves and full of red fruit on which rain drops were shining like a chandelier. I was intoxicated with happiness as if I had drunk wine, and this state lasted until I went to bed.

On the 6th [4 December] we entered Dublin a little after sunset. This three-day journey had taken us through a hilly country. The villages in this country resemble those of India. The roofs of the houses are thatched with straw, and there are not more than ten to twelve of them in each village. Some [roofs] are covered with sods, which have grass growing on them a span high: they remain green year round. The peasants and the common people in this country are so poor that the peasants of India are rich in comparison. Although they are obliged to travel over the stones that cover the roads, they never wear shoes, thus their [bare] arms and feet remain wet all the time and are as red as the feet of a Hindu woman [who has applied henna]. This poverty has two reasons: first, the high price of provisions, and, second, the abundance of children, who need a lot of food and clothing in so cold a climate. I was told that many of these people never taste meat or bread during their lives but subsist entirely on potatoes; and that, in the house of the rich farmers, sheep, dogs, pigs, chickens, and humans all live together in one place. While we were traveling, it frequently happened that young or old ran along the coach for a kos,[19] in the hope of obtaining a piece of bread. The country is well cultivated; it produces wheat, barley, peas, turnips, and, above all, potatoes. Therefore, whenever the potato crop is spoiled, the poor suffer a lot of hardship. The potatoes of this land are famous and exported to London. Rice, both of Bengal and America, can be procured everywhere, though at a high price: wherever I dined, my hosts would cook some rice dish for me, they and their other guests contenting themselves with bread, meat, and wine. In the villages, people eat barley bread or potatoes that have been boiled in meat juice. The animals are fed barley or dry straw, and when the grass is covered with snow they are given turnips. Land that is not suitable for tillage yields a type of clay that can be burned like cow's dung. Although it is not as good as coal, it is far better than cow dung and burns longer. The climate is so cold that even the poor have fire ovens in their homes.

Since we arrived in Dublin late at night, we found the inns full and thus had to go to a hotel frequented by lords and dukes where we had to pay a lot. On the 7th [5 December], by the advice of Mr. Eager who had come in the coach with us from Cork, I rented a lodging in English Street, near the College, at the house of a Mrs. Ball, an amiable widow who had several very fine daughters and sons. In this country it is customary to take lodgings by the week rather than by the month: I therefore took two rooms at a guinea a week; Captain Richardson did the same. I always breakfasted at home; the man-servant of the house bought us French bread, tea, and excellent butter. We dined at a restaurant; breakfast and dinner coming to two rupees per person. When the city's notables found out about my arrival, I received a lot of dinner invitations. Every gentleman who wished to invite me to his house first called, leaving an invitation if I was not in. Now I will write about Dublin, the major city in this land.

Dublin is situated on the sea shore, and its circumference is about twelve miles. Many of the houses are built of stone, and do not appear as if any mortar was used in their construction, the stones fitting so exactly to each other. Most houses, however, are built of brick and mortar, neatly laid together; the bricks are of a large size, and the mortar appears as a white border round their edges. All the houses in a street are of the same height; in the inside they are generally painted white and decorated in the usual European manner. Most of them have four stories, but a few have more. One floor is underground and contains the kitchen and rooms to store coal, ice, etc., keep the chinaware, and do the house's laundry. The ground floor has the women's living room and the reception room. The one above that is divided into bedrooms for the masters of the house, and the last floor, where

19. A kos, in Urdu *karoh*, is the equivalent of roughly two miles.

the ceilings are low, is allotted for the servants and the storage of grain ... The window curtains are either of chintz or silk. In every apartment there is a fire place made of marble. Inside the fireplace a fire container made of steel and brass has been fitted; it is so beautiful that in winter it looks like a vase and in the summer they put flowers in it. The walls of the rooms are covered with variegated paper, the carpets are woolen. The patterns of the wall paper, the carpets, and the curtains are so varied that in three years I never saw two houses with the same ones. Whatever the colors may be, subdued shades are preferred. The entrance to the house is low and narrow and close to the dining room, and if they did not put the owner's name and a number on it, it would be hard to find. This door is always shut. On the external side of most doors a ring-shaped [knocker] has been affixed, but next to some doors [there is] a chain, connected to a bell in the servants's quarters, and when one pulls at it someone will immediately come and open the door. In the servants' quarters there is a bell corresponding to every room in the house, enabling them to know where their presence is required.

The streets of this city are all paved with stone slabs and are divided into three portions: the two sides are covered with smooth stones and are [reserved] for pedestrians; the middle is paved with coarse stones and is used for horses and carriages. In most places tradesmen have shops on the two sides of the street, but in the neighborhoods of the elites instead of shops there is an iron railing which projects some yards into the street, allowing light and air to reach the lower floor, and heavy or dirty articles to be taken out or in through a door in the railing ...

It is not customary to bargain when making a purchase, and even uninformed strangers are not cheated. There is no need to describe the exquisite nature of goods and crafts, since everybody knows about them. Among the shops are milliners, which cater to women's needs, and also silversmiths, watch-makers, pastry shops, chemists, and fruiterers, all very clean and tidy. At the fruiterers there is an abundance of different types of pears, apples, grapes, cherries, oranges, lemons, and other fruits special to that land, and hundred types of dried fruits from different parts of the world such as almonds and walnuts. The pastry contains sweet or sour fruit fillings, is made with unbleached flour and butter, and is not sweet enough [for my taste]. They are placed in cardboard boxes and their variety is seemingly infinite. In this store they also sell different delicious soups and a concoction of lamb or chicken and spiced fruits wrapped in thin bread which they call "pies" or "tarts." People go to these shops to eat, and anyone who wants to have these foods in his own dining room buys them, as they are not prepared as well at home.

At night, both sides of the streets are lighted up by lamps suspended from posts of equal height which, with the addition of the numerous candles in the shop windows, render them as light as day. When we entered the city at night, we saw two long lines of light everywhere we went. The lights in the shops, especially the chemists which contained glass vases filled with different-colored liquids, reminded me of the imambara[20] at Lucknow, when illuminated, during the reign of the late Nawab Āsef al-Dowla.[21] This being the first town I had seen well lighted at night, it impressed me so much that later London did not make much of an impression on me. One of the ways in which shops attract customers is by placing over the doors a plank painted black, on which is inscribed, in gold letters, the names of the goods sold there.

The size of the crowds constantly walking in the parks and squares is astonishing. They have acquired such dexterity by habit that they never run against each other. Some girls, who, either from the coldness of the weather or their own cheerfulness, walk as though they are dancing, manage not to touch any one.

In this city there are so many carriages of different kinds that it is safe to say that from the day I arrived in Dublin until I left Paris three years later, the sound of coach wheels was never out of my ears, except when I was asleep or in the bedroom, for rooms are well insulated against street noise. One can get an idea of the number of carriages in Dublin by pointing out that there are a thousand one-horse carriages for the disposal of waste and seven hundred coaches for hire that take people from one place to another but do not leave the town. Then there are the nobility's coaches of which every married man must have one, and the mail coaches that take people to more distant destinations. To this one must add the small carts used to convey cargo. The rental price depends on the number of miles covered, and since there are milestones everywhere the passengers and the drivers never lose any time arguing about the prices. All these carriages are drawn by large horses that are peculiar to these two islands; they are also used for ploughing fields. Cows are only kept for their milk and butter, and bullocks for their meat. The sheep here do not have big tails, and their meat is fat and delicious. The chickens are the size of geese and lay large eggs.

The squares of this city are very extensive, and in the center of each there is a fountain over which a cupola made of stone is erected to shelter it

20. A building in which the martyrdom of the third Shiite Imam is commemorated annually by Shiites.

21. A reference to the Bara Imambara built by the ruler of Awadh in 1784. It is also called the Asafi Imambara.

from the sun. The water comes out of spigots shaped like a lion's head, and they all have keys that one must turn to get the water flowing. When one's cup is full, one turns the key again. In some of the squares there are platforms at the center of which they have placed statues of horses whose riders look like one of the kings in London. [verse] These fountains and statues have iron railings around them, and at night lamps are placed on them.

These stone statues are very widespread and valuable in these two islands as well as in France and Italy. Once in London I was present when a figure which had no head, arms, or legs, and basically consisted of nothing but a torso, was sold for 40,000 rupees. "This is indeed a strange thing!"[22] It is really astonishing that people possessing so much knowledge and good sense, and who laugh at the rulers of India for the gold and silver ornaments worn by their womenfolk, should be thus tempted by Satan to spend their money on for such useless purposes. They have appropriate statues for every situation: at doors or gates they have huge porters, inside the houses they have figures of women dancing with tambourines and other musical instruments, over the chimney-pieces they place small figurines of Greek goddesses, on tombs statues of the deceased, and in the gardens they put up demons, tigers, or wolves in pursuit of a jackal, in the hope that animals will be frightened and not come into the garden. What has been described was a type of garden, and at the center of some of these gardens there are squares, like the *chowks*[23] of India. The circumference of some [of these gardens] is half a mile, for some others it is a quarter mile. In its middle is a garden where people whose houses are close-by take walks in the morning and the evening. [drawing] These squares confer great elegance to the city; people meet each other in the mornings and the evenings and have conversations. Musicians gather and one can listen to their playing for a few pennies.

If people want more, they visit a park. This consists of extensive grounds enclosed by a wall. It contains brooks of water over which bridges made of marble or iron have been constructed, and it also has rows of shady trees. Animals can graze in it; deer are allowed to run wild and breed. Their flesh being highly prized, they are hunted with rifles. On one side of this park there is a building with gardens. Every city has two or three of these parks, and on the Sabbath they attract the old and the young.

The city of Dublin is even and pleasant, has a good climate, and a lot of space; it is better located than London. Around it there are hamlets and gardens where the rich spend their summers. At other times they visit them

---

22. Koran 38:5.

23. In South Asia a *chowk* refers to an open market area in a city at the junction of two roads.

for their fresh air and take walks ... On one side there is Phoenix Park, which without the slightest exaggeration I can call the most charming place I have seen in my life. The Dublin river runs through the middle of it between sloped verdant banks, and two bridges of white marble catch the eye ... Contemplating this beautiful sight, I understood the English who, in spite of India's grandeur, consider a sojourn in India degrading. Another captivating scene near Dublin is the seaside, where thousands of ships anchor. They have hundreds of wooden boxes containing two rooms and placed on four wheels which can be moved around. In the summer the rich use them to go out into the sea and bathe, which is very beneficial for health.

On this side there is a tower, which is built in the sea at a distance of half a kos. A pier forty yards in breadth connects it to shore. The utility of this tower is that at night they suspend a large oil lamp on top of it, thus enabling ships to come straight to the anchorage and avoid the dangerous and numerous underwater rocks and shoals. The pier fulfills two functions: the lighthouse keeper can reach it easily, and it protects the city from the stormy sea. There are many small dams up to a length of a thousand yards and numerous bridges over the branches of the sea that lie between Dublin and the other seaside towns. The river divides into two branches in Dublin and then pours into the sea. One branch, which is the size of the Gomti in Lucknow, flows in the center of the city. Both banks of it are lined with stone, and there are broad bridges over it. The edges of bridges have iron railings, to which numerous lamps are attached at night, illuminating the scene on a daily basis in a way seen in India and Iran only on big feasts.

In these three days I saw numerous canals in and around Dublin; on them wood, coal, and other goods are conveyed on small ships from one city to another. There is a new one connecting Dublin to Cork,[24] and its banks have been planted with trees. Running water, of which there is an abundance in this kingdom because of the mountains, joins this canal in many places, and together the waters flow through the green landscape. Every two or three miles a bridge containing a lock is constructed. Where it reaches the bridge, the canal gradually becomes so narrow that only one ship can pass through it. Then it widens again. Because of the locks they can fill the basin and if need be empty it onto the nearby fields. When a ship arrives the lock's gate is opened, and the water pulls the ship into the lock. Then the ship is fastened to horses on the banks of the canal, which pull the ship forward. On the other side of the Dublin this canal joins a large basin which has ... docks for the construction and repair of ships ...

24. This must be a mistake, for Cork is on the sea and does not need to be connected to Dublin by a canal. Charles Stewart substituted Limerick for Cork in his translation.

One of the famous buildings in Dublin is [Trinity] College, which is made all of stone and has an impressive entrance gate. In the middle of it stands a five-story building for the teachers, and on four sides there are ample rooms for students, of whom as many as 1,200 are present at any given time. All buildings have external decorations. One room, a hundred yards in length and twenty in width, contains the library. Its walls are lined with bookshelves that hold 40,000 volumes on all subjects, including the *Khamseh* of Nezāmi, the *Shāhnāmeh*, and a few other Persian books, all beautifully illuminated and wrapped in a brocade cover. In another building there is a museum, which houses a great number of curiosities, ... tastefully arranged on tables and glass showcases. Among these is a mummy that has been brought from the pyramids of Egypt. At the back of the College is an extensive meadow, boarded by a path and trees. Students walk and exercise there in the morning and evening. The headgear of these students and those of England is a skullcap made of black velvet. On the top of the skullcap a square piece of cardboard encased in the same black velvet has been sewed, and from this a flower made of black silk dangles down on one side.

At that time the head of the school was Provost Kearney.[25] First he took me on a guided tour of the school, then he gave a dinner reception for me. He and his wife are very generous, went out of their way in hospitality. [At his table] I also met Dr. Brown, the provost's deputy and a member of parliament who is very popular among the people of Dublin, and Dr. Hall, both of whom became such good friends that I would see them every day. Dr. Brown repeatedly invited me to dinner at his home outside the school. He is an angel in the guise of a human being, and has a wife just like himself: friendly, beautiful, refined, and endowed with a sense of humor and an easy smile. I composed a ghazal in her honor and sent it to her from London. [poem].

Next in rank among the public buildings, is the Parliament House. This is divided into two large apartments, one for the meetings of the grandees of the realm, the other for the King's administrators of this island.[26] The walls of this apartment are covered with tapestries depicting battle scenes[27]

25. John Kearney (1744–1813) was appointed provost of Trinity College in 1799. (Charles Stewart).

26. The building was the world's first purpose-built two-chamber parliament house, and the two parts mentioned by Mirzā Abu Tāleb were in fact the meeting places of the House of Commons and the House of Lords. Shortly after his visit, the Irish parliament was abolished and the Kingdom of Ireland was merged with the United Kingdom of Great Britain to become the United Kingdom of Great Britain and Ireland.

27. The tapestries represent the "Battle of the Boyne" and the "Defence of Londonderry." They were designed by Dutch landscape painter William Van der Hagen and woven by John Van Beaver and date from 1733. (Charles Stewart)

... First I thought they had been painted, but later I realized they had been woven. I had never seen anything like it and was astonished, but later I saw plenty of them in London ...

[I then visited] Custom House, a very large building. This is where the merchants' wares are brought and then bought and sold. There is also the Exchange Building, where merchants assemble to negotiate their deals and exchange news about commercial matters. It contains many tables at which, if they wish, they can take their meals if the deals have not been concluded before mealtime.

In this building I saw a winding clock,[28] which, like common clocks, has two hands and twelve spaces ... and shows the four directions. Afterwards I proceeded to the Courts of Law, and then to a building where the nobility of Dublin used to hold balls in the summertime but which is now used as barracks for Lord Cornwallis's troops.

The five buildings I have mentioned are constructed of beautifully hewn stone; they are adorned with mirrors, pictures, and chandeliers. The middle building is round or octagonal and is topped by a copula fifty yards high. It is so large that 4,000 people can stand in it. The copula has huge windows to the let the light in ...

There are many churches in every neighborhood, among which Christ Church stands out.[29] Its main nave is a hundred yards long and thirty yards wide, and wooden benches are placed on both sides of it. On the other side of the benches, on the three-story wall, there are galleries that can hold five to six people overlooking the pulpit and the preacher. This church, Dublin's oldest building, was built 600 years ago. It is customary for men and women to sit separately, and they are not allowed to mix. After the sermon and the music have started, people have to sit still and do nothing but listen. The music of this church is famous, and I also heard military bands play gentle music in the squares in the morning and in the evening.

Another [place I visited] is the parade, where the troops exercise. It consists of two wide spaces, each having a stone-paved square in the middle and quarters for the soldiers on the sides. One of them belongs to the cavalry and houses stables.

There are also a number of buildings called *pablek* [public], which means that they belong to everyone. Examples are hospitals, birth clinics, asylums, orphanages, and homes for military people who are invalids or old. Such places abound in Dublin. These institutions have plenty of servants, beds,

28. Mirzā Abu Tāleb speaks of a *sā'at-e bād*, a wind-clock, having no doubt confused the verb "to wind" with the homonymous noun denoting moving air.

29. This is Christ Church cathedral, one of Dublin's two medieval Roman Catholic cathedrals.

and other necessities, and all have a large kitchen where food is easily prepared for all, a spring of fresh water, a church for prayer, and a toilet which does not stink even though hundreds of people use it and do not always clean up after themselves. The buildings are built from stone and beautifully decorated inside. The institutions derive their income from foundations, from yearly donations of the rich, or from legacies of the deceased as specified in their testaments. One custom that I very much liked among the inhabitants of these two islands is that when a dying person thinks that he has more wealth than his heirs need, he bequeaths [some of] it to such institutions, or occasionally to his friends near or far. When I saw these philanthropic institutions, I forgave the parsimony of these people that I had noticed and disliked in India, for if one does not spend carefully, wealth will not accumulate for these purposes.

Coffee-houses, restaurants, taverns, and gambling houses abound, as do shops that have been set up by traders for their own benefit and for that of the public. There are two bath houses, whose roofs look like big ovens from the outside. I entered one and bathed with difficulty; its cellar was empty and it lacked a chimney. A furnace warms the water, but it has only one tub, and that is so small that it holds one person with difficulty and even then the water does not rise above one's waist. The people of Dublin do not bathe in the winter, and in the summer they wash themselves in the sea. These two bath houses are for the invalid and convalescents. Not only are there no bath attendants or barbers,[30] there is no one to serve and help [the customer]. Instead of washrags (kiseh) they use brushes made from horse hair. Everyone has to remove his filth with his own hands, [as there is no one to rub one's body clean].

Then there are two places for dancing and performing sleights of hand, and they are called "playhouse." Depending on how close the seats are to the stage their prices are different. The best places are thee shillings, equivalent to six Indian annas, the cheapest one shilling. This income is used to construct the necessary props, the costumes, lighting, as well as the monthly wages of the employees and the musicians. The rest constitutes the owner's profit, for the sake of which he has set up the playhouse. People who have nothing else to do go there every night except on Mondays, and stay until midnight. There are so many customers that I have heard that on some nights the playhouse generates an income of up to 1,500 rupees. All over Europe these buildings are either round or elliptic, as I have drawn. [drawing] To ensure that everybody can see the stage, the seats in what is called the "pit" are arranged on a slope. The place where the dancing takes place is called the "stage." It is so large that it can hold up to 200 people; canons on

30. The word used, *hajjām*, also means phlebotomist.

carts can be moved on it. A large curtain on which cities, mountains, meadows, and forests are depicted closes the stage. When one part of the acting,
dancing, or singing is finished, they close the curtain and behind it prepare
the next part. On stage there are screens depicting a variety of landscapes
that can be pushed together to provide a backdrop. The décor is more astonishing than the acting, and turns the experience into something like a
dream. All around the pit there are boxes with six chairs in them that are
entered from the back. In some theaters there are five floors of them, in others seven. Each box has a chandelier with four candles; on the ceiling of the
pit and around the stage they light so many lamps that the night becomes
bright like the day. Elite women do not sit anywhere except in the boxes,
which is why the members of the elite hire most of these, the owner [of the
playhouse] letting them at half-price for the duration of ten years. Above
the stage there is a room from which the throne of the fairies descends,
shrouded in vapor, and underneath it there is a similar room into which it
disappears. What I have described is the opera. But at Astley instead of having seats, the pit is covered with sand and is used for equestrian exercises,
its circumference being a hundred yards. Bronze chandeliers hang from the
ceiling, in them thick wicks burn in oil. When the stage is filled with acting
the chandeliers are at a very high elevation close to the roof, but during the
displays of horsemanship they are lowered. The owner of this theater is a
Mr. Astley, who also owns a similar house in London, which is also named
after him. When summer arrives, he leaves London for Dublin with his props
and spends four to five months here. Every two weeks he offers people a
new show.[31] When the performers are tired of acting and singing, they take
a break and the curtain is lowered.

Fifteen of Astley's good-looking performers, wearing colorful embroidered velvet uniforms that glitter like diamonds, bring two to three
well-trained horses fitted with colorful bridles to the stage and proceed to
ride them without a saddle. One, who is the best equestrian among them,
is dressed as a clown and stands at the center of the stage, pretending to
be frightened by the horses, making everyone laugh. Seemingly against his
will he is hoisted upon a horse and then performs tricks so astounding that
the mind rebels against accepting them for fact. For instance, he will stand
on the back of a horse and dance on it ... Or he will juggle with five or six
sharp knives, or skip ropes on the horse's back while it is galloping. Then
[another] performer stands on two horses simultaneously and performs the
same tricks. In another act a man wearing men's clothing is put in a sack,

---

31. Named after its founder Philip Astely, Dublin's *Astley's Theatre* was a located on Peter
Street. In London *Astley's Amphitheatre* was located on Westminster Bridge Road in Lambeth.

which is then tied at the top and put on a horse. When the sack is removed, he is wearing women's clothing. Sometimes ten to twenty people ride the horses and make them dance to music, in the manner of English women and men ... There is a man in that theater who is excellent at jumping: they put ten horses next to each other, he takes a run, and touches the first and then jumps over all ten. This man then hits a paper ball that has been hung at a height of 20 yards with his foot and then falls onto a mat without injuring himself.

One of the shows that I liked very much in that theater was the one about fairies and an Abyssinian magician called Harlequin. The daughter of a king, named Columbine, fell in love with the Abyssinian, and a fairy got wind of it and transported the girl's throne to her abode, on the Mountain of Qāf [at the end of the world]. The queen of the fairies visits the princess with her entourage, wakes her up, chastises and counsels her. Although [Colombine] is frightened, she still exhibits the signs of her love and longs to return ...

Another building is called Exhibition. On the ground floor and on the upper floor all sorts of displays can be found, of old things and new, which would take a long time to praise adequately. The proprietor took us to a back room, where he showed us a map of Gibraltar, which is in Spain on the shore of the Mediterranean. After this back room, which is dark and covered with a curtain, we reach a larger, well-lit room. It was as if we were standing on the shores of the Mediterranean: we saw the straits, the movement of the high waves, and the city and fortress of Gibraltar. Four French warships moved towards the harbor, and were shot at by cannon in the fortress. These ships looked exactly like real ones, and one could see their effect on the sea water and hear the noise of the canons of the fortress and the ships. Then a battle broke out between these ships and English ships. One could see masts being broken and sails falling into the sea and injured sailors falling into the sea. Finally one French ship caught fire, two sank, three were captured, and the rest fled. Next to the burned and sunk ships a dozen small ships were moving, rescuing people from the water. I could see the anxiety of the shipwrecked as they were hanging onto boards and swimming, and could not figure out the tricks used.

Now I will tell you something about the people of Ireland, who are called "Irish." Most of the people of this island are Roman Catholics, i.e., the pope's nation. A few are Anglicans, who are considered to be dissenters and philosophers. [The Irish] are neither as unjust as the Anglicans, nor as austere and fanatical as the Scots in the interpretation of the tenets of the Christian religion, and they value equality. They are superior to the English and the Scots in bravery, generosity, sociability, hospitality, and big-heartedness. Although they lack the gravitas of the English, they are smarter and more quick-witted than them. For instance, my landlady, Mrs. Ball, and her children always understood from my gestures what [I was trying to say] and provided me with whatever I needed. After a week or two I had acquired enough English to explain to them the meaning of some poetry, and although I mixed up words and made other mistakes, they understood the nuances and the humor of the Persian language by analogy and guess-work. When I decided to go to England, most of my friends were saddened; they told me that my insufficient mastery of English would be a problem there, as over there people would not understand me as well as they did [in Ireland]. And that is indeed what happened: after I had spent a year in England and my English had improved a hundred-fold, the English still did not understand what I was trying to say as well as the Irish did.

[In Dublin], sometimes when I was lost and asked someone for directions, he would, thinking that I would not understand his explanations, leave whatever he was doing and accompany me to the house I was looking for. One night I had to pay a visit at a considerable distance. The person I asked for help accompanied me to a point from which I could have found the house by myself. I thanked him and implored him to turn back. He refused and came farther along. I swore to him that I would be able to find my way. Since my destination was still far away and he had no intention of returning, I threatened to call of my visit off and go back myself. He understood and pretended to turn back, but I noticed that he was so worried about me that he followed me in the dark. I was not sure it was the same person that followed me, but I had no choice but to move on. When I arrived at the door I waited so that when he had caught up with me I could bid him farewell again, but when he saw that I had reached my destination he turned back and left. That is when I was certain that it had been the same person.

The Irish are so fond of spending money, and so generous with their friends, that there are few rich people among them. They live in moderation: unlike the English they do not surround themselves with luxury, and unlike the Scots they do not spend their time acquiring wealth and rank; they do not live in wealth while fearing poverty. That is why the Irish have not risen in rank and have advanced little in the sciences. In spite of these good character traits, they exaggerate in drink, and consume a lot of a highly potent liquor special to that realm called whisky. One evening I was invited to a big party. At six o'clock we sat down to dinner and our host immediately started to drink wine, insisting that I do likewise. When he realized my moderation, he had two water glasses filled with wine and ordered me to empty them.

After the table had been cleared, he toasted the King, the Queen, and the girls I liked and could not refuse toasting. At two o'clock in the morning he asked for more wine and started refilling our cups. Although I was so drunk that I could hardly walk, I got up and asked for permission to leave. He said that my early departure saddened him, and that if I stayed, we would have tea together after the wine. From the English I have heard that the Irish get drunk over dinner and start fighting to the point of killing each other, but in the time I spend there I did not once see any behavior that was contrary to good manners and humanity.

Let it be known that in England they draw amusing but meaningful pictures that show a person's main traits; these pictures are called "caricatures" and they are sold in shops and on street corners. Their aim is to reveal people's shortcomings and to make fun of ministers and the royal entourage. I saw three caricatures that showed the characteristics of all three nations. Every picture contained twenty images of the person caricatured as he progressed [through life]. When a Scot leaves his home to seek his fortune in London, he is wretched and poor. Since he itches a lot in Scotland, every time he sees a milestone or a tree on the way he scratches his back against it. He ekes out a living by carrying letters from one town to another for a few pennies. When he arrives in London, he works as a steward in someone's home, gains his confidence with his honest work, saves his wages, and then lends his savings to his employer with interest and gets rich. His progress continues as he meets an English widow, charms her, and ends up marrying her, thus acquiring rank and name. He then joins the civil service and acquires administrative skills until he become the King's prime minister. The Irishman joins the King's military, rises in the ranks due to his valor until he becomes a general, insults someone at a drunken party, and is killed in the ensuing duel. As for the Englishman, he is drawn as a bull and is called John Bull, on account of eating and drinking huge quantities, like a bull. If anyone attempts to prevent him from eating, he attacks him with his horns. His demeanor in society is as coarse and indelicate as that of a bull.

As for Irish women, although they are not as tasteful as English women and cannot compete with them in beauty and grace, and although they are not as well built and fulsome as Scottish women, they usually have beautiful faces and are paler than the other two, and they also have a warm disposition and many graces.

Now I will tell you about the events of my stay in Dublin. On my second day there I informed Lord Cornwallis that I was in town; he was glad and agreed to see me. At our meeting he was very kind and gave orders to his servants that they see to all my needs and take me around to show me the gardens and sights of the city. As long I was there I saw him once a week, and every time he regaled me with a new kindness and favor.

On Tuesday, 12 Rajab [10 December, 1799] Captain Richardson departed for London. Since I could not tear myself away from Dublin so soon, and since my companionship with the captain, with whom I always spoke Hindi, prevented me from improving my English, I decided to stay in Dublin. This decision turned out to be very beneficial. The people of Dublin, seeing me all alone and friendless, tried even harder than before to cater to all my needs, so much so that I spent my time with such joy as I had never experienced before in my life. Young and old were constantly assisting me. As soon as I left home, they would surround me and everyone would say something about me. One would venture that I was the Russian general that was being expected, another suspected that I was a German prince, yet another thought I was a Spanish grandee, but most took me for an Iranian prince. One day so many people gathered around me that a shopkeeper invited me into his shop until people dispersed. I went in and busied myself looking at the knives and scissors of which he was selling a great variety. The spectators now pressed themselves to the shop windows so much so that several panes broke. But there were so many of them that the shop owner could not ask anyone in particular to pay for the damage.

After two weeks it started snowing. Roofs and the top of walls became white, streets became rivers of silver ... I had never seen snow before and cannot begin to describe how much I enjoyed its sight. After two or three days, meadows, fields, and mountains were all covered in white. The snow was a yard high and turned into ice ...

What is ever more curious is that snowy days are not that cold. But on other days it was so cold that even when I was in a room with air-tight windows and wrapped in three layers of shawls, the cold air would hit me like an arrow. There is no escaping from the cold other than walking around, for even fires do not give much warmth. A wet sheet of paper resists the flames for a while, and just as Indian ventilators in the summer cool one side but have no effect on other places, the fires in this country heat one corner after a lot of prodding but leave the rest cold. I repeatedly burned my hand as I approached the fire. Since it was not giving any heat, I deemed it still far away and approached it until it burned my hand. Nonetheless, this cold does not cause any harm, nor is it incapacitating. The harsh winter in Ireland agreed with me better than other seasons. It was so invigorating that lethargy and sluggishness were inconceivable. In India a kurta consisting of a single layer of Dhaka [muslin] seemed too much, and walking half a kos made one tired. Now my clothes are, to put it bluntly, like a donkey's load, and yet I am so active that sometimes I start running, and there is not one day on which I do not walk six or seven miles. In India I could not help sleeping two or three times a day for a total of eight hours, if not I would be fatigued. But in the two months I stayed in Dublin I never slept for more than four hours, and that at night and at a stretch. I never felt ill.

I think it is this weather that is the origin of all the blessings and good things in these two islands. There are a number of reasons for this. First, it makes women beautiful and strengthens the bodies and souls of men. Second, it forces one to move in ways that lead to physical health and a joyful disposition, enabling one to be resilient and undertake difficult tasks that beget success. While I was there I was injured a number of times. One tenths of these injuries would have made me groan with pain in India, but here I did not even notice where and how I was bruised. Third, it causes them to be even-tempered, allowing them to be open to the arts and sciences. Men and women reach puberty at the age of 20, and until that age they entertain absolutely no thoughts that would detract them from the acquisition of science and art. Even after puberty, since the weather is cold, they cannot sit around idly but instead keep themselves occupied and do not waste any time on useless thoughts. I saw many fifteen-year-old boys and girls who, like the five- to six-year-olds in India, think of nothing but eating, sleeping, playing, and their school work. And I also saw many adults who had been successful in trade and in the arts and had amassed some wealth, but who were as simple as Indian children. Fourth, it causes houses and clothes to be designed in a way that is conducive to work. Fifth, it allows them to spend more time on useful things. To fight the cold, they have to put on so many layers of clothes that getting dressed or undressed takes at least an hour. This means that they sleep only at night, spending the rest of the time working or socializing. Since women's clothes are very tight, making love to them is uncomfortable and no fun. A married man approaches his wife only at night, and an unmarried man has no choice but to be celibate: since it is dangerous to mix with the women of the rabble, he only rarely has a chance to be with [a woman]. The truth of the matter is that since every man can enjoy the company of women during meals and evening parties, the heart is satisfied and sexual intercourse takes place only by consent. In India, on the contrary, since clothes are wide and unfastened, a man can have a woman as soon as he is stimulated, and thus he wastes time and loses his bodily strength.

After a few days the ponds and rivers froze, and I saw an astonishing art known as "skating," which my reader's mind will have trouble accepting. A foot-long piece of iron that has the breadth of a finger and the width of a knife's blade is anchored in a wooden sole that has been fastened to a shoe's bottom. A man puts his weight on one leg and moves his shoe. Since the ice is even and slippery, and the blades conducive to sliding, the man darts forth like an arrow and advances more quickly than a horse. If he wants to stop, he places the other foot at a bit of a distance from the first, distributes his weight equally on both legs, and that will make him stop. In the beginning, even remaining upright on these skates is difficult, and one repeatedly falls down. But a person who has mastered this art, can outrun 100 or 200 people trying to catch him from behind ... The benefits of skating are twofold. The rich are able to work up a sweat, which they might otherwise not do in the winter. And the poor can easily move between villages and towns and transact business. I heard that in Holland people travel hundreds of miles in this way. Old women put a basket of eggs on their heads, a child in their arm, and travel twenty miles in one hour to get to the city, and having sold their eggs, return to their village in the same way before dark.

From the sixth of Rajab [4 December 1799] until the nineteenth of Sha'ban [16 January 1800], I spent 44 happy days in that lovely city in the company of devoted friends. Although we had not seen enough of each other, on the eve of Thursday I bade them farewell and boarded a ship to go to England. Dr. Brown, Captain Whaley, Mr. Ball, and a dozen other people accompanied me to the harbor, which is a few miles from the city. They recommended me to the ship's captain and then parted with me and returned despondent.

Now I will relate something about the many dear Dubliners who were good to me. One of these was Sir George Shee.[32] He and his wife Lady Shee are wise, competent, and mild-mannered. He had resided for many years in India, and was for some time paymaster at Farrukhabad as an employee of the Government of Ireland. Then he returned to England, where he worked in the Treasury and made a name for himself. He is intimate with Lord Cornwallis, showed me the greatest hospitality, and was always good enough to be my interpreter with his Lordship.

Lord Carleton is a judge in Ireland. He and Lady Carleton invited me twice.[33] Their humanity is such that no one has ever been hurt by them. Their house was magnificently furnished, especially Lady Carleton's apartment. There were so many precious objects that I cannot adequately relate

32. Sir George Shee (1754–1825) of the East India Company married Lady Elizabeth Maria Shee (1764–1838; née Crisp) at Hugli near Calcutta in 1783. Shee was appointed Resident and Collector of Revenues at Farrukhabad, where he remained until 1782. Shee returned to Ireland in 1788, secured a baronetcy in 1794, and supported the Act of Union in 1800. (Charles Stewart)

33. Hugh Carleton (1739–1826), Viscount Carleton, was an Irish judge and politician who married his second wife, Mary Carleton, (d.1810; née Buckley), in 1795. (Charles Stewart)

what I saw: china dishes inlaid with gold, marble busts, chests, tables, musical instruments, and paintings. Among them were two lamps whose lanterns were of white cloth while the oil reservoir was of gold and which gave light like Venus. Its light bore no resemblance to that given by candles and was so abundant that at night all manner of delicate activities could be carried out in its glow. On the dining table the plates were all of gold and silver, and the dishes and sweets were so plentiful that I could hardly taste half of them.

The Duke of Leinster,[34] one of the grandees of Ireland, is a man of great character and has several beautiful and well-mannered daughters. When the people of Ireland rebelled against their King a few years ago, the brother of this duke led them;[35] he wanted to be king. In the end he was captured and died in prison, but the duke himself was not involved. [The Duke's] home is one of the most superb houses in Dublin, and it has an exceptional façade and gate.[36] In it there is a hall where 500 people can dine. It contains a staggering number of paintings and other pieces of decoration, including marble busts and tables whose tops depict flowers and bushes made with stones of different colors in so smooth a manner that one cannot see any cracks between them.[37] I heard that some of the paintings cost 1,000 guineas, and most of them 500 guineas.

I also met Colonel Wombwell,[38] one of the good people of the age, who had lived a long time in Lucknow as paymaster. He was an old friend of mine, and my joy at seeing him was all the greater in that I had not expected to see him in this country and that he spoke my language. After our meeting I would either be at his house or he at mine; sometimes, suspecting that I needed something, he would visit me two or three times a day. We visited different parts of Dublin in his coach, and every day he would spend three hours horse riding. Colonel Wombwell had had an Indian wife whom he had loved very much. When they boarded a ship in Bengal to return home, his wife was so frightened by the waves of the stormy sea that she took a boat to go back to the shore. But a sudden storm caused the boat to capsize and she drowned. This was the first sorrow that befell the colonel. When he reached England, three small daughters that he had sent ahead died as well. He then married another daughter to a nephew of his, and since he did not

34. William Robert Fitzgerald (1749–1804), second Duke of Leinster.

35. Lord Edward FitzGerald (1763 – 1798) took a leading role in the United Irishmen Rebellion. He died of wounds received while resisting arrest on a charge of treason.

36. Leinster House is now the seat of the parliament of the Republic of Ireland.

37. The author is describing *pietra dura*, a form of inlay with stones of different colors.

38. Sir George Wombwell (1769–1846), second baronet of Wombwell, was known primarily for his race horses. His father was an extensive East India proprietor and was Director of the East India Co. from 1766 to 1768 and from 1775 to 1778.

plan to remarry and had no other relatives, it was decided that his daughter and son-in-law would move into his household and that she would be the lady of the house. But that daughter also fell ill and died. Overwhelmed by sorrow, he fell ill and became bed-ridden for a while. He had been rather corpulent [in India], but when I saw him again he had lost so much weight that I hardly recognized him. He avoided company and was constantly moving about in pursuit of changes of scenery. He has built himself a very well appointed house in Norfolk bordering on the estate of the Duke of Norfolk, among whose friends he is counted. He had come to Dublin when the Norfolk Volunteer Regiment was sent to assist Lord Cornwallis. Later I repeatedly saw him in London, and our final parting took place in Paris, the capital of France. "Volunteers" are troops that the English noblemen raise and fit out in wartime to protect the realm. They learn the ways of the army and exercise every day. Since the colonel did not have a house in this city, he would often take his meals in the regimental mess with the other officers. He invited me to join him a number of times, and on these occasions I saw some of the finest-looking eighteen- or nineteen-year-old young men I have ever seen ... It transpired that Norfolk is a land of beauty and superior in this respect to the other parts of England, for I saw a girl who had just arrived from Norfolk the likes of whom I had never encountered in Ireland. The chickens, turkeys, and other poultry, as well as the vegetables of Norfolk are also famous.

Mrs. Fleming has developed the art of hospitality to a degree that the rest of humanity cannot even come close to match. When she heard that I had repeatedly met her husband at the house of my friend Mr. W. A. Brooke [in India], she asked through an intermediary to meet me. After that she often invited me to parties at her home, and when she was invited to someone else's house she arranged for me to get an invitation as well and I would accompany her. Twice she took me to the Playhouse. When I entered her home, all the world's bounties available in Dublin were spread before me on the dining table. Together with her fifteen-year-old son, who is as clever and pleasant as his mother, and her three daughters, who are as beautiful as the houris of paradise, she saw to my needs in every conceivable way. One of the things that made me happy was her showing me the picture of my dear friend, Mr. Brooke, which I had seen in Bengal and enjoyed looking at again. In the course of our conversation it transpired that she very much missed her husband and her other two daughters, who were in India. Pictures of him were hanging on two opposite walls in her house, and a little portrait of him was worn by their little daughter around the neck. She would use any excuse to bring up his name, and would say things like: "this apple is from a tree he planted," "he would have his meals at this table," "the wheat of this bread comes from Mr. Fleming's country house," or "Mr. Fleming liked this sweet." I felt sorry for Mr. Fleming to be far away from such a woman. On one occasion she asked me whether Mr. Fleming was enjoying himself in Calcutta. I answered: "How can a man enjoy himself when he is separated from a woman like you?" She liked my answer and smiled, but did not believe me, saying that I was only trying to console her. When I was about to leave for England, she wrote a letter to a relative of hers in Chester recommending me to him.

At the house of Mrs. Fleming I met Mr. Aron (?). Since his brother was married to the sister of my friend Mr. Brooke, he invited me twice, and on both occasions he and his wife went out of their way to see to please me. [...]

Now I will relate how distinguished Irish and English people live in their homes. When they throw a dinner party in the evening, the house is quiet. The coaches outside cannot be heard and the servants are silent – it is as if fairies and demons produce the food out of thin air. One would think that there is no other building in town, since all windows are shut and curtains are closed. [...] The servants come in only to bring the food. After the meal it is the hosts themselves who light the candles, pour the wine, make tea or coffee, and tend to the fire in the fire place. If they need the servants, they pull silken cords, of which there is one on each side of the fire place: one for calling manservants, the other for the maids. The servants' quarters are so far away that the cord-puller does not hear the sound of the bells [activated by the cords], and I was always astonished when the servants actually appeared upon being called, even though I had experienced it hundreds of times. At table, when two people talk to each other, the others remain silent. When one stops talking, the other will speak. Most of the time everybody speaks softly.

It is not customary to attend a dinner party without having been invited. Otherwise, if someone wants to call on a friend, he will go to his house and at the door hand the servant a piece of square cardboard on which his address is written, after which he waits. If the master of the house is in and has time, he gives permission for the caller to come in.

I met Mr. White at the home of Mrs. Fleming. He invited me twice. When I first saw him, the simplicity of his attire led me to think that he was an ordinary person, but I then found his house as well appointed as the houses of lords and dukes. His generosity and hospitality were boundless; he had different courses and expensive wines served for six to eight hours, including fruits, ices, and a supper after midnight. [...] One of the good fortunes that he has been blessed with is his wife, the daughter of Sir John, who is very beautiful and pleasant and has six sisters. Mrs. White plays a musical instrument very well, and one of her sisters sings beautifully like David, so much so that her voice cannot be distinguished from the sound of an instrument. Until that day I had not heard English singing of that quality and had concluded that the beauty of their music comes from instruments alone.

General Valancey is an officer of artillery,[39] he is petty and haughty. He is fascinated with Hebrew, Arabic, Persian, and other languages. He has stated that Hindi and the Irish languages are closely related.

Lords Shannon and Newcomen are also among the good people [I met].[40] Mrs. Humphries, whose husband died in India and who has a beautiful son and a beautiful daughter, repeatedly invited me. I met most of the great ladies of Dublin at her house, where they entertained me with their playing and singing. Her son was a bright fellow who had taken a liking to me. One day I was at his house when a servant dropped a tray with about fifty precious tea and coffee cups, breaking them all. He did not pay attention to the mishap and kept talking to me. This story, and the other traits of the Irish that I have related above, and what I [later] experienced in London, were contrary to everything Captain Williamson had told me, causing me much anxiety all the way from Bengal to the Cape. Here are a few examples of what he said:

Once, when, inexperienced as I was, I put a piece of bread on the table and proceeded to cut it carefully, he turned to me and said: "If you do this in London, your hostesses will fear that you damage their tables and be so upset that they will not invite you again." On other occasions, when I spilled a bit of sauce on the table while cutting some meat or when I put some left-overs in the wrong dish, he told me with disgust: "the way you eat, no one will dine with you in London." The fact of the matter is, however, that wherever I went in Dublin and London people were forgiving and encouraged me to eat in my own way, with my hand. Besides, in the mess I visited I often saw them put a big soup tureen filled with barley soup on a table, and everybody would eat directly out of it without being fussy about each others' hands and mouths. He also said that in London nobody will show one the way without being paid, or spend half a shilling to help someone. I have already told the story of [how I asked for directions and was helped]. As for generosity: in both cities people invited me out on the pretext of having a walk, and then took me to places of entertainment. Before I knew it,

39. Charles Vallancey (c.1726–1812), antiquary and general, developed an improbable argument suggesting that Irish civilization was ultimately descended from Eastern origins. (Charles Stewart)

40. Richard Boyle (1728–1807), second Earl of Shannon, was then First Lord of the Treasury in Ireland. Sir Thomas-Gleadowe Newcomen (1776–1825), Viscount Newcomen, was a wealthy banker in Dublin. (Charles Stewart)

they had spent four to five shillings so that I would enjoy myself. Most of them gave me gifts of books, knives, eye-glasses, watches, and other English presents. Some insisted on offering me one or two thousand gold rupees, but I refused the offers since I had no need of such assistance. [Captain Williamson] also warned me that "if you expect us to feed you meat, you will die of hunger in London." But what I found was that everybody was eager to show generosity of this sort to their friends. What is more, they considered it a good deed and were grateful to their guests, especially the host and his wife, who are so busy caring for their guests that on the day of the reception they themselves deprive themselves of food. I tell these stories so as to reveal the difference between the character of the English of India and the real character of the English. [...]

Mr. Griffith and his wife spent a long time in India, where they amassed some wealth. They have bought a lot of land around Dublin and are engaged in agriculture. In spite of their wealth they live like India's Gujaratis.[41] Then there is Mr. South (?), a judge in Dublin, who has an attractive wife with the most beautiful mouth and lips I have ever seen. Most Irish people have bad teeth, and when she smiles one notices that she is missing a tooth. This adds so much to the beauty of her lips and teeth that I composed a poem in her honor. [verse]

Mr. Rich (Roach?) is also in a high position in the courts. [...] I was a guest in his house a number of times and on these occasions his wife played the harp for me. I was so enraptured with her playing that no sensation remained in my body and reason left my head. [...]

Mr. Ball, the eldest son of my landlady, and his uncle Mr. Allen repeatedly invited me to breakfast and lunch and were generous with me in all sorts of ways. Mr. Ball runs the post house and lives separate from his mother. His wife is beautiful and has the same good taste as [the rest of the] family. Since the ship I was to take to cross the Irish Sea was a packet-boat and thus under the supervision of Mr. Ball, he arranged for me to have a cabin to sleep in. On board the ship I had good friends like Mr. Eager, Captain Daley, Captain Days, who was a young man of sixteen or seventeen and so beautiful that I gave him the title "heavenly youth,"[42] Mr. Fitzmaurice, and Mr. Harkey. They guided me throughout the entire trip and tried to teach me English. If I tried to expand on their good qualities my tale would become too long. But I composed a poem to celebrate the joy of meeting them, and sent them an English translation of it after I arrived in London. [verse]

41. In India rich Gujaratis have the reputation of living frugally.
42. In English, transliterated into the Arabic alphabet. A reference to Koran 76:19, 56:17, 52:24.

9

An Irish Visitor to the Court of the Shah of Persia in 1835:

Extract from the Unpublished Diary of Sir Francis Hopkins of Athboy

David James

Introduction

I N THE EARLY MORNING of 27 July 1835 the steam vessel *Pluto* left Falmouth harbor bound for Constantinople, the Black Sea, and ultimately Odessa in Southern Russia. Among her passengers that morning she carried His Majesty's Ambassador Extraordinary to the Shah of Persia, Mr. Henry Ellis, and his staff.

As the first representative of the Crown in Tehran for fifteen years, Ellis was eminently suited for his task. He was an able diplomat and had already seen service in Persia in 1814 where he had been Minister Plenipotentiary. He was in addition an oriental traveler of some standing, having accompanied Lord Amherst to China in 1816 and on the return journey experienced the privations of a shipwreck and a voyage to Java in an open boat.[1]

Ellis's mission was to persuade the Persian Government to accept an addition to the 1814 Anglo-Persian Treaty and to negotiate a trade agreement. However it was also hoped that the presence in Tehran of a fully-accredited representative of the Crown would revitalize relations between the two powers.[2]

During the Napoleonic Wars, particularly when it looked as if France and Russia might threaten India, Anglo-Persian relations had been good and although these declined somewhat towards the end of that period never-

1. S.v. "Sir Henry Ellis," *Dictionary of National Biography*, vol. 6: 697.
2. See M. E. Yapp "Control of the Persian Mission 1822–1836," *University of Birmingham History Journal* 7 (1960): 162–79, where the question of Anglo-Persian relations during this period is discussed.

theless a treaty was signed in 1814 which promised physical and financial aid to Persia in the event of a Russian attack. But in the changed situation of Europe following the Napoleonic Wars, to a Britain pursuing a policy of friendship towards Russia an Anglo-Persian alliance and the treaty of 1814 were a distinct embarrassment. It was to lessen this embarrassment that in 1822 Canning decided to transfer control of the British Mission in Tehran to the Government of India on the grounds that Britain's European and Asian policies were quite separate. However the treaty with its uncomfortable promises still remained.

Following the Russo-Persian War of 1827 the Envoy in Tehran, Sir John Malcolm, effected a diplomatic "coup" by buying out the awkward clauses of the treaty. The Persian Government found itself urgently in need of money to prevent a Russian advance on Tehran so for 20,000 *tumāns* (about £18,000) Malcolm had the 3rd and 4th clauses abrogated.

But the War of 1827 gave rise to a new situation in Persia. First, because the Persians turned their attention away from confrontation with Russia to Afghanistan, which an army under the command of the Persian Crown Prince, Abbās Mirza, invaded in 1833. Secondly, because the Treaty of Turk-manchai which ended the 1827 War increased Russian influence in Persia. These developments were regarded with some apprehension by the Indian authorities who realized that any extension of Persian hegemony over Afghanistan would mean the presence of Russian agents south of the Hindu Kush.

These apprehensions were also felt in London where the alteration of the Anglo-Persian Treaty was now perhaps regretted. It was decided to upgrade the Envoy in Tehran, John Campbell, who was Chargé dAffaires, by knighting him. Campbell was also authorized to advance money to Abbās Mirza which would enable him to secure his succession without having to rely on Russian aid. But the measures proved ineffective, so the British Government in another attempt made Campbell Consul-General and suggested an addition to the treaty of 1814 declaring support for the territorial integrity of Persia. Campbell was also to negotiate a trade agreement.

When Campbell's efforts continued to meet with no success the British Government decided to transfer control of the Mission back to the Crown and to send out a new representative, Henry Ellis.

The time was quite appropriate for Ellis's arrival.[3] Abbās Mirza had died some months before, leaving his 25 year-old son Mohammad Mirza to take his place, as Crown Prince. But when Fath Ali Shah died soon afterwards, Mohammad Mirza's claim was disputed by his uncles and fighting broke out

---

3. P. M. Sykes, *A History of Persia* (London: Macmillan, 1915), vol. 2, 427.

between the parties concerned. It was thanks largely to a British officer, Henry Lindsay Bethune, who commanded Mohammad Mirza's troops, that the latter defeated his rivals and ascended the throne in 1834 with the title of Mohammad Shah.

Despite this rise in Britain's standing and the obvious necessity of having a properly accredited ambassador at the Persian Court, Ellis's mission had great difficulty in getting started. In the first place Ellis, though able, was at the same time vain and ambitious and refused to go without full ambassadorial rank. Furthermore although the East India Company readily agreed to the transfer of the British Mission in Tehran it baulked at the prospect of paying for it, which was what the Government wanted, and upon being pressed insisted upon a financial limit of a mere £ 12,000. Finally before the Mission had set out the Whigs were returned to office and the Mission was made complimentary, to last only two months, though this time was later extended. [4]

On board the *Pluto* that morning, whether by design or accident, was a young Irishman who was traveling to the East with the apparent intention of visiting Baghdad. Although he was not officially part of Ellis's staff,[5] he seems to have become a temporary member of the Ambassador's suite, for he accompanied Ellis to Tehran and was with him when he had his audience with Mohammad Shah.

The *Pluto* arrived in Constantinople on 23 August where the party disembarked, remaining in the Ottoman capital until September 1. During that time they inspected the city and were presented to the Sultan, Mahmud II (1808–1839). On September 1 they left on board the *Pluto* for the Black Sea port of Trebizond where they arrived two days later. They then continued overland to Tehran, an exhausting journey on horseback lasting more than a month.

On November 6 Ellis and his staff were presented to Mohammad Shah in the Royal Palace. The following day while Ellis got down to negotiations with the Persian Prime Minister, Haji Mirza Āghāsi, the young Irish traveler left for India, having changed his mind about visiting Baghdad.

Throughout his travels the young man kept a detailed diary. It spans a period of almost two years, commencing on 27 July 1835 and ending on 28 June 1837. The entries in the diary cover his journeyings in Turkey, Persia, Central India and his return to Dublin via Egypt, Rhodes, Turkey, Greece, Italy, France, and England.

There is no name on the diary and personal information in the entries

---

4. See Yapp "Control of the Persian Mission 1822–1836": 174–76.

5. The accounts of Ellis's Mission and the names of all those who went to Tehran in 1835 were published in a Parliamentary Paper in 1846. (683) XXXI 477.

is meager. However, after comparing what information there is with the records in the Genealogical Office, Dublin Castle, it seems certain that the author was Sir Francis Hopkins of Athboy who was born in 1813 and died at Madeira in 1847. He was the son of Sir Francis Hopkins, M.P., First Baronet of Athboy, who received his title for putting down disturbances in the area in 1794 and died in 1814.[6]

Reproduced below is Hopkins's interesting account of his journey to Tehran in 1835 and audience with the Shah. It begins on September 30, when he crossed the Turkish-Persian border, and ends with his visit to the Royal Palace a month later ... The diary is at present the property of Patrick Casey of Blackrock, and was acquired some years ago by his father in the course of a visit to Westmeath. I would like to thank Mr. Casey for allowing me to reproduce this extract.

The Diary

SEPTEMBER 30TH 1835   CROSSING THE TURKISH-PERSIAN
                                                 FRONTIER

Five hours to Kilissi, a miserable village, through a hilly country. Crossed the boundary between Turkey and Persia.

OCTOBER 2ND   THE PLAIN OF KHOY

The *Ilchi*[7] sent on Capt. Stoddart[8] with the Tartar to Qara Ā'ineh to notify our arrival to Yusuf Khan, the Persian authority nearest the frontier. Pretty girls in spite of their rags. Aqa Bey, Chief of the Khorāsānlu Tribe with a large party of followers came out to meet the Ambassador at a mile's distance from the village of Qara Ā'ineh, firing pistols, flourishing their swords. Six hours to Ajawuk, another *pīshvāz*.[9] Dr. Riach[10] came in this afternoon accompanied by the *Mehmāndār*,[11] Hajji Bejim Khan, with tents etc. and the servants from the Embassy from Tehran.

3RD

Started at half-past seven, but as the *Mehmāndār* pleaded fatigue we only went as far as Pereh [today known as Feruraq]. Seven hours. The

6. Ms. 112 p. 3. The Hopkins Pedigree to 1847.
7. Persian for "ambassador."
8. Captain Charles Stoddart, Military Secretary to the Embassy.
9. A reception party.
10. A physician, evidently acting as a secretary at the time.
11. A Persian officer in charge of entertaining foreign visitors.

road makes a gradual descent through a long ravine for about an hour
and a half's distance before entering the plain of Khoy. The son of the
Governor of Khoy came out to meet us a few miles from Pereh. Good
quarters here but exposed to air.

4TH   KHOY

At eleven o'clock we put foot in the stirrup. A numerous *esteqbāl*[12]
met us on entering the town. We proceeded to a palace that had
been prepared for our reception. After dinner Yahyā Khan arrived to
succeed Hajji Bejim Khan in his duties as *Mehmāndār*.

5TH

Went over the bazaars. Sr. Gilbaldi, a Sardinian merchant, dined with
us.

6TH

A long lecture read by the Ambassador to the Governor Hatim Khan
for his breach of manners in not returning his visit yesterday. We had
nearly arrived at our station when the Governor's son came up with
us stating that he had orders from his father to bring back a letter of
forgiveness from the *Ilchi* and, if necessary, to go as far as Tehran to
obtain it.

On our arrival at the village we found tents pitched for each
individual of the party. The contrast they afforded to the dust and
filth we had hitherto been accustomed was most pleasing.

7TH   LAKE URMIA

Four *farsakhs*[13] to Tasuj. The road entered a narrow defile almost
immediately after leaving the village, on reaching the extremity of
which, Lake Urmia[14] burst upon the view, which from this point is
very beautiful. The water is exceedingly salty so much that it is said
that no fish can live in it.

The desert to the plain is very rough and rugged. Here the
Ambassador got into the carriage which the Prince staying at Tasuj
had sent forward for his use. It was an old lumbering Italian-looking
coach of some fifty years old or upwards.

On our arrival at Tasuj His Highness Faridun Mirza, brother of the
Shah signified his wish to see the *Ilchi*. We accordingly went to his

---

12. A welcoming party.

13. A measurement of 3.5 miles according to Sir John Malcolm, *Sketches of Persia: From the
Journals of a Traveller in the East* (London: J. Murray, 1828), vol. 2, 9.

14. Lake Urmia, 4,230 ft. above sea level.

house at four o'clock and found His Highness seated on a chair in a small room. He conversed with the Ambassador for about an hour, gave us tea from a handsome English tea service. He is a little dark complexioned man, handsome and in the expression of the features bore a strong resemblance to the prints I had seen of Abbās Mirza.[15]

The wind blew strongly in the night and we found the tents rather cold.

8TH   HAJJI SAYYID

The Ambassador having heard that the *Vali-Ahd*, or heir-apparent, a boy of four years of age,[16] was staying at a village but little out of our route, he determined to pay him a visit. (I ought to mention that yesterday a fine horse of the Turkoman breed arrived as a present from the Shah to the *Ilchi*.)

The village where the young Prince was staying was distant seven *farsakhs* from Tabriz,[17] whither most of the inhabitants had fled to avoid the Cholera which was raging violently at this time. Having arrived rather earlier than we were expected, the child was not dressed or ready to give his audience, so we passed away the time in partaking of our *Mehmāndār*'s breakfast. We made an excellent meal with our fingers, and stepping across the road which divided the house we were in from that of the heir-apparent we were at once ushered in to his presence.

The little boy sat with great dignity at the top of the room, he is without exception the most beautiful child I ever saw, and it was most ludicrous to see the manner in which he wiped his mouth after drinking a cup of tea, passing his hand across his chin as if it was already covered with a beard. The *Ilchi* made him a *pishkesh* (a present) of an opera glass as a remembrance of his visit. He had his little *Nasaqchibāshi*, or Earl Marshal, a child of his own age and son of a nobleman of the Afshar Tribe who accompanied us from Tasuj.

This district is famous for its fruit and to its goodness we can testify as the *Vali-Ahd* sent a large present of it to the *Ilchi*.

After leaving the young heir we rode on ten miles to Shebastar where we found everything prepared for us in a very nice house. Capt. Sheil[18] arrived from Urmia this evening.

15. The Persian Crown Prince who died in 1833, aged 46.

16. Presumably Nāser al-Din Mirza whao was born in 1831, later Nāser al-Din Shah, r. 1848–1896.

17. From Abbās Mirza onwards it was the custom of the Crown Prince to reside in Tabriz.

18. Capt. Justin Sheil. Later Secretary to the Legation and Chargé d'Affaires. See also chapter 10.

9TH   TABRIZ

Started at sunrise. The road lay over an immense plain all the
way to Tabriz. We meandered at least a *farsakh* out of the road in
consequence of trying to make a short cut.

The *Beylerbey*,[19] Messrs. Bonham, Buyers, Nisbett and Strange,[20] and
a numerous *esteqbāl* met us about a mile from the town. A guard-of-
honor was placed at the Embassy house and continued there during
our stay and a salute of fifteen guns was fired on entering the town.

The walls of the town struck us as having a very oriental
appearance, from the shape of the battlements and the blue and green
glazed tiles which ornamented the gates.

10TH

Went over the bazaars. Inspected Sir Henry Bethune's[21] stud but did
not become a purchaser.

11TH

Bought a horse from Capt. Sheil for 60 tomans.[22] Called on the
Beylerbey. Walked round the walls of the town, they are about three
miles and a quarter in circumference.

12TH

Rode out with Messrs. Buyers and Strange to the ruins of an old fort
or castle situated on the east side of the town and said to have been
constructed by the Caliph Hārun al-Rashid.[23] The ground they cover
is extensive and from the summit of a mound in the center, there
is a good view of the green oasis which characterizes Tabriz and its
suburbs. Coal has lately been discovered among the hills here but of so
bad a quality as not to make it worthwhile to work it.

13TH

Rode out to the powder mills in the morning before breakfast. They
are about three miles to the south of the town. As a specimen of the
great care and caution observed in this establishment, I may observe
that one of the workmen was comfortably smoking his *ghalyān* (a
pipe) in a room where the powder was being pounded from large

19. Turkish; meaning the governor of a province in Persia at this time. See Frederic
Shoberl, *Persia* (London: R. Ackermann, 1822), vol. 1, 59.

20. British officers training die Persian Army.

21. Capt. Henry Lindesay Bethune 1787–1851. British officer who commanded troops loyal
to Mohammad Shah in the civil war which erupted in 1834 after the death of Fath Ali Shah. He
retired in 1839 but returned to Persia as traveler and died in Tabriz in 1851.

22. A *tumān* was worth about £0.90 in 1822.

23. R. 786–809 A.D.

into small grain! All the ingredients for making gunpowder are found within a distance of four marches from Tabriz.

Went to the palace and gardens occupied formerly by Abbās Mirza. There are here some curious attempts at fresco painting.

14TH

The remaining curiosities worthy of mention in Tabriz are the Ark,[24] an old building the date of whose execution is not ascertained, but which is supposed to have been either a mosque of citadel, and is now an arsenal, and a ruined mosque[25] of large dimensions to the south of the town. Mr. Perkins whom we met at Erzerum arrived today.

15TH

Two Russian newspapers arrived yesterday with the London news of the 1st of September.

16TH

Left Tabriz at twelve o'clock and seven *farsakhs* to Sadrābād. By some mal-arrangement the baggage did not come up so we had to sleep upon the ground under a single canvas tent. It was excessively cold.

17TH

Crossed the plain of Ujān. Here Fath Ali Shah[26] used to hold his summer encampments. To the center is a summer palace which formerly belonged to Abbās Mirza. At a distance it bore some resemblance to an English abbey, from the square tower rising in the center of the building. A fatiguing dusty march of seven hours to Tikmeh Dāsh. The country about here is very salt, the surface of the ground being covered as with a hoar frost.

18TH

Seven hours to Turkmanchai over an uninteresting road. Met a party of pilgrims bound for Mecca. This village is situated in a valley and is famous for the excellence of its bread.

19TH

A mule load having been missed we halted here today. In this village was signed the treaty which gave the Aras a boundary between Russia and Persia. [27]

---

24. Mosque of Ali Shah. Built in the fourteenth century and turned into an arsenal by Abbās Mirza.

25. Perhaps the "Blue Mosque" built in 1465.

26. R. 1797–1834.

27. Treaty of Turkmanchai 1828.

20TH   MIYĀNEH

Six *farsakhs* to Miyāneh. The country improved in appearance. Great
quantities of the castor oil plant. After marching three hours we came
upon the bed of the River Qezel Uzun which we followed to Miyāneh.
On our entrance to the town we were greeted by several *pahlavān*s or
wrestlers who marched a little distance in advance, naked to the waist
brandishing immense clubs and singing in chorus. This town has long
been famous for its poisonous bugs, mentioned by Sir John Mandeville[28]
as a place "wherein no Christene man may dwelleth long tyme but
dyeth soon and no man knowe the cause." However as our tents were
pitched a short way beyond the town we had not any opportunity of
confirming by our own experience the reports of previous travelers.

Our *Mehmāndār* Yahyā Khan displayed his dress sword to us in the
evening; a most magnificent toy at first sight. The straps supporting
the scabbard to the belt were covered with emeralds an inch-square
and in the center of the buckle of the belt was a ruby the size of
a crown piece. These stones however almost all full of flaws, and
although they made a magnificent appearance by candlelight would
not be very valuable in England where the value of a stone depends on
the water and not on the size.

21ST

At the distance of two or three miles from Miyāneh the river is
crossed by a bridge of twenty-one arches and shortly afterwards
the road commences the ascent of the Qāfelān Kuh Mountain. After
gaining the summit the remains of a causeway attributed to Shah
Abbās[29] are visible and on the left are the ruins of a fortress, very
formidable in the times of the bow and arrow the Persians of our
parry told us. At the foot of this gorge flows a rapid river which is
crossed by a handsome bridge of three arches,[30] under the shade or
one which was dry we breakfasted with Yahyā Khan. A few miles
beyond this Mr. Brown was murdered.

22ND

Six *farsakhs* to Timurkhāneh cold morning, entered the Province of
'Erāq-e Ajam. Exchanged my white horse for Stuart's[31] grey.

28. Sir John Mandeville, *The voiage and travayle of Sir John Maundeville knight: which treateth
of the way toward Hierusalem and of marvayles of Inde with other islands and countreys*, annotated by
J. Ashton (London: Pickering & Chatto, 1887).

29. R. 1587–1629.

30. Qāfelān Kuh Bridge. Built in the twelfth century, restored by Shah 'Abbās and again in
the eighteenth century.

31. Captain Stuart. Private Secretary to the Ambassador.

23RD

Availed ourselves of permission to take a bath this morning. Halted today as Mirza Bābā,[32] the Persian secretary to the mission, was suddenly taken ill and unable to proceed. Lost my signet ring. A messenger arrived from Capt. Farrant[33] stating that he was lying ill at Soltāniyeh, two stages distant, of the smallpox. The Ambassador immediately sent Dr Bell[34] forward to attend him.

24TH   ZANJĀN

The Mirza not feeling sufficiently well to march this morning Dr. Riach remained behind with him. We started in a shower of rain which lasted nearly all the way to Zanjān, a town said to contain 12,000 inhabitants.

Just inside the gates of the town we were met by a third *Mehmāndār*, Mohammad Khan Dombolī, the Vizier of Zanjān, and twenty five horse of Capt. Farrant's lancers organized and disciplined in the European manner. We found our tents pitched about a mile beyond the town and before dismounting the Ambassador made the troops go through the lance exercise, which they performed in a very creditable manner.

25TH   SOLTĀNIYEH

Entered upon the plain of Soltāniyeh and marched six *farsakh*s to a village of the same name. The green-glazed dome of the ruined mosque here being visible for a long distance.[35]

Here is one of the summer palaces of the Shahs of Persia, One of His present Majesty's uncles was here and made us his guests. The palace is an unsightly building upon a high mound or rising ground, and reminded me – why or wherefore I know not – of the Italian style. The remainder of Capt. Farrant's Lancers joined us a short distance before reaching Sultaniyeh. In the quarter allotted to the Ambassador, round the walls of the apartment are some amusing paintings of Fath Ali Shah spearing deer with his crown and armlets and full court costume on,[36] ridiculously out of drawing. Other full-length portraits of different members of the royal family were not so bad for Persia.

The Prince invited us for dinner at half an hour after sunset. We found him a very polished, handsome man, with an ease of

32. There is no mention of Mirza Baba in the published accounts.
33. Captain Francis Farrant. Later Military Attaché and Secretary to the Legation.
34. Surgeon of the Embassy.
35. Probably the Mausoleum of Oljeitu, r. 1294–1313.
36. Fath Ali Shah was particularly fond of seeing his portrait, usually resplendent with enormous beard and wasp waist.

manners and a well-bred politeness that could not be surpassed in any European court. The floor of the room in which we dined was covered with white linen cloths or napkins embroidered at the edge with gold, and as a tablecloth in the center of the room a handsome shawl was spread instead of chintz the usual covering. I thought the servants would never cease laying down dishes, which to the number of fifty or sixty loaded the table. It was rather an infliction to us of the suite to be obliged to sit an hour and a half after dinner, listening to the conversation of the *Ilchi* and the Prince without understanding a syllable.

Dr. Bell returned and stated that Capt. Farrant had had an attack of modified smallpox, but was now going on very well. Soltāniyeh must have been at one time a considerable town as the extent of the remains and mud walls indicate, but it contains now but few inhabitants.[37]

26TH & 27TH

Whilst we were partaking of the *Mehmāndār*'s breakfast this morning, a message arrived from Dr. Riach announcing the death of Mirza Baba. A long ride of nine *farsakh*s, not made much better by being led at least three miles out of our way by attempting a short cut. Numberless deserted villages which we passed this day attest the desolation which Persia has undergone these last few years from plague and pestilence and war.

Six *farsakh*s to a small village. The prospect from the roof of the house I was lodged in exactly came up to the ideas I had formed in England of a Persian landscape.

28TH   QAZVIN

Marched five *farsakh*s through a rich plain intersected with numerous water ducts or *qanats*[38] to Kazvin which is situated at a short distance from the foot of a large range of mountains running east and west.[39] The outskirts of the town, for a mile and a half on every side, are gardens of vine and fruit trees. The town guards, carrying small round embossed shields and long heavy sticks terminating in an egg-shape,[40] and five feet long, met us at a short distance from the city gates. We were conducted to the "Kolāh Farangi,"[41] a palace built by one of the

---

37. Soltāniyeh was after 1306 the capital of the Mongol Ilkhanid dynasty.
38. Underground irrigation channels.
39. Alborz Mountains.
40. A *gorz*, or mace.
41. Turkish: meaning the "Tower of the Franks," i.e., Europeans.

Safavid kings[42] and so called from its containing two or three pictures of Europeans – ambassadors most probably – painted in gaudy colors on the walls.

29TH

Halted here today and visited Prince Soltān Mirza and the Vizier of the town.

30TH

A very fatiguing march of nine *farsakhs*. A short time before reaching our *manzel*, abode, we met Sir John Campbell[43] and Capt. Todd. All along the plain from Qazvin, at intervals of a quarter of a mile, is a chain of mud forts. Observed also a great number of artificial tumuli, some of considerable height.

31ST   SOLEYMĀNIYEH

Nine *farsakhs* to Suleymāniyeh. Took up our abode in the Royal Palace. In a room in the inner court are portraits of Fath Ali Shah and numerous members of the Royal Family, tolerably well painted. Adjoining this chamber and at the corner of the square is a high tower with a pretty view from the top.

The apartments in which we were lodged were those usually occupied by the ladies, whose summer bed stood in a comer of the court. It was raised about five feet from the ground, and sufficiently large to accommodate twenty of the fair.

NOVEMBER 1ST 1835

Remained at Soleymāniyeh all day. To the east of the town flows the River Karateh, in winter a considerable river but in summer nearly dry.

2ND

Rode five *farsakhs* to Kand [Kan], a beautiful little village about two *farsakhs* from Tehran.

3RD   TEHRAN

Long negotiations as to the rank of the persons who were to come out with the *esteqbāl* to meet the Ambassador prevented our starting out until three o'clock. The *Ilchi* having stated his wishes on the subject of an *esteqbāl* in these terms: "Either give me a proper reception or I will enter the capital after the manner of Europe, privately." This manner

42. The Safavid dynasty ruled Persia from 1502 to 1736.
43. Consul General in Tehran.

of reasoning was conclusive, and every preliminary having being
settled to his liking the Ambassador mounted the horse which had
been sent from the Royal Stables for his use and proceeded towards
Tehran.

The trappings and bridle of the animal were most magnificent;
the bridle was one mass of precious stones and exceedingly large
diamonds, of no great value certainly, inasmuch as they were full of
flaws, and perhaps even inferior to the Bristol diamonds, but at a
distance presented a most magnificent appearance. A cordon of pearls
and precious stones was suspended from his neck, the housings and
saddle cloth were of spangled cloth of gold inlaid with turquoises,
pearls etc., and the bit and stirrup were of the same metal.

On reaching the Royal Tents which had been pitched about four
miles out of the city, we found the Minister of Foreign Affairs, Mirza
Mas'ud, and all the officers of the regiments at present in Tehran,
with numberless grandees of the Persian court assembled near the
tents. These, with all the mounted population of the city made a train
of considerable magnitude.

The Russian Mission met us a few hundred yards from the gates of
the town. At the gates of the "Palace," as the Embassy house is here
called, a triple line of soldiers were ranged on each side of the street
as a guard of honor, forming an avenue of a hundred yards in length.

Several of the principal persons who had come out to meet us
dined at the "Palace," and the first toast proposed by the Ambassador
was, "*Salāmat-e Āl-e Mohammad Shāh!*"[44]

Our huzzas[45] and "three-times threes"[46] seemed to amuse our
guests not a little.

The party broke up in high spirits; not a thing had gone wrong and
it was universally agreed that a better *esteqbāl* had never been given to
any ambassador before.

4TH & 5TH

The luxury of not being obliged to rise by candle light and march for
ten hours was fully appreciated by all the party. This was a decided
day of rest.

Count Simonitch,[47] the Russian Envoy, visited the Ambassador with
his suite.

---

44. Salutations to the House of Mohammad Shah.
45. Also 'Huzzah,' a shout used to express joy, encouragement, or triumph (editor's note).
46. Three cheers repeated three times (editor's note).
47. General Count Simonitch, the Russian Ambassador.

6TH

We had this day an audience with the Shah....

* * *

At this point in the diary there is inserted a translation of the "Dastur-e [?]," or 'Program of Ceremonies' to be observed by the Ambassador on his approach to the "Throne of the Center of the Universe." This had been sent to Ambassador Ellis several days before his arrival in Tehran.

The first part of the program involved the official reception of the Ambassador by the Beylerbey, Fath Ali Khan, at the Royal Tents some distance from the capital. He would then proceed to the Residency, accompanied by the nobles and grandees of the welcoming party (the *Esteqbāl*) and there would find Hajji Ali 'Askar waiting to receive him. This as we have seen had already been carried out on the 3rd of the month.

On the day of the audience, one or two days later, the Ambassador would be conducted to the Palace through streets which had been specially cleaned for the occasion. After the Ambassador and his suite had arrived at the Palace they would receive an official salute from all the troops assembled therein and be conducted to one of the Royal Apartments where the Deputy Master of Ceremonies, Mohammad Qoli Khan, would inform the Ambassador of the forms of introduction. The Ambassador would then present himself before the King of Kings and, reading from a prepared speech, would make an elaborate profession of friendship towards His Illustrious Majesty on behalf of the British Government. The Shah would then reply to the Ambassador and the latter would be permitted to withdraw to the apartment of the Prime Minister (Hajji Mirza Āghāsi who came to power in May 1835) where he would refresh himself. He would then be conveyed to the Residency with all due pomp and ceremony.

The following day the Ambassador would have discussions with the Persian Foreign Minister.

[DIARY RESUMED (6TH NOVEMBER)]

... At two o'clock this day we mounted the horses which according to the program had been sent from the Royal Stables, proceeding through narrow streets and a part of the bazaar which terminated at the outer gate of the Ark.

After passing an open space we crossed the bridge of the citadel, and were conducted into a very large square filled with troops and numerous pieces of cannon with artillerymen on duty. Dismounting from our horses and traversing the whole length of the square, we

turned under a narrow and dark archway and entered through it at
once upon the quarter of the Palace. It showed a spacious area, shaded
with trees and intersected with water. Rows of lofty *chenār* (plane
trees) and other trees divide this immense court up into several
avenues. That which runs along the midst of court is the widest;
enclosing a narrow piece of still water stretching from end to end and
animated here and there with a few little *jets d'eau*. To the center is
the building where His Majesty generally sits to receive the homage of
his subjects, which contains the Marble Throne.

Passing through this court we entered a similar one, at the
extremity of which was the apartment in which His Glorious Majesty
sat to receive us. When we had approached to within fifty yards of
the Royal person we left our slippers on the pavement of the court,
and advanced bowing and bowing until we reached the building, and
ascending a flight of steps we were ushered into the presence of the
King of Kings.

The apartment in which we stood was open from the roof of the
building nearly to the earth, and supported on two sides by twisted
columns of white marble fluted with gold. The interior of the saloon
was profusely decorated with carving, gilding, arabesque painting,
and looking glass, which latter material was in a manner interwoven
with all the other wreathing ornaments, gleaming and glittering in
every part from the vaulted ceiling to the floor.

The throne on which the Shah sat was the famous Takht-e Tāvus,
the Peacock Throne which Nāder Shah[48] tore from under the Mughal
Emperors at the sacking of Delhi;[49] it is raised a few steps from the
ground. On the right of the Shah stood four pages holding; first the
crown, secondly the shield and scepter, and two swords of state, the
scabbards of which were one mass of diamonds. The crown itself is of
an ugly bucket shape and so heavy that it cannot be worn more than a
few moments without intolerable pain to the Regal brows.[50]

Mohammad Shah wore a black lambskin cap with two or three
aigrettes fixed on for the occasion. He is six and twenty years and of
unprepossessing features. He speaks in such a rapid and unintelligible
manner that even those who are constantly with him find it difficult
to understand him.

After the Ambassador's speech which occupied about twenty
minutes, His Majesty requested him to be seated, and after asking

48. R. 1736–47.

49. In 1738.

50. Now in the vault of the Central Bank of Iran in Tehran with the Persian Crown Jewels
(editor's note).

a few questions as to the journey, he made a signal to retire, and according to custom we adjourned to the apartments of the Prime Minister and teaed, coffeed, piped, and sweetmeated in the usual manner, which indispensable forms being terminated, we were conveyed to the Residence with honors and ceremonies similar to those described.

In the magnificence of the Persian Court I was much disappointed, having expected to find some remains of that Asiatic Splendor which in Europe is supposed to accompany the persons and courts of Eastern monarchs. For with the exception of the regalia itself there is not a thing worth looking at at the Persian Court, His Glorious Majesty proclaiming his opinion that a line of soldiers is a more noble sight than all the pageantry of trains of jeweled and coroneted nobles.

Conclusion

On the 17th the author proclaims his intention of leaving for India as soon as possible with a Capt. Ruddell as a companion.[51] On the following day he continued on his travels which were to take him to India, the Red Sea, Egypt, and back by way of Rhodes to Turkey and Greece. He then sailed for Italy and made his way across Europe to Dublin, where he arrived on the 23rd of May 1837.

51. Capt. Ruddell is not mentioned in the published accounts but according to the author of the diary he was one of the Ambassador's secretaries.

10

An Irishwoman in Tehran, 1849–1853

Identity, Religion, and Empire

Brendan McNamara

MY OBJECTIVE IN THIS CHAPTER is to explore an episode of Irish-Iranian socio-cultural interaction that has not previously been investigated from an Irish perspective. I will not go too far back in time to cover the wondrous possibilities suggested by Lady Francesca Esperanza Wilde, when she contends that Ireland was at one time infused with Iranian cultural influences as a result of a great movement of people that arrived on these shores from the East.[1] My focus is on a migration of the reverse kind but does involve a Lady who, along with her husband, sojourned for almost four years in Tehran. The Lady's husband was the British "Envoy Extraordinary and Minister Plenipotentiary" to the court of the Shah and he held that position for four years up to his marriage in 1847, and further until 1853 when he left his post on grounds of ill-health.[2] She is not generally known as being Irish though she certainly was, as indeed was her husband.

My study focuses on the story of Mary Woulfe Sheil and (to a lesser extent) Justin Sheil, the British Minister, and explores issues of identity and religion, and how they influenced the approach taken by Lady Sheil when she penned her well-known travelogue *Glimpses of Life and Manners in Persia*,[3] published in 1856 and regarded as the first travelogue written by a woman about Persia.[4] My initial objective was to interrogate the text for what it

---

1. Lady Francesca Speranza Wilde, *Ancient Legends, Mystic Charms, and Superstitions of Ireland* (London: Ward & Downey, 1887), 4.

2. Information drawn from, Stephen Wheeler (rev. James Lunt), "Sheil, Sir Justin (1803–1871)," *Oxford Dictionary of National Biography* (Oxford: Oxford University Press, 2004), vol. 50, 171; and W. T. (William Torrens) McCullagh, *Richard Lalor Sheil* (London: Hurst and Blackett, 1855). Justin Sheil held other consular positions in Tehran prior to 1844.

3. Lady Mary Leonora Woulfe Sheil, *Glimpses of Life and Manners in Persia* (London: John Murray, 1856).

4. *Encyclopaedia Iranica* vol. 11, s.v. "Great Britain-vii: British Travelers to Persia" (by Denis Wright) 246–52. See also Mansour Bonakdarian, "Iranian Studies in the United Kingdom in the Twentieth Century," *Iranian Studies* 43:2 (April 2010): 270. "Persia" will be used throughout as the contemporary country designation for the period under consideration.

tells us about the Sheils as well as for what it might reveal about Persia during a most fascinating period in its history. I was interested in investigating to what extent the text embodies a typical example of cultural "othering" in colonialist travel writing. Is it, as has been contended, an "exoticizing" narrative,[5] less concerned with nineteenth-century Persia but more with the discourse current at that time at the heart of the Empire? What soon became clear is that the text exposes a great deal about the Sheils and that discourse, but offers little towards advancing cultural literacy with respect to mid-nineteenth-century Persia. *Glimpses* would seem an apt title and in that sense one could cite a well-known advertising catchphrase that declaims about a particular paint, "it does exactly what it says on the tin." There is, though, on further examination, some evidence that an identifiable combination of factors, relating to identity and religion, imbues the text with a subtlety and complexity manifesting as an underlying criticism of empire, and the religion of empire, hitherto un-scrutinized.[6]

Before we examine these possibilities it will be important to know a little more about the Sheils' "Irishness."[7]

The Woulfes and the Sheils

Mary Leonora Woulfe Sheil was born in 1825, the only daughter of Stephen and Frances Woulfe of Tiermaclane, near Ennis in County Clare. The family was of Norman origin and first came to Ireland at the end of the twelfth century. They held extensive lands in the Corbally area of Limerick, now a suburb of the city. A branch of the family settled in County Clare and through the centuries maintained their Catholic faith. Mary's father, Stephen, a graduate of the famous Jesuit college at Stoneyhurst, and Trinity College, Dublin, was a leading figure in law and government in Ireland and held the highest official positions of any Catholic of his time. He successively held the posts of Solicitor-General (1836), Attorney-General (1837) and Chief Baron of the Exchequer (1838).[8] Stephen Woulfe was an ally of Daniel O'Connell and ac-

5. See Farah Ghaderi, "'A Living Tableau of Queerness': A Postcolonial Study of Lady Sheil's Travel Account on Persia," in *Journal of Teaching English Language and Literature Society of Iran* 2 (2008): 123–43.

6. The terms "culture," "othering," and "identity" are not fully discussed here, though it is understood that taken together they indicate concepts that are fairly polysemic. See Fred Dervin, "Cultural Identity, Representation, and Othering," in John Jackson, ed., *Routledge Handbook of Intercultural Communication* (London: Routledge, 2011), Chapter 11.

7. For a discussion on "Irishness" see Brian Graham, "Ireland and Irishness: Place, Culture and Identity," in Brian Graham, ed., *In Search of Ireland; A Cultural Geography* (London: Routledge, 1997): 1–17.

8. See Brendan Mc Namara, "Lady Mary," in *Connections: Early Links Between the Bahá'í Faith*

tive, at least in the early stages, in the campaign for Catholic Emancipation but later they had a falling out and became estranged.[9] He died suddenly in 1840 when he was at the pinnacle of his career.

The Sheils were another prominent Irish Catholic family of this period.[10] Justin Sheil was born in 1803, just a few miles outside Waterford city, on the County Kilkenny side of the River Suir. Justin's father, Edward, was a successful businessman who made his fortune in Spain. When changes to land legislation in the late eighteenth century extended the length of time a Catholic could hold a lease, Edward returned to Ireland and built a house on the banks of the Suir, downriver from the city of Waterford. *Bellevue* boasted magnificent views and was part of a picturesque landscape eulogized in Spenser's classic poem *The Faerie Queene*. The Sheils lived a life of privilege, though the children had an upbringing that was rigorous and disciplined. They had their own tutor in house (a refugee French priest) and their education was staunchly Catholic. The Sheils were domiciled at *Bellevue* until 1809 when, as a result of bad investments, Edward Sheil lost his fortune and the family had to sell the estate, moving to more modest accommodation in Dublin.[11]

Justin's elder brother, Richard Lalor Sheil, is more famous in Irish history. He was a prominent playwright, a close collaborator of "the Liberator" (as Daniel O'Connell was known in Ireland), and an ardent proponent of civil liberties. He was second only to O'Connell in the campaign for Catholic Emancipation in Ireland and when this was achieved in 1829 he soon after won a seat in Parliament where he distinguished himself as an orator of note. Richard later dropped out of the campaign to bring about further changes in the status quo in Ireland and became "Master of the Mint" in the Whig government in the late 1840s, being derided by some as an office seeker. He was embroiled in no small scandal when, during his tenure at the treasury, he was responsible for the production of a new florin coin, the equivalent of two old shillings. For reasons of space and simplicity the old refrains "Defender of the Faith" and "By God's Grace" were omitted from

---

and Ireland (Cork: TK Publications, 2007), 26. The Woulfes were clearly well integrated into local life by the nineteenth century. Stephen's mother was a McNamara.

9. Ibid., 26. See also Patrick M. Geoghegan, *King Dan: The Rise of Daniel O'Connell 1775-1829* (Dublin: Gill & MacMillan, 2008) for a review of O'Connell's quest for Catholic Emancipation.

10. It is thought that the Sheils were descended from the ancient *O'Siadhail* Ulster family. See Michael C. O'Laughlin, *Families of Co. Donegal, Ireland* (Kansas: Irish Roots Cafe, 2001), 117.

11. Information and quote from the McCullagh, *Richard Lalor Sheil*, 7. The French priest was a certain Abbé de Grineau from Languedoc.

under the Sovereign's likeness, creating quite a furor given Mr. Sheil's Catholic background and the Queen's position as Head of the Church of England. Though it was all rather an innocent set of circumstances, the new coin was soon dubbed the "godless" or "graceless" florin![12]

Justin Sheil was sent to Stonyhurst for his education before entering the East India Army in 1820 at the age of seventeen. He thus began his military and (eventually) diplomatic career which would see him reach the rank of captain by the age of twenty-seven and three years later become part of a body of officers commissioned to train the Persian Army. In 1836 he became Secretary to the British Legation in Tehran and in 1844 he succeeded Sir John McNeill as envoy and minister at the court of the Shah. All through this time he was rising through the ranks and ended his distinguished career a Lieutenant-General, as well as a Knight of the Realm.[13]

These families were linked by educational background, professionally and as prominent Irish Catholic families of their era, involved in the quest for Catholic Emancipation. A modern reading would probably see them characterized as "West Britons," given the anatomy of Irish identity constructed after the struggle for independence at the beginning of the twentieth century. The archetypal qualifications for being "Irish," in the new Ireland, included that one should be Gaelic-speaking, a peasant, living in the west of Ireland and Catholic. Some leading figures in the Irish revolution, in carving out this particular conception of ideal Irish identity, went so far as to denounce Jews, freemasons, and others whose cultures did not correspond to their ideal, implicitly Catholic, notion of society, holding views which resonated with those being expressed at that time in right-wing circles in France and other European countries.[14] The Sheils would hardly recognize themselves in the mirror of this retrospective "othering" in the construction of the new Ireland, but they were sufficiently attuned to issues of identity and religion in their service to government, and with respect to their place in society, to position themselves for the best possible beneficial outcome in their liaison with Persia, and to engage in a discourse that involved, ironically, "othering" of the Persian milieu they encountered.

12. See Sinead Strugeon, "Sheil, Richard Lalor," in James Mc Guire and and James Quinn, eds., *Dictionary of Irish Biography: From the Earliest Times to the Year 2002* (Cambridge: Cambridge University Press and Royal Irish Academy, 2009), vol. 8, 893–95.

13. See Wheeler, "Sheil, Sir Justin (1803–1871)," 171.

14. For this discussion I have drawn on Mary E. Daly, "Cultural and Economic Protection and Xenophobia in Independent Ireland, 1920s-1970s," in Borbála Farago and Moynagh Sullivan, eds., *Facing the Other: Interdisciplinary Studies on Race, Gender and Social Justice in Ireland* (Newcastle: Cambridge Scholars Publishing, 2008), 6–18.

Glimpses of Life and Manners in Persia

In 1847 Justin Sheil, then 44 years old, and Mary Woulfe, 22, were married while Justin was home on leave from his assignment and the couple set out for Persia together in August of 1849.[15] Lady Sheil's published record of their sojourn at the court of the Shah is presented as a diary account of the family's travels, first as husband, wife, and entourage, and returning with the addition of three young children born to Lady Sheil while there.[16] Additional notes on "Russia, Koords, Toorkomans, Nestorians, Khiva and Persia" are appended from the pen of Justin Sheil, probably to lend gravitas and gain acceptance for the volume once published. Without attempting a chapter by chapter analysis (and leaving aside almost entirely the Minister's appended notes), a recurring theme is readily discernible. Lady Sheil's descriptions seem to represent classic expressions of cultural "othering," a "stereotypical representation from a colonizing location."[17] Persia is a decayed land, requiring a civilizing influence. The position of women is intolerable and no proper rule of law extends protection or administers justice.[18] Persians are a "strange people,"[19] Lady Sheil avers, and the mortality amongst children is "immense, owing to neglect, ignorance and laziness."[20] She finds the government despotic and the people "a curious combination of bigotry and tolerance, or perhaps indifference."[21] Life is cruel and manners quite abhorrent and, on taking her leave of the Orient, she expresses full agreement with Morier that the "people are false, the soil is dreary and disease is in the climate."[22] The inference is clear. The burden for improving matters rests squarely on the shoulders of the English and it is only in the extension of the benefits of the British Empire that Persia will prosper.[23]

In discussing the history of Islam in America, GhaneaBassiri describes how – in constructing an idea of what it meant to be "American" in the nineteenth century – a variety of responses "conflated industrial progress, commercial capitalism, egalitarian and enlightenment ideals, science,

---

15. *Connections*, 26–27.

16. The party included, along with the Sheils, three Irish servants, one French, and the family pet, a terrier named Crab. See *Connections*, 27. The children were Frances (b.1850), Edward (b.1851) and Mary (b.1852). Ibid., 31.

17. Ghaderi, "'A Living Tableau of Queerness'": 130.

18. *Glimpses*, 145–47 and 168–69.

19. Ibid., 253.

20. Ibid., 149.

21. Ibid., 196 and 140.

22. Ibid., 289.

23. See, for example, Ibid., 164 where Lady Sheil explains the benefits to a village under the "protection" of the British Mission.

rationality, the white race and Protestant Christianity to argue for the superiority of Anglo-American, liberal Protestantism." He summarizes this as the conflation of race, religion and progress, while allowing that these were not seen, in the late nineteenth century, as distinct analytical categories which could be examined together in defining a specific national identity. It is, though, a useful template, he argues, in viewing how others sought to position their own identity in attempting to belong and lay claim to a share of the unfolding "American dream." A similar discourse, he contends, surrounded the attempts to justify European imperialism in Muslim countries and was used to legitimate the civilizing or modernizing project of colonization.[24] Lady Sheil's discourse and observations can, therefore, be located within the matrix of the conflation of race, religion, and progress, the predominant discourse justifying colonization. In this reading, Persia, its people and religion, are backward and European culture paramount. The account is intended to fix her reader's understanding of the orient/occident where western identity is superior and civilizing missions justified.[25] It paints "a queer tableau of Persia"[26] and provides for her readers a biased ethnography justifying the civilizing goals of the colonizer. It has further been described as a typical "gendered construction of the other Persian land,"[27] inviting colonial despoliation.[28]

English and Catholic

There are anomalies, though, deserving of consideration in applying this categorization. One anomaly is that Lady Sheil was, as highlighted at the outset, not English but Irish and overtly Catholic. In her diary, whilst not hiding her Catholicism, Lady Sheil does abjure her Irishness and identifies herself very definitely as English. She has "English ideas,"[29] lays claim to a reputation for "English probity"[30] and considers that she "must be the first Englishwoman

24. See Kambiz GhaneaBassiri, *A History of Islam in America* (New York: Cambridge University Press, 2010), 95–100. Persia was not of course a colony at this juncture but both the British and the Russians were vying for influence in what became known as the "Great Game." See Ghaderi, "'A Living Tableau of Queerness'": 126.

25. See Ghaderi, "'A Living Tableau of Queerness'": 129. Ghaderi draws on and cites Edward Said, *Orientalism* (London: Routledge, 1978), 22.

26. Ghaderi, "'A Living Tableau of Queerness'": 129.

27. Ibid., 130.

28. For an interesting discussion on analyzing discourse in the context in which it arises, see Kate Zebiri, "The Redeployment of Orientalist Themes in Islamophobia," *Studies in Contemporary Islam* 10 (2008): 1–43.

29. *Glimpses*, 212.

30. Ibid, 238

who has been in Mazendaran."[31] Her servants though are unmistakably Irish and "ignorant," as she describes them in reporting an incident when attending Mass being conducted by a Catholic Armenian clergyman, the Irish maids are scandalized to find the priest's wife and daughters in attendance.[32] Lady Sheil's reasons for positioning herself in this manner may be a response to what she experienced and observed in Ireland and purposefully designed so that her diary might be well received once published at the heart of the Empire. In other words, she sought to represent herself as outside her own colonized milieu, at least with respect to her nationality if not her religion.

Why she would feel the need to abnegate her nationality, but feel secure in publicly asserting her Catholicism, requires some explanation. In his exposition of how Irish people were regarded in Victorian Britain, and in particular how that view was represented in Victorian caricature, Curtis contends that Irish people were explicitly discriminated against on the basis of race as well as religion.[33] This racism applied, in his view, to Irish Catholic immigrants to Britain and to Irish Catholics still domiciled in Ireland. But, according to Curtis, the Victorian "Paddy" construct took on more than one guise and English caricaturists created a veritable "topography of Irish facial features"[34] as an expression of underlying racist intent. The most benign of these typologies was the tall muscular Northern Irish Protestant, in particular the loyal Ulsterman, who appeared in caricature as handsome with a high facial angle, almost resembling a respectable Englishman. The second type was the rustic small farmer or laborer, variously dubbed, Mick, Tim, Thady or Paddy. This was the dull, politically innocent, orthognathous Paddy, a figure of amusement for English tourists with his incessant, illogical line of conversation. This figure was politically neutral and regarded as more or less harmless. Thirdly, English cartoons portrayed the prognathous and somewhat hairy, unshaven, plebeian Irishman, definitely classified as "Paddy," a supporter of home Rule but not an advocate of violence. This Paddy's protrusive mouth and jaw did suggest a somewhat less than human figure, but he was still an object of some fun even when drunk and disor-

31. Ibid., 262.

32. See Ibid., 3 and 233.

33. See L. Perry Curtis Jr., *Apes and Angels: The Irishman in Victorian Caricature* (Washington, DC: Smithsonian Institution, 1997). For counter arguments see, for example, Graham Davis, "Little Irelands," in Roger Swift and Sheridan Gilley, eds., *The Irish in Britain* (London: Pinter, 1989), 104–33. Gilley is one of Curtis's main detractors, discounting race as an issue in discrimination of Irish people, contending that religion was the main factor. See his "English Attitudes to the Irish in England, 1789–1900," in Colin Holmes, ed., *Immigrants and Minorities in British Society* (London: George Allen and Unwin, 1978), 81–110.

34. Ibid., xxi.

derly. The forth basic type was a different representation altogether. Simian Paddy supported the use of force in the cause of Irish freedom from Britain. A cross between a dangerous ape and a primitive man he appeared with a hairy muzzle-like upper lip, concave nose, low facial angle and sharp teeth. Violent and bent on revenge for all the injustices visited upon his native land, simian Paddy appeared in the guise of a troglodyte.[35] In print there was a similar representation of Irish Catholics, as in Bretherton's diatribe which contains the following choice comments,

> The Irish as a race ... have no care for material possessions; they are inefficient and untrustworthy in business; they hate stable government and hate the law ... Unfortunately the man-eaters of Kerry and the Troglodytes of Tipperary are inspired to an even greater degree - being more completely Hibernian - by the same superabounding national conceit ... [which] drives the natives to murder. You have only to remember that the Hibernian proper has the slave mentality, and will act accordingly. He is a mixture of childishness and ferocity. He is basely superstitious, callous to suffering, credulous, excitable, thriftless, untruthful, dirty, pettily dishonest, destructive, cunning [sic] imitative, tortuous, devoid of moral courage, and intensely vain ...[36]

In short, the Irish are very much like Lady Sheil's Persians! Where Lady Sheil would have been located in this typology, had she "outed" herself as Irish, is not so readily discernible. Curtis does not provide us with a fifth classification, though one can be imagined, as occupied perhaps by loyal Irish Catholic landowners and figures such as O'Connell and his close supporters. Residing within this fifth declension (and however she might have appeared in caricature), one could conclude that Lady Sheil would not have escaped at least some of the opprobrium as expressed in these blatantly anti-Irish sentiments. What is of interest here is that, if this was the lens through which Irish Catholics were viewed at the heart of the Empire, it was not, as Curtis contends, how English Catholics were regarded. English Catholics, though regarded as inferior, were not as corrupt, immoral, superstitious and (significantly), politicized, as were Irish Catholics, the presumption being that Catholicism itself had been corrupted by the ignoble Paddy.[37] Lady Sheil makes no attempt to disguise her Catholicism and is careful to repre-

---

35. This is a synopsis of Curtis's analysis of how Irishmen appeared in caricature in Victorian publications. Ibid., xxi-xxii.

36. C.H. Bretherton, *The Real Ireland: 1878-1939* (London: A.C Black, 1925), 2, 13, 32 and 46, quoted in Curtis, Jr., *Apes and Angels: The Irishman in Victorian Caricature*, 115.

37. Ibid.,115 and 191 n190.

sent herself as English and Catholic within the pages and in the publication of her travelogue. Set against the conflation of race, religion and progress, Lady Sheil positions herself towards the outer edges of what might be accepted. Her relative youth was no bar to her adoption of a sophisticated, nuanced self-representation, but can be easily understood in the context of the political/religious tapestry of her background.

Critique of Empire

It is clear that religion played a central role in the life of the Sheil family, not only in their family background, formation and the involvement of their families with the quest for Catholic Emancipation. The family's religiosity is evidenced by the fact that, in later times, two of the ten Sheil children entered Catholic orders as nuns, another became a religious brother and one a priest.[38] While in Persia, Lady Sheil was acutely aware of matters religious and was concerned that the family could access Catholic rites.[39] Her observations on religion in Persia, which are many in her narrative, are therefore of great interest and more so for being more than a little contradictory. For all her "othering" of Persia and Persians she makes some strident statements about religious freedom and practice amongst the Muslim populace. She finds "Freedom of speech in Persia ... on an equality with freedom of religion."[40] Attending a dramatic Ashura presentation (depicting the martyrdom of the Imam Hussein which she describes in great detail), Lady Sheil finds herself impelled to join in the weeping of the other attendees.[41] At another time she allows that the Muezzin's call to prayer excites a "combination of feelings, of dignity, solemnity, and devotion, compared with which the din of bells becomes insignificant," and she juxtaposes this against the "solemn awe" inspired by the "keening as it sweeps afar over the dales and hills of Munster, announcing a Gael has been gathered to his fathers."[42] Even so, she concludes, the call to prayer is an imposing thing to hear ... St. Peter's and St. Paul's together can produce nothing equal to it."[43] She goes farther

38. Honor, Grace, Justin, and Denis. Fr. Denis Sheil was the last novice ordained by Cardinal Newman and later Superior of Newman's Oratory in Birmingham. See *Connections*, 33. Another son, Edward Sheil (born in Persia in 1851), was an Irish nationalist MP for many years. See *Irish Times* 7 July 1915, at http://0search.proquest.com.library.ucc.ie/hnpirishtimes/docview /515979575/131D1D757337483B70A/1?accountid=14504, accessed on 15 September 2011 at 9.00am.

39. See, for instance, *Glimpses*, 210 and 233.

40. Ibid., 200.

41. Ibid., 125–30.

42. Ibid., 85.

43. Ibid., 85.

with a comment on equality of opportunity, using for an example the then Prime Minister, the Amir-Nezām, Mirza Taqi Khan (d.1852),

> ... in Persia and other Mahommedan countries there is a large fund of personal equality, and obscurity of descent is not an obstacle to advancement.[44]

Set against her other scathing assessments, one is tempted to conclude that these comments are more an oblique criticism of the position of her own religious faith in the Empire (perhaps even in her own homeland) and indeed a criticism of Empire itself, over and against the position she adopts within the paradigm of contemporary discourse as suggested by GhaneaBassiri's matrix of conflation.[45] Lady Sheil's critique is not in the same vein as the type of counter-Orientalist or anti-imperialist discourse variously engaged in by Blunt and Browne; her criticisms are more subtle and insinuated from the cover of an established identification with one side of a binary orientalist discourse and are proffered within the purlieus of a commentary on religion and religious matters.[46]

Another example of this underlying critique of empire is found in Lady Sheil's descriptions concerning the episode of the Bab and the Babi upheavals.[47] Her recounting of the story is broadly sympathetic, if containing a number of factual inaccuracies, repeating some of the general misconceptions concerning the Bab and his followers current at the time.[48] She describes the Babis as an "amiable sect"[49] and the Bab as a "celebrated person."[50] She writes that the Bab's execution "was on the point of becoming a most remarkable event, which would probably have overturned the throne and Islamism in Persia,"[51] owing to the mysterious circumstances attending the aborted first attempt to carry out the deed. She goes on to recount events following the attempt on the life of the Shah by three young Babis in 1852, and the subsequent pogrom that resulted in wholesale executions of

44. Ibid., 201.

45. I am grateful to Farah Ghaderi for discussions that developed these points.

46. On Blunt, Browne, and others see Geoffrey Nash "Politics, Aesthetics and Quest in British Travel Writing on the Middle East," in Tim Youngs, ed., *Travel Writing in the Nineteenth Century: Filling the Blank Spaces* (London: Anthem Press, 2006), 55–65.

47. *Glimpses*, Ch.XI, 171–81 and 273–82. In her diary, Lady Sheil also comments on Sunnism (84–85) and Zoroastrians ("Gebrs")(Ch. IX).

48. See Moojan Momen, ed., *The Bábí and Bahá'í Religions, 1844-1944: Some Contemporary Western Accounts* (Oxford: George Ronald, 1981), 5.

49. *Glimpses*, 176.

50. Ibid., 176.

51. Ibid., 177–78. See also Shoghi Effendi, trans. and ed., *The Dawn-Breakers: Nabíl's Narrative of the Early Days of the Bahá'í Revelation* (Wilmette: US Bahá'í Publishing Trust, 1932), 501–20.

Babis, some of whom were given over to "different departments of state"[52] to be dispatched in a variety of inventively cruel ways. Even the court doctor [Ernest] Cloquet, Lady Sheil recalls, was invited to show his loyalty by taking part but excused himself with the retort that he "had killed too many people professionally to permit him to increase their number by any voluntary homicide on his part."[53] The fate of the celebrated Babi poetess, Qurrat al-'Ayn, is also included in Lady Sheil's chronicle of these events and her execution is described as a "cruel and useless deed."[54] It is perhaps in her final summation, recounting that the Babis had garnered some popular sympathy for their fate, that Lady Sheil expresses her most overt critique of the status quo in Britain. "It thus appears," she writes, "that *even in Persia,* a vague undefined feeling of liberality in religion is taking root."[55]

Sources and Gender

Lady Sheil was, of course, greatly circumscribed as a woman in making direct contact with Persians and her travelogue relies to a great extent on second-hand information, through her husband (the Minister), from the household staff, and from expatriate visitors to the Mission. For her information on the story of the Bāb, for example, she borrowed greatly from her husband's diplomatic dispatches to the Foreign Office in London. There are some details that are not taken from this source, including her pen-picture of the Bab.[56] Interestingly, from the perspective of socio-cultural links between Persia and Ireland, it has been suggested that her description of the Bab was communicated to her by a certain Dr. William Cormick, who was domiciled in Tabriz at the time of these events and who attended the Bab on a number of occasions, in his capacity as a physician, both before and following the Bab's interrogation and bastinadoing in Tabriz in 1848.[57] Cormick was the son of an Irishman from County Kilkenny, Dr. John Cormick (from a Catholic family), who arrived in Persia in 1810 in the second mission of Sir John Malcolm.[58] Like his father before him, William was seconded as physician to the fam-

---

52. *Glimpses,* 277.

53. Ibid., 278. The said doctor was later poisoned in mysterious circumstances having drunk from a bottle of liquor provided by a servant which caused his demise some ten days later.

54. Ibid., 281. See also Sabir Afaqi, ed., *Tahirih in History: Perspectives on Qurratu'l Ayn from East and West* (Los Angeles: Kalimat Press, 2004).

55. Ibid., 282. Emphasis added.

56. *The Bábí and Bahá'í Religions,* 9.

57. *Glimpses,* 176 and 178.

58. *Connections,* 5.

ily of Abbās Mirza and later to the family of the Crown Prince, Nāser al-Din Mirza, the future Nāser al-Din Shah. When the crown-prince was appointed Governor of Azerbaijan in 1847, Cormick went with him. He did not return to the capital on the prince's accession to the throne, being replaced in his role as family physician to the new Shah by the Frenchman, Cloquet.[59] In a letter Cormick wrote to a friend he contains a similar portrayal of the Bab as that of Lady Sheil, composed from his own first-hand encounters.[60] Cormick has left no corpus of papers or records (that we know of) from which we might discern his views with respect to culture and life in Persia and no correspondence with the Sheils is extant. It is, though, of interest to us that another person of Irish background living in Persia was most likely in communication with Lady Sheil during her sojourn, from whom she garnered some of the information contained in her diary, and that both found themselves in the maelstrom of momentous events.

Lady Sheil did make efforts to learn Persian and, by her own account, acquired sufficient proficiency to allow her to have direct communication with a few Persian ladies whom she would occasionally visit.[61] On two occasions she had tea with the Queen Mother, visited various female relatives of the Shah and was invited to call on the wife of the Prime Minister.[62] On one visit to the palace, the Queen Mother gave her a tour of various inner apartments during which they encountered the Shah, unattended, seated in a garden. After a convivial conversation, the Shah himself conducted the party to view the new portions of the royal complex of which, it is said, he was greatly proud.[63] Lady Sheil's interviews do open an insight into the position or role of women close to the government of Persia at that time. To some extent the women she met are represented in terms of the colonizing stereotype, as "locked in the matrix of oriental constructions."[64] They appear as voiceless, frivolous, and eroticized. In accessing areas no male travel writer of her time could hope to enter, Lady Sheil does adopt what can be described as a masculine stance and observes with an "imperial gaze,"[65] but

59. Ibid., 7. There are a number of Cormick family graves in the Armenian cemetery in Tabriz though William retired to England and died there in 1873. Cormick is known to have been in Ireland to visit relatives in 1841 (personal communication from Cormick's great-granddaughter, Mrs. Vicky Uffindell).

60. *The Bábí and Bahá'í Religions*, 74–82.; *Connections*, 1–21. Cormick was the only person of European background known to have met and spoken to the Bab. See *The Dawn-Breakers*, Introduction, xxxi-xxxiii.

61. *Glimpses*, 124.

62. Ibid., 131, 134, 202, and 284.

63. Ibid., 202.

64. Ghaderi, "'A Living Tableau of Queerness'": 133.

65. Ibid.

not entirely. The Queen Mother is recognized as being very clever and is "supposed to take a large share in the affairs of government."[66] The Grand Vizier's wife, whom Lady Sheil met prior to her departure from Persia, is not only remarkably intelligent but also "highly esteemed and respected."[67] Lady Sheil finds the few Persian women she became acquainted with generally lively and clever, "restless and intriguing,"[68] able managers of their husband's and son's affairs, though the instrument of their influence, she avers, is "incessant talking and teasing."[69] There is here a hint of an alternative paradigm for the position of women in the upper echelons of Persian society.[70]

Glimpses Reviewed

A lengthy review of Lady Sheil's travelogue, which appeared in a magazine published in late 1856, gives us some indication as to how her exposition was received in London.[71] At first fairly flattering, the review slowly begins to take Lady Sheil to task; for her stark description of the Persian landscape which must be an exaggeration resulting from ennui or discomfort while traveling;[72] for her lack of understanding with respect to the difference between Sunni and Shia; and for her over-estimation of the progeny of Fath Ali Shah. Momentum is built until her account of Agha Mohammad Khan, which highlights how the ruler's ferocity was tempered with a solicitous, benign behavior towards his subjects, is enough to convince the reviewer that the paragraph has been "penned by someone under Dr. Conoly's care at Hanwell," Conoly being a well-known Victorian psychiatrist and Hanwell his asylum near London.[73] Interestingly, nowhere in the review is she described as Irish though her husband the Minister is, when a paragraph contained in his "Notes" (appended to the travelogue) is cited and derided as having only possibly been penned by "someone suckled on the Emerald Isle."[74] She is,

66. *Glimpses*, 131.

67. Ibid., 284.

68. Ibid., 134.

69. Ibid.

70. See Charles Forsdick, "Hidden journeys: Gender, genre and twentieth-century travel literature in French," in Jane Conroy, ed., *Cross-Cultural Travel: Papers from the Royal Irish Academy Symposium on Literature and Travel* (Galway: National University of Ireland, 2002), 315–23.

71. *Fraser's Magazine for Town and Country*, Vol. 54 (December 1856): 220–30. Unattributed.

72. Ibid., 223.

73. See Andrew Scull, *Social Order / Mental Disorder: Anglo-American Psychiatry in Historical Perspective* (Berkeley: University of California Press, 1989), 164–213.

74. *Fraser's Magazine for Town and Country*: 229.

though, chided for her "Romanistic zeal"[75] in comparing Catholic Lent to the Muslim Ramadan. Having succeeded in avoiding any anti-Irish backlash, and experiencing only a relatively mild rebuke for her Catholicism, Lady Sheil is excoriated for something she might have foreseen would stand against her in her new-found role as a published commentator on the Orient; she is put down because she is a woman. The review continues,

> Lady Sheil will forgive us – like a good wife – when we say that the most valuable portion of her book is the 'Additional Notes' by her husband ...

And even then, the Minister's contributions (our anonymous critic concludes), "merit a separate paper and an abler pen"! The reviewer's parting description of the narrative as a "pleasant volume"[76] is of little compensatory value.

Conclusion

Lady Sheil's travelogue can be seen as a typical example of orientalist, Victorian travel writing, culturally and racially "othering" her adopted milieu. Her position as wife of the British Minister to Tehran, at a time when Britain was maneuvering for increased influence in Persia, renders her position far from neutral and her *Glimpses of Life and Manners* can be understood as an attempt to fix her reader's acceptance for the need of a civilizing intervention in that country. Factors that have not been considered previously do bear on her narrative, and a nuanced criticism of empire can be discerned as an outcome of a combination of influences relating to her own national and religious identity. Her "Irishness" and Catholic faith, in particular, need to be considered when assessing her contribution to the discourse of the time, which can be described in terms of GhaneaBassiri's matrix of the conflation of race, religion, and progress. In the end she provides us with a fascinating occasion of socio-cultural interaction between Persia and Ireland in the mid-nineteenth century.[77]

75. Ibid., 229.
76. Ibid., 230.
77. Lady Sheil died near Dublin in the year 1869, aged forty-four, and is interred in Glasnevin cemetery O'Connell Gardens section, grave D82.

Bibliography

[Mirzā Abu Tāleb Khān Esfahāni]. *Masir-e Tālebi, yā safarnāmeh-ye Mirzā Abu Tāleb Khān*. Edited by Hoseyn Khadiv Jam. Tehran: Sherkat-e sahāmi-ye ketābhā-ye jibi, 1973.

Afaqi, Sabir, ed. *Tahirih in History: Perspectives on Qurratu'l Ayn from East and West*. Los Angeles: Kalimát Press, 2004.

Ahl, Frederick. "Uilix Mac Leirtis: the Classical Hero in Irish Metamorphosis." In *The Art of Translation: Voices from the Field*. Edited by Rosanna Warren. Boston: Northeastern University Press, 1989: 173–98.

Aʿlam, Hūšang. "Crane." *Encyclopaedia Iranica* 6 (1993): 398.

Amanat, Abbas. *Resurrection and Renewal: The Making of the Babi Movement in Iran, 1844-1850*. Ithaca, NY: Cornell University Press, 1989.

Anklesaria, Behramgore Tehmuras, ed. and trans. *Zand-Ākāsīh: Iranian or Greater Bundahišn*. Bombay: Rahnumae Mazdayasnan Sabha, 1956.

Ansari, Abdul Haq. "Ibn ʿArabī: The Doctrine of *Wahdat al-Wujūd*." *Islamic Studies* 38:2 (1999): 149–92.

Anvar, Leili. "The Radiance of Epiphany: The Vision of Beauty and Love in Hafiz's Poem of Pre-Eternity." In *Hafiz and the Religion of Love in Classical Persian Poetry*. Edited by Leonard Lewisohn. London: I. B. Tauris, 2010, 123–39.

Ashman Rowe, Elisabeth. *Vikings in the West: The Legend of Ragnarr Loðbrók and His Sons*. Studia Medievalia Septentrionalia 18. Vienna: Fassbaender, 2012.

Atherton, James S. *The Books at the Wake: A Study of Literary Allusions in James Joyce's Finnegans Wake*. Mamaroneck, NY: P. P. Appel, 1974.

Aubert, Jacques Aubert. "Lacan and the Joyce-Effect." *Joyce Studies in Italy* 1 New Series/14 Old Series (2013): 79–88.

The Bab, Seyyed Ali Mohammad Shirāzi. *The Báb. Bayán-i Fársí*. Tehran: Azali Publication, 1946. Available online at htp://www.h-net.org/~bahai/areprint/bab/G-L/I/INBA62.pdf.

The Bab, Seyyed Ali Mohammad Shirāzi. *Montakhabāt-e āyāt az āthār-e Ḥaḍrat-e Noqteh-ye Ulā*. Chandigarh: Carmel Publishers, 2007.

The Báb, Sayyed ʿAlí Muhammad Shírází. *Selections from the Writings of the Báb*. Haifa: Bahá'í World Centre, 1976.

Bahá'í Prayers: A Selection of Prayers Revealed by Bahá'u'lláh, The Báb, and 'Abdu'l-Bahá. Wilmette, IL: Baha'i Publishing Trust, 1982.

Ballantyne, Tony. *Orientalism and Race: Aryanism in the British Empire* (Houndmills: Palgrave, 2002).

Balsamo, Gian. *Joyce's Messianism: Dante, Negative Existence, and the Messianic Self*. Columbia:University of South Carolina Press,2004.

Baudelaire, Charles. "The Salon of 1845." In *The Art of Paris 1845-1862: Salons and Other Exhibitions Reviewed by Charles Baudelaire*. Edited and translated by Jonathan Mayne. Oxford: Phaidon Press, 1965, 1-32.

Bayat, Mangol. *Mysticism and Dissent: Socioreligious Thought in Qajar Iran*. Syracuse: Syracuse University Press, 1982.

Bazargan, Susan. "W. B. Yeats: Autobiography and Colonialism." *Yeats: An Annual of Critical and Textual Studies* 13 (1995): 201-24.

Beja, Morris. "Epiphany and the Epiphanies." In *A Companion to Joyce Studies*. Edited by Zack Bowen and James F. Carens. Westport, CT: Greenwood Press, 1984: 707-725.

Bergin, Osborn and R. I. Best, ed. and trans. "Tochmarc Étaín." *Ériu* 12 (1934-8): 137-96.

Berlin, Isaiah. *The Roots of Romanticism*. Princeton: Princeton University Press, 1999.

Best, Richard, ed. and trans. "The Adventures of Art Son of Conn, and the Courtship of Delbchaem." *Ériu* 3 (1907): 149-73.

Bhabha, Homi. *The Location of Culture*. London and New York: Routledge, 1994.

Bicknell, Herman. *Háfiz of Shíráz: Selections from His Poems*. London: Trübner, 1875.

Biegstraaten, Jos. "Khayyam, Omar xi. Impact on Literature and Society in the West." *Encyclopaedia Iranica*.

Bishop, John. *Joyce's Book of the Dark, Finnegans Wake*. Madison, WI: University of Wisconsin Press, 1986.

Boedeker, Deborah. *Aphrodite's Entry into Greek Epic*. Leiden: Brill, 1974.

Bonakdarian, Mansour. "Iranian Studies in the United Kingdom in the Twentieth Century." *Iranian Studies* 43:2 (2010): 265-93.

———. "Erin and Iran Resurgent: Irish Nationalists and Iranian Constitutional Revolution." In Iran's *Constitutional Revolution: Politics, Cultural Transformations and Transnational Connections*. Edited by H. E. Chehabi and Vanessa Martin. London: I. B. Tauris, 2010, 291-318 and 467-76.

———. "Iranian Nationalism and Global Solidarity Networks 1906-18: Transnationalism, Globalization, and Nationalist Cosmopolitanism." In *Iran in the Middle East: Transnational Encounters and Social History*. Edited by H. E. Chehabi, Peyman Jafari and Maral Jefroudi. London: I. B. Tauris, 2015, 77-119.

Bowen, Zack R. and James F. Carens, eds. *A Companion to Joyce Studies*. Westport, CT: Greenwood Press, 1984.

Böwering, Gerhard. *The Mystical Vision of Existence in Classical Islam: The Qur'anic Hermeneutics of the Sufi Sahl At-Tustari (d. 283/896)*. Berlin: de Gruyter, 1980.

Boyce, Mary 1984. *Textual Sources for the Study of Zoroastrianism*. Manchester: Manchester University Press.

Breatnach, Caoimhin. "The Transmission and Text of *Tóruigheacht Dhiarmada agus Ghráinne*: A Re-Appraisal." In *The Gaelic Finn Tradition*. Edited by Sharon J. Arbuthnot and Geraldine Parson. Dublin: Four Courts, 2012, 139–50.

Bretherton, C. H. *The Real Ireland: 1878-1939*. London: A. C. Black, 1925.

Brown, Norman O. "The Apocalypse of Islam." *Social Text* 8 (1984 - Winter 1983): 155–71.

[Burrage, Charles Dana, ed.] *Twenty Years of the Omar Khayyám Club of North America*. [Boston]: Rosemary Press, 1921.

Bushrui, Suheil and Bernard Benstock, eds. *James Joyce, an International Perspective: Centenary Essays in Honour of the Late Sir Desmonde Cochrane*. Irish Literary Studies 10. Gerrards Cross, Buckinghamshire & Totowa, NJ: C. Smythe; Barnes and Noble Books, 1982.

Bushrui, Suheil. "Joyce in the Arab World." In *James Joyce, an International Perspective: Centenary Essays in Honour of the Late Sir Desmonde Cochrane*. Edited by Suheil Bushrui and Bernard Benstock. Irish Literary Studies 10. Gerrards Cross, Buckinghamshire & Totowa, NJ: C. Smythe ; Barnes and Noble Books, 1982: 232–237.

——. "Yeats's Arabic Interests." In *In Excited Reverie: A Centenary Tribute*. Edited by A. Norman Jeffares and K. G. W. Cross. London: Macmillan, 1965, 280–314.

Calder, George, ed. and trans. *Imtheachta Aeniasa: the Irish Aeneid*. London: Irish Texts Society, 1907.

Campanile, Enrico. "Old Irish Bóand." *Journal of Indo-European Studies* 12 (1985): 477–9.

——. *La ricostruzione della cultura indoeuropea*. Pisa: Giardini, 1990.

Campbell, Bruce F. *Ancient History Revived: A History of the Theosophical Movement*. Berkeley: University of California Press, 1980.

Campbell, David, ed. and trans. *Greek Lyric*. 5 vols. Cambridge: Harvard University Press, 1982–93.

Campbell, Joseph and Henry Morton Robinson. *A Skeleton Key to Finnegans Wake: Unlocking James Joyce's Masterwork*. Novato, CA: New World Library, 2005 [first published 1944].

Card, James Van Dyck. *An Anatomy of "Penelope".* Rutherford, NJ: Fairleigh Dickinson University Press & London: Associated University Presses, 1984.

Card, James Van Dyck. "'Contradicting': The Word for Joyce's 'Penelope'." *James Joyce Quarterly* 11:1 (October 1, 1973): 17–26.

Carey, John. "Myth and Mythography in *Cath Maige Tuired*." *Studia Celtica* 24–5 (1989–90): 53–69.

——. "Eithne in Gubai." *Éigse* 28 (1995): 160–4.

Catana, Leo. "The Coincidence of Opposites: Cusanian and Non-Cusanian Interpretations." *Bruniana & Campanelliana* 17:2 (2011): 381–400.

Clarke, H. Wilberforce, trans. *The Dīvān-i Hāfiz.* Bethesda, MD: Ibex, 1998.

Cohen, David. "Suibhne Geilt." *Celtica* 12 (1976): 113–24.

Cole, Juan Ricardo. *Modernity and the Millennium: The Genesis of the Baha'i Faith in the Nineteenth-Century Middle East.* New York: Columbia University Press, 1998.

Conroy, Jane, ed. *Cross-cultural Travel: Papers from the Royal Irish Academy Symposium on Literature and Travel.* Galway: National University of Ireland, 2002.

Cook, Arthur. "The Cretan Axe-cult outside Crete." *Transactions of the Third International Congress for the History of Religions.* 2 vols. Edited by Percy Allen and John de Monins Johnson. Oxford: Clarendon Press, 1908: 2.184–94.

Corbin, Henry. *En Islam iranien: aspects spirituels et philosophiques.* 4 vols. Paris: Éditions Gallimard, 1971–72.

Cullingford, Elizabeth Butler. *Gender and History in Yeats's Love Poetry.* Cambridge: Cambridge University Press, 1993.

Curtis Jr., L. Perry. *Apes and Angels: The Irishman in Victorian Caricature.* Washington, DC: Smithsonian Institution, 1997.

Dāneshvar, Simin. *Savushun,* 9th ed. Tehran: Khārazmi, 1357 [1978].

Daneshvar, Simin, translated by M. R. Ghanoonparvar. *Savushun: A Novel about Modern Iran.* Washington, DC: Mage Publishers, 1990.

Darmesteter, James, trans. *The Zend-Avesta.* 3 vols. Oxford: Clarendon Press, 1880–87.

Daryaee, Touraj. "Kāve the Black-Smith: An Indo-Iranian Fashioner?" *Studien zur Indologie und Iranistik* 22 (2001): 9–21.

Davidson, Olga. *Poet and Hero in the Persian Book of Kings.* 3rd edition. Boston: Ilex Foundation, distributed by Harvard University Press, 2013.

——. *Comparative Literature and Classical Persian Poetics: Seven Essays.* 2nd edition. Boston: Ilex Foundation, distributed by Harvard University Press, 2013.

———. "Persian/Iranian Epic." In *A Companion to Ancient Epic*. Edited by J. M. Foley. Oxford/Malden MA: Blackwell, 2005: 264–276.

Davis, Dick. *The Rubaiyat of Omar Khayyam: Translated by Edward FitzGerald*. London: Penguin, 1989.

———. *Panthea's Children: Hellenistic Novels and Medieval Persian Romances*. New York: Bibliotheca Persica, December 2002.

———, tr. *Shahnameh: The Persian Book of Kings* (by Abolqāsem Ferdowsi). New York: Viking, 2006.

———. Introduction to the translation of Fakhraddin Gorgani's *Vis and Ramin*. London: Penguin Classics, 2009), xxi-xxiv.

Dehbāshi, Ali, ed. *Safarnāmeh-ye Hāj Sayyāh beh Farang*. Tehran: Nashr-e Nāsher, 1363 [1984].

Dervin, Fred. "Cultural Identity, Representation, and Othering." In *Routledge Handbook of Intercultural Communication*. Edited by John Jackson. London: Routledge, 2011.

Denham, Robert. *Northrop Frye : Religious Visionary and Architect of the Spiritual World*. Charlottesville: University of Virginia Press, 2004.

Dobbs, Margaret, ed. and trans. "Altromh Tighi da Medar." *Zeitschrift für celtische Philologie* 18 (1930): 189–230.

Drachmann, Anders, ed. *Scholia vetera in Pindari carmina*. 3 vols. Leipzig: Teubner, 1903–27.

Dumézil, Georges. *Horace et les Curiaces*. Paris: Gallimard, 1942.

———. *Servius et la Fortune: essai sur la fonction sociale de louange et de blâme et sur les éléments indo-européens du cens romain*. Paris: Gallimard, 1943.

———. *Mythe et épopée*. 3 vols. Paris: Gallimard, 1968–73.

———. *Heur et malheur du guerrier: aspects mythiques de la fonction guerrière chez les Indo-Européens*. Paris: Presses Universitaires de France, 1969.

Dunbabin, Thomas. *The Western Greeks*. Oxford: Clarendon Press, 1948.

Duncan, Lilian, ed. and trans. "Altram Tige Dá Medar." *Ériu* 11 (1932): 184–225.

Eco, Umberto. *The Aesthetics of Chaosmos: The Middle Ages of James Joyce*. Cambridge, MA: Harvard University Press, 1989.

Ellmann, Richard. "The Backgrounds of Ulysses." *The Kenyon Review* 16:3 (1 July 1954): 337–386.

———. *Yeats: The Man and the Masks*. London: Faber and Faber, 1961.

———. *James Joyce*. New and rev. ed. New York: Oxford University Press, 1982.

Erdődi, József. "Finnische *sampo*, Ai. *skambha*." *Indogermanische Forschungen* 3 (1932): 214–19.

Ernst, Carl W. *The Shambhala Guide to Sufism*. Boston and London: Shambhala, 1997.

Farago, Borbála and Sullivan, Moynagh, eds. *Facing the Other: Interdisciplinary Studies on Race, Gender and Social Justice in Ireland*. Newcastle: Cambridge Scholars Publishing, 2008.

Faraone, Christopher. *Talismans and Trojan Horses: Guardian Statues in Ancient Greek Myth and Ritual*. Oxford: Oxford University Press, 1992.

———. "Rushing into Milk: New Perspectives on the Gold Tablets." In *The "Orphic" Gold Tablets and Greek Religion: Further Along the Path*. Edited by Radcliffe Edmonds. Cambridge: Cambridge University Press, 2011: 310–30.

Fargnoli, Nicholas A. and Michael Patrick Gillespie. *Critical Companion to James Joyce: A Literary Reference to His Life and Works*. New York, NY: Facts on File, 2006.

Farzād, Mas'ud. *Jāme'-e Nosakh-e Hāfez*. Shiraz: Enteshārāt-e Dāneshgāh-e Pahlavi, Kānun-e Jahāni-ye Hāfez-Shenāsi, 1347/1968.

Fischer, Michael H. *The First Indian Author in English: Dean Mahomed (1959-1851) in India, Ireland, and England*. Delhi: Oxford University Press, 1996.

Fisher, Michael H. *Counterflows to Colonialism: Indian Travellers and Settlers in Britain 1600-1857*. Delhi: Permanent Black, 2004.

FitzGerald, Edward. *Rubáiyát of Omar Khayyám*. Edinburgh and London: Foulis, 1905.

Flavius Philostratus, Heroikos, translated by Jennifer K. Berenson Maclean and Ellen Bradshaw Aitken. Atlanta: Society of Biblical Literature, 2001.

Ford, Patrick. "The Well of Nechtan and 'La Gloire Lumineuse'." In *Myth in Indo-European Antiquity*. Edited by Gerald James Larson. Berkeley: University of California Press, 1974: 67–74.

———, ed. *Math uab Mathonwy*. Belmont: Ford and Bailie, 1999.

Foster, Roy F. *W. B. Yeats: A Life - Vol. 1: The Apprentice Mage, 1865-1914*. New York and Oxford: Oxford University Press, 1997.

Fox, Richard G. "East of Said." In *Edward Said: A Critical Reader*. Edited by Michael Spinkler. Oxford: Blackwell, 1992, 144–56.

Fragner, Bert G. *Die Persophonie: Regionalität, Identität und Sprachkontakt in der Geschichte Asiens*. Berlin: Das Arabische Buch, 1999.

Frame, Douglas. *The Myth of Return in Early Greek Epic*. New Haven: Yale University Press, 1978.

Frye, Northrop, in *The American Scholar* 30:4 (Autumn 1961): 606.

———. *The Educated Imagination*. Bloomington: Indiana University Press, 1964.

———. *Anatomy of Criticism*. Princeton: Princeton University Press, 1973.

———. *The Great Code: Bible and Literature*. New York & London: Harcourt Brace Jovanovic, 1982.

———. "Cycle and Apocalypse in *Finnegans Wake*." In *Myth and Metaphor: Selected Essays, 1974-1988*. Edited by Robert Denham. Charlottesville and London: University Press of Virginia, 1990: 356–374.

———. *Words with Power: Being a Second Study of the Bible and Literature*. New York: Viking, 1990.

Gallais, Pierre. *Genèse du roman occidental: Essais sur Tristan et Iseut et son modèle persan*. Paris: Tête de feuilles, 1974.

Geoghegan, Patrick M. *King Dan: The Rise of Daniel O'Connell 1775-1829*. Dublin: Gill & MacMillan, 2008.

Ghaderi, Farah. "'A Living Tableau of Queerness'": A Postcolonial Study of Lady Sheil's Travel Account on Persia." *Journal of Teaching English Language and Literature Society of Iran* 2 (2008): 123–43.

Ghaemmaghami, Omid. "The Báb's journey to the Kaaba." In *A Most Noble Pattern: Collected Essays on the Writings of the Báb, Sayyid 'Alí Muhammad Shírází*. Edited by Todd Lawson and Omid Ghaemmaghami. Oxford: George Ronald, 2011: 175–195.

GhaneaBassiri, Kambiz. *A History of Islam in America*. New York: Cambridge University Press, 2010.

Ghanoonparvar, M. R. *In a Persian Mirror: Images of the West and Westerners in Iranian Fiction*. Austin: University of Texas Press, 1993.

Gignoux, Philippe and Ahmad Tafazzoli, ed. and trans. *Anthologie de Zādspram: Édition critique du texte pehlevi*. Paris: Association pour l'avancement des études iraniennes, 1993.

Gilbert, Robert G. *The Golden Dawn Scrapbook: The Rise and Fall of a Magical Order*. York Beach, Maine: Samuel Weiser, 1997.

Gillespie, Michael Patrick. *The Aesthetics of Chaos: Nonlinear Thinking and Contemporary Literary Criticism*. Gainesville, FL: University Press of Florida, 2003.

Glasheen, Adaline. *A Census of Finnegans Wake: An Index of the Characters and Their Roles*. London: Faber and Faber, 1957.

Goethe, Johann Wolfgang von. *West-östlicher Diwan*. Leipzig: Insel-Verlag, 1937.

Goodrick-Clarke, Nicholas. "3. The Dublin Hermetic Societies (1885–1939)." In *Dictionary of Gnosis and Western Esotericism*. Edited by Wouter J. Hanegraaff. Leiden: Brill, 2006, 555–58.

Gorski, William T. *Yeats and Alchemy*. Albany: State University of New York Press, 1996.

Graham, Brian, ed. *In Search of Ireland: A Cultural Geography*. London: Routledge, 1997.

Gray, Elizabeth, ed. and trans. *Cath Maige Tuired: The Second Battle of Mag Tuired*. Naas: Irish Texts Society, 1982.

Gruffydd, William, ed. and trans. *Math vab Mathonwy.* Cardiff: University of Wales Press, 1928.

Günther, Sebastian. "Day, Times of." In *Encyclopaedia of the Qur'an.* Edited by Jane Dammen McAuliffe. Leiden: Brill Academic Publishers, 2001, vol. 1: 499–504.

———. "Muhammad, the Illiterate Prophet: An Islamic Creed in the Qur'an and Qur'anic Exegesis." *Journal of Qur'anic Studies* 4:1 (2002): 1–26.

Gwynn, Edward, ed. and trans. *The Metrical Dindsenchas.* 5 vols. Dublin: Academy House, 1903–35.

———. "An Old-Irish Tract on the Privileges and Responsibilities of Poets." *Ériu* 13 (1942): 1–60, 220–36.

H. F. N. [?]. "Review of M. Mansoor: *The Story of Irish Orientalism.*" *The Dublin Magazine* 20:4 (1945): 60.

Hagan, Edward A. "Aryan Myth: a Nineteenth-Century Anglo-Irish Will to Power." In *Ideology and Ireland in the Nineteenth Century.* Edited by Tadgh Foley and Seán Fole. Dublin and Portland, OR: Four Courts Press, 1998, 197-205.

Halliday, Fred. "Orientalism and Its Critics." *British Journal of Middle Eastern Studies* 20:2 (1993): 145–63.

Hanaway, William L. "Persian Travel Narratives: Notes Toward the Definition of a Nineteenth-Century Genre." In *Society and Culture in Qajar Iran: Studies in Honor of Hafez Farmayan,* Edited by Elton L. Daniel. Costa Mesa, CA: Mazda, 2002: 249–268.

Harper, Prudence. "The Ox-headed Mace in Pre-Islamic Iran." *Acta Iranica* 24 (1985): 247–59.

Hart, Clive. *A Concordance to Finnegan's Wake.* Minneapolis: University of Minnesota Press, 1963.

Haudry, Jean. *La religion cosmique des Indo-Européens."* Paris: Les Belles Lettres, 1987.

Hayden, Mary, ed. and trans. "The Songs of Buchet's House." *Zeitschrift für celtische Philologie* 8 (1912): 261–73.

Helmstadter, Richard J. and Bernard Lightman, eds. *Victorian Faith in Crisis.* London: Macmillan, 1990.

Henry, Patrick. "The Caldron of Poesy." *Studia Celtica* 14–15 (1979–80): 114–28.

Higbie, Carolyn. *The Lindian Chronicle and the Greek Creation of Their Past.* Oxford: Oxford University Press, 2003.

Hillers, Barbara. *"Sgél in Mínaduir:* Dädalus und der Minotaurus in Irland." In *Übersetzung, Adaptation und Akkulturation im insularen Mittelalter.* Edited by Erich Poppe and Hildegard Tristram. Münster: Nodus, 1999: 131–44.

Hodgson, Marshall G. S. *The Venture of Islam: Conscience and History in a World Civilisation*, Vol. 3. Chicago: Chicago University Press, 1974.

Holmes, Colin. ed. *Immigrants and Minorities in British Society*. London: George Allen and Unwin, 1978.

Humbach, Helmut, Josef Elfenbein and Prods Oktor Skjærvø, ed. and trans. *The Gāthās of Zarathushtra, and the Other Old Avestan Texts*. 2 vols. Heidelberg: Winter, 1991.

Ibrahim, Vivian. "The Mir of India in Ireland: Nationalism and Identity of an Early 'Muslim' Migrant." *Temenos: Nordic Journal of Comparative Religion* 46:2 (2010) 153–73.

Inden, Ronald. "Orientalist Constructions of India." *Modern Asian Studies* 20:3 (1986), 401–46.

——. *Imagining India*. Bloomington: Indiana University Press, 1990.

Islam, Shamsul. "The Influence of Eastern Philosophy on Yeats's Later Poetry." *Twentieth Century Literature* 19:4 (1973): 283–90.

Iyer, Raghavan and Nandini Iyer, eds. *The Descent of the Gods: Comprising the Mystical Writings of G. W. Russell "A. E."* Gerrards Cross: Colin Smythe, 1988.

Joyce, James. *Dubliners*. Harmondsworth: Penguin in association with J. Cape, 1956.

——. *Critical Writings of James Joyce*. Edited by Ellsworth Mason and Richard Ellmann. New York: Viking Press, 1959.

——. *A Portrait of the Artist as a Young Man*. New York: The Viking Press, 1956.

——. *Ulysses*. New York: Modern Library, 1961.

——. *Selected Letters of James Joyce*. Edited by Richard Ellmann. New York: Viking Press, 1975.

——. *Finnegans Wake*. London: Penguin, 1992.

James Joyce Quarterly, Special Issue: "ReOrienting Joyce." 35:2–3 (Winter-Spring 1998).

Jamison, Stephanie. *The Rig Veda between Two Worlds*. Paris: Collège de France, 2007.

Janda, Michael. *Eleusis: das indogermanische Erbe der Mysterien*. Innsbruck: Institut für Sprachen und Literaturen der Universität Innsbruck, 2000.

Jay, Elisabeth. *Faith and Doubt in Victorian Britain*. London: Macmillan, 1986.

Johnston Graf, Susan. "Heterodox Religions in Ireland: Theosophy, the Hermetic Society, and the Castle of Heroes." *Irish Studies Review* 11:1 (2003): 51–59.

Jung, C. G. *Mysterium Coniunctionis: An Inquiry into the Separation and Synthesis of Psychic Opposites in Alchemy*. Princeton, NJ: Princeton University Press, 1977.

Justi, Ferdinand. *Iranisches Namenbuch*. Marburg: Elwert, 1895.

Kager, Maria. "The Bilingual Imagination of Joyce and Nabokov." Paper presented at the 18th Trieste Joyce School, June 29- July 5, 2014.

Kawami, Trudy. "Greek Art and Persian Taste: Some Animal Sculptures From Persepolis." *American Journal of Archaeology* 90 (1986): 259-67.

Khaleghi-Motlagh, Djalal. "Barmāya." *Encyclopaedia Iranica* 3 (1988): 809.

——, ed. *Shāhnāmeh*. 8 vols. New York: Bibliotheca Persica, 1988-2008.

Khan, Gulfishan. *Indian Muslim Perceptions of the West During the Eighteenth Century*. Karachi: Oxford University Press, 1998.

Kellens, Jean. "Qui est Gāuš Tašan?" In *Proceedings of the Second European Conference of Iranian Studies*. Edited by B. G. Fragner, C. Fragner, G. Gnoli, R. Haag-Higuchi, M. Maggi and P. Orsatti. Rome: Instituto Italiano per il Medio ed Estremo Oriente, 1995: 347-57.

King, Richard. *Orientalism and Religion: Postcolonial Theory, India and "the Mystic East"*. London: Routledge, 2002.

Kinsella, Thomas, trans. *The Táin: From the Irish Epic Táin Bó Cúailnge*. Oxford: Oxford University Press, 1969.

Kotwal, Firoze and Jamsheed Choksy. "Jiwām." *Encyclopaedia Iranica* 14 (2008): 664-66.

Kuhn, Adalbert. "Die Sprachvergleichung und die Urgeschichte der indogermanischen Völker." *Zeitschrift für Vergleichende Sprachforschung auf dem Gebiete des deutschen, griechischen und lateinischen* 4 (1855): 81-123.

Lamb, Charles. *The Adventures of Ulysses, Edited with Notes for School*. Boston: Ginn & Company, 1886.

Lambden, Stephen. "An Episode in the Childhood of the Bab." In *In Iran*. Edited by Peter Smith. Studies in Bábí and Bahá'í History volume 3. Los Angeles: Kalimát Press, 1986: 1-31.

Landolt, Hermann, "Walayah." In *Encyclopedia of Religion*. 2nd edition, Edited by Lindsay Jones. Detroit: MacMillan Reference USA, 2005, vol. 14: 9656-62.

Larrington, Carolyne. "Þóra and Áslaug in *Ragnars saga loðbrókar*: Women, Dragons and Destiny." In *Making History: Essays on the* Fornaldarsögur. Edited by Martin Arnold and Alison Finlay. London: Viking Society for Northern Research, 2011, 53-68.

Larsen, Timothy. *Crisis of Doubt: Honest Faith in the Nineteenth Century*. Oxford: Oxford University Press, 2006.

Lawson, Todd. "Interpretation as Revelation: The Qur'án Commentary of Sayyid 'Ali Muhammad Shirazi, the Báb." In *Approaches to the History of the Interpretation of the Qur'án*. Edited by Andrew Rippin. Oxford: Oxford University Press, 1988: 223-253.

——. "The Terms Remembrance (*dhikr*) and Gate (*bab*) in the Báb's Commentary on the Sura of Joseph." In *Studies in Honor of Hasan M. Balyúzí*. Edited by Moojan Momen. Studies in the Babí and Baha'í Religions, volume 5. Los Angeles: Kalimat Press, 1989: 1–63.

——. "The Báb's Epistle on the Spiritual Journey towards God." In *The Baha'i Faith and the World Religions: Papers Presented at the Irfan Colloquia*. Edited by Moojan Momen. Oxford: George Ronald, 2005: 231–247.

——. "Orthodoxy and Heterodoxy in Twelver Shiʿism: Aḥmad Al-Aḥsāʾī on Fayḍ Kāshānī (the *Risālat al-ʿIlmiyya*)." In *Religion and Society in Qajar Iran*. Edited by Robert Gleave. London: RoutledgeCurzon, 2005: 127–154.

——. "Duality, Opposition and Typology in the Qur'an: The Apocalyptic Substrate." *Journal of Qur'anic Studies* 10:2 (2008): 23–49.

——. *Gnostic Apocalypse in Islam: Qur'an, Exegesis, Messianism, and the Literary Origins of the Babi Religion*. London and New York: Routledge, 2012.

——. "The Súrat al-ʿAbd of the *Qayyúm al-asmá'* (Chapter 109): A Provisional Translation and Commentary." In *A Most Noble Pattern: Collected Essays on the Writings of the Báb, ʿAlí Muhammad Shírází (1819-1850)*. Edited by Todd Lawson and Omid Ghaemmaghami. Oxford: George Ronald, 2012: 116–145.

——. "Typological Figuration and the Meaning of 'Spiritual': The Qur'anic Story of Joseph." *Journal of the American Oriental Society* 132:2 (2012): 221–244.

——. "The Qur'an and Epic." *Journal of Qur'anic Studies* 16:1 (2014): 58–92.

—— and Omid Ghaemmaghami, eds. *A Most Noble Pattern: Collected Essays on the Writings of the Báb, ʿAlí Muhammad Shírází (1819-1850)*. Oxford: George Ronald, 2012.

——. *Exegesis as Mystical Encounter*. Leiden: Brill, forthcoming.

——. "Paradise in the Quran and the Music of Apocalypse." In *Roads to Paradise: Eschatology and Concepts of the Hereafter in Islam. Volume I: Foundations and the Formation of a Tradition. Reflections on the Hereafter in the Quran and Islamic Religious Thought*. Edited by Sebastian Günther and Todd Lawson. Leiden: Brill, 2015, 1: 49–94.

Leach, E. R. "Critical Introduction" to M. I. Steblin-Kamenskij, *Myth* (translated by M. P. Coote). Ann Arbor, 1982: 1–20.

Leavitt, John. "The Cow of Plenty in Indo-Iranian and Celtic Myth." In *Proceedings of the Eleventh Annual UCLA Indo-European Conference*. Edited by Karlene Jones-Bley, Martin Huld and Angela Della Volpe. Washington: Institute for the Study of Man, 2000: 209–24.

Lennon, Joseph. *Irish Orientalism: A Literary and Intellectual History*. Syracuse: Syracuse University Press, 2004.

Lernout, Geert. *Help My Unbelief: James Joyce and Religion*. New York: Continuum, 2010.

Lewisohn, Leonard, ed. *Hafiz and the Religion of Love in Classical Persian Poetry*. London: I. B. Tauris, 2010.

———. "The Mystical Milieu: Hafiz's Erotic Spirituality." In *Hafiz and the Religion of Love in Classical Persian Poetry*. Edited by Leonard Lewisohn. London: I. B. Tauris, 2010, 31–73.

Liebrecht, Felix. "Die Ragnar Lodbroksage in Persien." *Orient und Occident* 1 (1862): 561–67.

Lincoln, Bruce. "The Myth of the 'Bovine's Lament.'" *Journal of Indo-European Studies* 3 (1975): 337–62.

———. *Priests, Warriors and Cattle: A Study in the Ecology of Religions*. Berkeley: University of California Press, 1981.

———. *Theorizing Myth: Narrative, Ideology and Scholarship*. Chicago: University of Chicago Press, 1999.

Lipiński, Edward. *Itineraria Phoenicia*. Leuven: Peeters, 2004.

Loloi, Parvin. *Hâfiz, Master of Persian Poetry: A Critical Bibliography. English Translations Since the Eighteenth Century*. London: I. B. Tauris, 2004.

———. "Hafiz and the Language of Love in Nineteenth-Century English and American Poetry." In *Hafiz and the Religion of Love in Classical Persian Poetry*. Edited by Leonard Lewisohn. London: I. B. Tauris, 279–94.

Louden, Bruce. "Bacchylides 17: Theseus and Indo-Iranian Apam Napat." *Journal of Indo-European Studies* 27 (1999): 57–78.

Lyon Macfie, Alexander. *Orientalism: A Reader*. Edinburgh: Edinburgh University Press, 2000.

———. *Orientalism*. London: Longman, 2002.

Macalister, Robert, ed. and trans. *Lebor Gabála Érenn: The Book of the Taking of Ireland*. 5 vols. Dublin: Irish Texts Society, 1938–56.

MacEoin, Denis. "Orthodoxy and Heterodoxy in Nineteenth-Century Shiʿism: The Cases of Shaykhism and Babism." *Journal of the American Oriental Society* 110:2 (April 1990): 323–29.

———. *The Sources for Early Bābī Doctrine and History: A Survey*. Leiden: E. J. Brill, 1992.

———. *The Messiah of Shiraz: Studies in Early and Middle Babism*. Boston: Brill, 2009.

Madigan, Daniel. *The Qur'ân's Self-Image: Writing and Authority in Islam's Scripture*. Princeton, NJ & Woodstock, Oxfordshire UK: Princeton University Press, 2001.

Mādigān ī hazār dādistān. Costa Mesa: Mazda, 1997.

Magoun, Francis, trans. *The Kalevala, or Poems from the Kalevala District*. Cambridge, MA: Harvard University Press, 1963.

Malcolm, Sir John. *Sketches of Persia: From the Journals of a Traveller in the East.* London: J. Murray, 1828, vol. 2.

Mandeville, Sir John. *The voiage and travayle of Sir John Maundeville knight: which treateth of the way toward Hierusalem and of marvayles of Inde with other islands and countreys.* Annotated by J. Ashton. London: Pickering & Chatto, 1887.

Mansoor, Menachem. *The Story of Irish Orientalism.* Dublin: Hodges, Figgis & Co., 1944.

Márkus-Takeshita, Kinga Ilona. "From Iranian Myth to Folk Narrative: The Legend of the Dragon-Slayer and the Spinning Maiden in the Persian Book of the Kings." *Asian Folklore Studies* 60 (2001): 203–14.

Martin, Richard P. "Epic as Genre." In *A Companion to Ancient Epic.* Edited by John Miles Foley. Malden, MA: Blackwell Publishing, 2005: 9–19.

Matasović, Ranko. *A Theory of Textual Reconstruction in Indo-European Linguistics.* New York: P. Lang, 1996.

McCarthy, Justin Huntly. *Ghazels from the Divan of Hafiz.* London: Nutt, 1893.

———. *Hafiz in London,* London: Chatto & Windus, 1886.

McCourt, John, ed. *James Joyce in Context.* Cambridge: Cambridge University Press, 2009.

McCullagh, W. T. (William Torrens). *Richard Lalor Sheil.* London: Hurst and Blackett, 1855.

McHugh, Roland. *The Sigla of Finnegans Wake.* London: Edward Arnold, 1976.

———. "Mohammad in Notebook VI.B.31," *A Wake Newslitter: Studies in James Joyce's Finnegans Wake* n.s. 16:4 (August 1979): 51–58.

McInerney, Jeremy. *The Cattle of the Sun: Cows and Culture in the World of the Ancient Greeks.* Princeton: Princeton University Press, 2010.

McIntyre, J. Lewis. *Giordano Bruno.* London: Macmillan, 1903.

McLuhan, Marshall. *Understanding Media: The Extensions of Man.* New York: McGraw Hill, 1964.

McNamara, Brendan, ed. *Connections: Early Links Between the Bahá'í Faith and Ireland.* Cork: TK Publications, 2007.

McTurk, Rory. *Studies in* Ragnars Saga Loðbrókar *and its Major Scandinavian Analogues.* Medium Aevum Monographs, New Series, 15. Oxford: Society for the Study of Mediaeval Languages and Literature, 1991.

Mehran, Marsha. *Pomegranate Soup.* New York: Random House, 2005.

———. *Rosewater and Soda Bread.* New York: Random House, 2008.

Meineke, August, ed. *Fragmenta Comicorum Graecorum.* 5 vols. Berlin: Reimer, 1839–57.

Melia, Daniel. "Some Remarks on the Affinities of Medieval Irish Saga." *Acta Antiqua Academiae Scientiarum Hungaricae* 27 (1979): 255–261.

Melikian-Chirvani, A. S. "The Wine-Bull and the Magian Master." In *Recurrent Patterns in Iranian Religions: From Mazdaism to Sufism*. Edited by Philippe Gignoux. Paris: Association pour l'avancement des études iraniennes, 1992: 101–34.

Micallef, Roberta and Sunil Sharma, eds. *On the Wonders of Land & Sea: Persianate Travel Writing*. Boston: Ilex Foundation, 2013.

Mieder, Wolfgang, ed. *A Dictionary of American Proverbs*. New York: Oxford University Press, 1992.

Miles, Brent. *Heroic Saga and Classical Epic in Medieval Ireland*. Cambridge: D. S. Brewer, 2011.

Mills, George Harper. *Yeats's Golden Dawn*, London: Macmillan, 1974.

Mills, Margaret Harper. "Yeats's Religion." *Yeats: An Annual of Critical and Textual Studies* 13 (1995): 48–71.

Minorsky, Vladimir. "Vis u Ramin: A Parthian Romance." *Bulletin of the School of Oriental and African Studies* 11 (1943–46): 741–63; 12 (1947–1948): 20–35; 16 (1954): 91–92;

———. "New Developments," *Bulletin of the School of Oriental and African Studies* 25 (1962): 275–86.

Mittwoch, Eugen. "Ayyām al-ʿArab," *Encyclopaedia of Islam*, Second Edition. Edited by P. Bearman, Th. Bianquis, C. E. Bosworth, E. van Donzel, W. P. Heinrichs. Brill Online, 2014. Reference. University of Toronto. 16 September 2014.

Mohl, Jules, ed. *Le livre des rois* I-VII. Paris: Imprimerie nationale, 1838–1878.

Molé, Marijan. *La légende de Zoroastre selon les textes pehlevis*. Paris: Klincksieck, 1967.

Momen, Moojan, ed. *The Bábí and Baáʾí Religions, 1844-1944: Some Contemporary Western Accounts*. Oxford: George Ronald, 1981.

———. "The Trial of Mullá ʿAlí Bastámí: A Combined Sunní-Shíʿí Fatwá against the Báb." *Iran* 20 (January 1982): 113–43.

Monette, Connell. "Indo-European Elements in Celtic and Indo-Iranian Epic Tradition: the Trial of Champions in the Táin Bó Cúailgne and the Shahnameh." *The Journal of Indo-European Studies* 32 (2004): 61-78.

Morris, Sarah. *Daidalos and the Origins of Greek Art*. Princeton: Princeton University Press, 1992.

Morsalvand, Hasan, ed. *Heyratnāmeh: Safarnāmeh-ye Abolhasan Khān Ilchi beh Landan*. Tehran: Mo'asseseh-ye Khadamāt-e Farhangi-ye Rasā, 1364 [1985].

Motadel, David. "Iran and the Aryan Myth." In *Perceptions of Iran: History, Myths and Nationalism from Medieval Persia to the Islamic Republic*. Edited by Ali Ansari. London: I. B. Tauris, 2014, 119-45.

Murray, Kevin, ed. and trans. *Baile in Scáil: the Phantom's Frenzy.* London: Irish Texts Society, 2004.

Nabokov, Vladimir Vladimirovich. *Pale Fire.* New York: Knopf, 1992.

Nagy, Gregory. "The Sign of Protesilaos." *MHTIC. Revue d'anthropologie du monde grec ancien* 2 (1987): 207–213.

———. *Pindar's Homer: The Lyric Possession of an Epic Past.* Baltimore: Johns Hopkins University Press, 1990.

———. *Greek Mythology and Poetics.* Ithaca NY: Cornell University Press, 1990.

———. *Homeric Questions.* Austin TX: Texas University Press, 1996.

———. "The Library of Pergamon as a Classical Model." In *Pergamon: Citadel of the Gods.* Edited by Helmuth Koester. Harrisburg PA: Trinity Press International, 1998: 185–232.

———. "The Sign of the Hero: A Prologue." In *Flavius Philostratus: Heroikos.* Translated with an introduction and notes by Jennifer K. Berenson and Ellen Bradshaw Aitken. Atlanta: Society for Biblical Literature, 2001, xv-xxxv. Also available online at chs.harvard.edu

Nagy, Joseph Falaky. "Orality in Medieval Irish Narrative: An Overview." *Oral Tradition* 1:2 (1986): 272–301.

———. "Hierarchy, Heroes and Heads: Some Indo-European Structures in Greek Myth." In *Approaches to Greek Myth.* Edited by Lowell Edmunds. Baltimore: Johns Hopkins University Press, 1990: 199–238.

———. "How the Táin Was Lost." *Zeitschrift für celtische Philologie* 49–50 (1997): 603–609.

Nasser Deyhim, Mehrbanoo, trans. *An Iranian in Nineteenth Century Europe: The Travel Diaries of Haj Sayyah, 1859-1877.* Bethesda, MD: IBEX Publishers, 1998.

Nguyen, Martin. "Exegesis of the ḥurúf al-muqattaʻa: Polyvalency in Sunni Traditions of Qurʼanic Interpretation." *Journal of Qurʼanic Studies* 14:2 (October 2012): 1–28.

Nikolaeva, Natalia. "The Drink of Death." *Studia Celtica* 35 (2001): 299–306.

Ní Shéaghdha, Nessa, ed. and tr. *Tóruigheacht Dhiarmada agus Ghráinne: The Pursuit of Diarmaid and Gráinne.* Irish Texts Society 48. Dublin: Published for the Irish Texts Society by the Educational Company of Ireland, 1967.

O'Brien, Joan. *The Transformation of Hera: A Study of Ritual, Hero and the Goddess in the* Iliad. Lanham: Rowman and Littlefield, 1993.

Ó Cathasaigh, Tomás. "*Cath Maige Tuired* as Exemplary Myth." In *Folia Gadelica.* Edited by Pádraig de Brún, Seán Ó Coileáin and Pádraig Ó Riain. Cork: Cork University Press, 1983: 1–19.

———. "Mythology in *Táin Bó Cúailnge.*" In *Studien zur Táin Bó Cúailnge.* Edited by Hildegard Tristram. Tübingen: Gunter Narr Verlag, 1993: 114–32.

———. "Tóraíocht Dhiarmada agus Ghráinne." In *An Fhiannaíocht*. Edited by Pádraig Ó Fiannachta. Léachtaí Cholm Chille 25. Maynooth: An Sagart, 1995, 30–46.

Ó hAodha, Donncha, ed. and trans. "The Irish Version of Statius' *Achilleid*." *Proceedings of the Royal Irish Academy* 79 (1979): 83–138.

Ó hÓgain, Dáithí. *Myth, Legend and Romance: An Encyclopaedia of Irish Folk Tradition*. New York: Prentice Hall, 1991.

O'Keeffe, James, ed. and trans. *Buile Suibhne Geilt*. London: Irish Texts Society, 1913.

Olmsted, Garrett. *The Gods of the Celts and the Indo-Europeans*. Budapest: Archaeolingua, 1994.

O'Laughlin, Michael C. *Families of Co. Donegal, Ireland*. Kansas: Irish Roots Cafe, 2001.

O'Rahilly, Cecile, ed. and trans. *Táin Bó Cúailnge from the Book of Leinster*. Dublin: Dublin Institute for Advanced Studies, 1967.

———, ed. and trans. *Táin Bó Cúailnge: Recension I*. Dublin: Dublin Institute for Advanced Studies, 1976.

O'Rahilly, Thomas. *Early Irish History and Mythology*. Dublin: Dublin Institute for Advanced Studies, 1946.

Pakzad, Fazlollah, ed. *Bundahišn: Zoroastrische Kosmogonie und Kosmologie*. Tehran: Centre for the Great Islamic Encyclopedia, 2005.

Pickford, C. E. Review of Pierre Gallais, *Genèse du roman occidental: Essais sur Tristan et Iseut et son modèle persan*, *Medium Ævum* 46 (1977): 144–46.

Poe, Edgar Allan. *Collected Works. Volume 1: Poems*. Edited by Thomas Ollive Mabbott. Cambridge MA: Belknap Press of Harvard University Press, 1969.

Qāḍī, Wadād, al-. *The Primordial covenant and human history in the Qur'an*. The Margaret Weyerhaeuser Jewett Chair of Arabic Occasional Papers. Edited by Ramzi Baalbaki. Beirut: American University of Beirut, 2006.

Radjaie, Ali. *Das profan-mystische Ghasel des Hafis in Rückerts Übersetzungen und in Goethes Diwan*. Würzburg: Ergon Verlag, 1998.

Rafati, Vahid (translated by Omid Ghaemmaghami). "Colours in the Writings of the Báb." In *A Most Noble Pattern: Collected Essays on the Writings of the Báb, 'Alí Muḥammad Shírazí (1819–1850)*. Edited by Todd Lawson and Omid Ghaemmaghami. Oxford: George Ronald, 2012: 33–51.

Rahman, Fazlur. *Major Themes of the Qur'an*. Minneapolis, MN: Bibliotheca Islamica, 1980.

Ringer, Monica M. "The Quest for the Secret of Strength in Iranian Nineteenth-Century Travel Literature: Rethinking Tradition in the *Safarnameh*." In *Iran and the Surrounding World 1501-2001: Interactions in*

Culture and Cultural Politics. Edited by Nikki Keddie and Rudi Matthee. Seattle: University of Washington Press, 2002: 146–161.

Rippin, Andrew. "Occasions of Revelation." In *Encyclopaedia of the Qur'an.* Edited by Jane Dammen McAuliffe. Leiden: Brill Academic Publishers, 2003, vol. 3: 69–73.

Robinson, Samuel. *A Century of Ghazels, or a Hundred Odes, Selected and Translated from the Diwan of Hafiz.* Whitefish, MT: Kessinger Publishing.

Ross, Anne. "Esus et les trois 'grues.'" *Études Celtiques* 9 (1961): 405–38.

Rubanovich, Julia. "The *Shāh-nāma* and Medieval Orality: Critical Remarks on the 'Oral Poetics' Approach and New Perspectives," *Middle Eastern Literature* 16:2 (2013): 217–26.

Russell, George. *The National Being,* New York: Macmillan, 1930.

Said, Edward. *Orientalism.* London: Routledge, 1978.

Saiedi, Nader. *Gate of the Heart: Understanding the Writings of the Bab.* [Waterloo, Ont.]: Wilfrid Laurier University Press and the Association for Baha'i Studies, 2008.

Sayers, William. "Bargaining for the Life of Bres in *Cath Maige Tuired.*" *Bulletin of the Board of Celtic Studies* 34 (1986): 26–40.

Schimmel, Annemarie. *A Two-Colored Brocade: The Imagery of Persian Poetry.* Chapel Hill: University of North Carolina Press, 1992.

Schlauch, Margaret, tr. *The Saga of the Volsungs, The Saga of Ragnar Lodbrok, together with The Lay of Kraka.* New York: The American-Scandinavian Foundation, W. W. Norton & Company, 1930.

Schwartz, Martin. "Gathic Compositional History, *Yasna* 29, and Bovine Symbolism." In *Paitimāna: Essays in Iranian, Indo-European, and Indian Studies in Honor of Hanns-Peter Schmidt.* Edited by Siamak Adhami. Costa Mesa: Mazda Publishers, 2003: 195–249.

Scull, Andrew. *Social Order / Mental Disorder: Anglo-American Psychiatry in Historical Perspective.* Berkeley: University of California Press, 1989.

Sergent, Bernard. *Celtes et Grecs.* 2 vols. Paris: Payot, 2000–2004.

Seyed-Gohrab, Ali-Asghar. "The Erotic Spirit: Love, Man and Satan in Hafiz's Poetry." In *Hafiz and the Religion of Love in Classical Persian Poetry.* Edited by Leonard Lewisohn. London: I. B. Tauris, 2010, 107–21.

Shahbazi, A. Shapur. "Haftvād." *Encyclopaedia Iranica* XI (2002): 534–36.

Shakespeare, William. *As You Like it.*

Shayegan, M. Rahim. *Aspects of History and Epic in Ancient Iran: From Gaumāta to Wahnām.* Hellenic Studies 52. Washington: Center for Hellenic Studies, 2012, 139–55.

Sheil, Lady Mary Leonora. *Glimpses of Life and Manners in Persia.* London: John Murray, 1856.

Shoberl, Frederic. *Persia*. London: R. Ackermann, 1822, vol. 1.

Shoghi Effendi, trans. and ed., *The Dawn-Breakers: Nabíl's Narrative of the Early Days of the Bahá'í Revelation*. Wilmette, IL: US Bahá'í Publishing Trust, 1932.

Sick, David. "Mit(h)ra(s) and the Myths of the Sun." *Numen* 51 (2004): 432–67.

Sims-Williams, Patrick. *Irish Influence on Medieval Welsh Literature*. New York: Oxford University Press, 2011.

Skjærvø, Prods Oktor. "Eastern Iranian Epic Traditions III: Zarathustra and Diomedes – An Indo-European Epic Warrior Type." *Bulletin of the Asia Institute* 11 (2000): 175–82.

Smith, Peter. *The Babi and Baha'i Religions: From Messianic Shiism to a World Religion*. Cambridge: Cambridge University Press, 1987.

Society for the Preservation of the Irish Language. *Annual Report for 1898*. Dublin: Society for the Preservation of the Irish Language, 1898.

Sohrabi, Naghmeh. *Taken for Wonder: Nineteenth-Century Accounts from Iran to Europe*. New York: Oxford University Press, 2012.

Spooner, Brian and William L. Hanaway. "Introduction: Persian as *Koine*: Written Persian in World-Historical Perspectice." In *Literacy in the Persianate World: Writing and the Social Order*. Edited by Brian Spooner and William L. Hanaway. Philadelphia: University of Pennsylvania Museum of Archaeology and Anthropology, 2012: 1–68.

Stewart, Charles, trans. *The Travels of Mirza Abu Taleb Khan in Asia, Africa, and Europe during the years 1799, 1800, 1801, 1802*. London: Hurst, Rees, and Orme, 1810.

Stokes, Whitley, ed. and trans. "The Bodleian *Dinnshenchas*." *Folklore* 3 (1892): 465–516.

———. "The Prose Tales in the Rennes *Dindsenchas*." *Revue Celtique* 15 (1894): 272–336, 418–84 and *Revue Celtique* 16 (1895): 31–83, 135–67, 269–312.

———, ed. *Acallamh na Senórach*. In *Irische Texte: Mit Übersetzungen und Wörterbuch*. Edited by Whitley Stokes and Ernst Windisch. Vierte Serie. 1. Heft. Leipzig: Hirzel, 1900.

———, ed. and trans. "The Songs of Buchet's House." *Revue Celtique* 25 (1904): 18–38, 225–7.

Strugeon, Sinead. "Sheil, Richard Lalor." In *Dictionary of Irish Biography*. Edited by James McGuire and James Quinn. Cambridge: Cambridge University Press and Royal Irish Academy, 2009, vol. 8.

Sykes, P. M. *A History of Persia*. London: Macmillan, 1915, vol. 2.

Tafazzoli, Ahmad. "Ferēdūn." *Encyclopaedia Iranica* 9 (1999): 531–33.

Tindall, William York. *The Literary Symbol*. New York: Columbia University Press, 1955.

———. *A Reader's Guide to James Joyce*. New York: Noonday Press, 1959.

Tondriau, Julien. "Dionysos, dieu royal: du Bacchos tauromorphe primitif aux souverains hellénistiques Neoi Dionysoi." In *Mélanges Henri Grégoire*. 4 vols. Bruxelles: Secréteriat des Éditons de l'Institut, 1949-53: 4.441-66.

Torrey, Bradford, ed. *The Writings of Henry David Thoreau, Journal, vo. 2, 1850-September 15, 1851*. Boston and New York: Houghton Mifflin and Company, 1906.

Tymoczko, Maria. *The Irish Ulysses*. Berkeley: University of California Press, 1994.

———. "Sir Henry Ellis," *Dictionary of National Biography*, vol. VI, p. 697.

Uther, Hans-Jörg. *The Types of International Folktales: A Classification and Bibliography, Based on the System of Antti Aarne and Stith Thompson*, 3 vols. Folklore Fellows Communications 284–86. Helsinki: Suomalainen Tiedeakatemia, Academia Scientiarum Fennica, 2004.

Van Berg, Paul-Louis. "Spit in My Mouth, Glaukos: A Greek Indo-European Tale about Ill-gotten Knowledge." In *Proceedings of the Sixteenth Annual UCLA Indo-European Conference*. Edited by Karlene Jones-Bley et al. Washington: Instutite for the Study of Man, 2005: 72–96.

Van Duzer, Chet. *Duality and Structure in the Iliad and Odyssey*. New York: Peter Lang, 1996.

Vendryes, Joseph. "Sur un passage du comique Philémon: le *Tarvos Trigaranos* en Grèce." *Revue Celtique* 28 (1907): 123–7.

Voelker, Joseph C. "'Nature It Is': The Influence of Giordano Bruno on James Joyce's Molly Bloom." *James Joyce Quarterly* 14:1 (October 1, 1976): 39–48.

Walbridge, Linda, ed. *Most Learned of the Shia: The Institution of the Marja' Taqlid*. New York: Oxford University Press, 2001.

Walters, Vivienne. *The Cult of Mithras in the Roman Provinces of Gaul*. Leiden: Brill, 1974.

Watkins, Calvert. "*Is tre fír flathemon*: Marginalia to *Audacht Morainn*." *Ériu* 30 (1979): 181–98.

———. *How to Kill a Dragon: Aspects of Indo-European Poetics*. Oxford: Oxford University Press, 1995.

———. "The Milk of the Dawn Cows Revisited." In *East and West: Papers in Indo-European Studies*. Edited by Kazuhiko Yoshida and Brent Vine. Bremen: Hempen, 2009: 225–39.

Weir, David. *James Joyce and the Art of Mediation*. Ann Arbor: University of Michigan Press, 1996.

Welburn, Andrew. *From a Virgin Womb: The Apocalypse of Adam and the Virgin Birth*. Leiden: Brill, 2008.

West, Edward, trans. *Pahlavi Texts*. 5 vols. Oxford: Clarendon Press, 1880–97.

West, Martin. *Indo-European Poetry and Myth*. Oxford: Oxford University Press, 2007.

Wheeler, Stephen (rev. James Lunt). "Sheil, Sir Justin (1803–1871)." *Oxford Dictionary of National Biography*. Oxford: Oxford University Press, 2004, vol. 50.

Widengren, Geo. *Die Religionen Irans*. Stuttgart: Kohlhammer, 1965.

Wilberforce Clarke, Lieut-Col. Henry. *The Divan, Written in the Fourteenth Century by Khwaja Shamsud-Din Muhammad-i-Hafiz-i Shirazi otherwise known as Lisanu-l-Ghaib amd Tarjumanu-l-Asrar*. Calcutta, 1891.

Wilde, Lady Francesca Speranza. *Ancient Legends, Mystic Charms, and Superstitions of Ireland*. London: Ward & Downey, 1887.

Woolf, Virginia. *To the Lighthouse*. Oxford: Oxford University Press, 2006.

———. *Mrs. Dalloway*. Peterborough, Ont.: Broadview Press, 2013.

Wright, Denis. "Great Britain vii: British Travelers in Iran." *Encyclopaedia Iranica* 11: 246–52..

Yapp, M. E. "Control of the Persian Mission 1822–1836." *University of Birmingham History Journal* 7 (1960): 162–79.

Yared, Aida. " 'In the Name of Anna': Islam and *Salam* in Joyce's *Finnegans Wake*." *James Joyce Quarterly*, ReOrienting Joyce 35, no. 2–3 (Winter-Spring 1998): 401–38.

Yeats, William Butler. *Reveries over Childhood and Youth*, London: MacMillan, 1916.

———. *Essays and Introductions*, London: Macmillan, 1961.

———. *Explorations: Selected by Mrs W. B. Yeats*. London: Macmillan, 1962.

———. *Yeats's Poems*. Edited by A. Norman Jeffries, London: Macmillan, 1989.

———. *The Collected Works, Vol. 2: The Plays*. Edited by David R. Clark and Rosalind E. Clark. Basingstoke: Macmillan, 2001.

———. *The Speckled Bird: An Autobiographical Novel, with Varian Versions*. Edited by William H. O'Donnell. Basingstoke: Palgrave Macmillan, 2003.

———. *Early Essays*. Edited by George Bornstein and Richard J. Finneran. New York: Scribner, 2004.

Youngs, Tim, ed. *Travel Writing in the Nineteenth Century: Filling the Blank Spaces*, London: Anthem Press, 2006.

Zarandí, Nabíl. *The Dawn-Breakers: Nabíl's Narrative of the Early Days of the Bahá'í Revelation*. Translated by Shoghi Effendi. Wilmette, IL: Bahá'í Publishing Trust, 1974.

Zebiri, Kate. "The Redeployment of Orientalist Themes in Islamophobia." *Studies in Contemporary Islam* 10 (2008): 1–43.

Zenker, Rudolf. "Die Tristansage und das persische Epos von Wis und Ramin." *Romanische Forschungen* 29 (1911): 322–69.

Zia-Ebrahimi, Reza."Self-Orientalisation and Dislocation: The Uses and Abuses of the Aryan Discourse in Iran." *Iranian Studies* 44:4 (2011): 445–72.

Newspapers

Frazer's Magazine for Town and Country, December 1856.
Irish Independent, 1 January 2015
The Irish Theosophist, 15 January 1893
The Irish Times, 20 July 1859
The Irish Times, 27 February 1877
The Irish Times, 15 November 1878
The Irish Times, 10 January 1879
The Irish Times, 6 June 1881
The Irish Times, 8 March 1883
The Irish Times, 17 June 1899
Lucifer: Theosophical Monthly, 15 January 1893

Web sources

Cole, Juan R. I. "Individualism and the Spiritual Path in Shaykh Ahmad Al-Ahsa'i." *Occasional Papers in Shaykhi, Babi and Baha'i Studies* 1, no. 4 (1997): http://www.h – net.org/~bahai/bhpapers/ahsaind.htm.

Dumas, Firoozeh. "Funny in Farsi" http://www.randomhouse.com/high-school/RHI_magazine/pdf3/Dumas.pdf

Lawson, Todd. "Coincidentia Oppositorum in the Qayyūm Al-asmā': The Terms 'Point' (*nuqta*), 'Pole' (*qutb*), 'Center' (*markaẕ*) and the Khutbat al-Tatanjiya," *Occasional Papers in Shaykhi, Babi and Baha'i Studies* 5, no. 1 (2001): http://www.h – net.org/~bahai/bhpapers/vol5/tatanj/tatanj.htm.

Momen, Moojan. "Perfection and Refinement: Towards an Aesthetics of the Bab." http://irfancolloquia.org/pdf/lights12_momen-aesthetics.pdf. (Revision, August, 2014 of original article published in *Lights of 'Irfan* 12 (2011): 221–43.)

Wikipedia http://en.wikipedia.org/wiki/Gilbert_schema_for_Ulysses

Yared, Aida. "Introducing Islam in Finnegans Wake: The Story of Mohammed in VI.B.45." *Genetic Joyce Studies* 1 (Spring 2001). Online at: http://www.geneticjoycestudies.org/

O'Siadhail Family History. http://www.surnamedb.com/Surname/O%27Shiel.

Articles in the *Encyclopaedia Iranica* are available at http://www.iranicaonline.org

Unpublished sources

National Library of Ireland, Yeats Papers, "From Hafiz" [NLI MS 30,049]
The Bab, Sayyed ʿAlī Muhammad Shīrāzī. *Tafsīr sūrat Yūsuf.* Baha'i World
    Centre Library, uncatalogued. [References are to a paginated photo-
    copy.]